Geoffrey Ashe is well-known for his Arthurian studies, notably *The Quest for Arthur's Britain*, which he edited, *Camelot and the Vision of Albion*, and *King Arthur's Avalon*. His researches have led him into the wider field of what have been called 'collective mystiques', and it is from this interest that have come such books as *The Ancient Wisdom*, *The Virgin* (a study of the cult of the Virgin Mary), and his new book, *Miracles*, which is also to be published in Abacus. He is the author of a novel, *The Finger and the Moon*.

Geoffrey Ashe lives at Glastonbury on the Tor, in the house formerly occupied by the magician Dion Fortune, now a rendezvous for travellers and researchers.

THE ANCIENT WISDOM

Geoffrey Ashe

ABACUS

First published in Great Britain
by Macmillan London Limited 1977
Copyright © Geoffrey Ashe 1977

Abacus edition published in 1979
by Sphere Books Ltd
30/32 Gray's Inn Road, London WC1X 8JL

Set in VIP Times

*Printed in Great Britain by
Hazell Watson & Viney Ltd,
Aylesbury, Bucks*

Contents

List of Plates

List of Illustrations

CHAPTER ONE

A Posture of Defiance

1

Western society has been witnessing a rebirth of the occult, the esoteric, the magical. With it has come a flood of speculative, world-ranging literature which purports to be scientific, but rejects normal science very much as occultists do: books about flying saucers, unknown human powers, a long-ago colonization of earth by alien astronauts. The phenomenon is complex and many-faceted. No sharp distinctions can be drawn between one part of it and another. They all overlap, and they add up to what some sceptics have called a 'flight from reason'.

As the wave rose in the early 1970s, it became a cliché of book-reviewers to ask with a pained air why so many people, especially at junior levels, were engrossed in exploded mumbo-jumbo and nonsensical fantasy. Any reviewer who had really wanted to find out (not many did) would have hit on at least one reason which ought to have been obvious. Attention was drawn to it by a notable psychologist, Viktor Frankl. I do not think I can improve on the words in which I enlarged on it myself, in an imagined lecture by another psychologist, a fictitious one. The quotation is from my novel *The Finger and the Moon*.

'More and more of our patients complain of a sense of meaninglessness in life. More and more often, the reason is the outlook of science. Or what has come through to them as the outlook of science. Sometimes it's called reductionism . . .

'Thinking people tend to feel that science has cut

1

Man down. It's explained away everything that matters in terms of smaller, meaner things that don't matter. Religion is *nothing but* wish-fulfilling fairytales. Love is *nothing but* body chemistry. Art is *nothing but* a surge of conditioned reflexes . . .

'Science leaves Man shut-in, futile, doomed . . . It feeds on the work of its countless laboratories, to trap people in closed systems – chemical, or biological, or physical systems – where all colour has gone and all hope is lost.'

Faced with a questioner urging that the revival of magic and so forth was a 'flight from reason', my imaginary psychologist counter-attacked.

'You claim to speak for scientific, progressive humanism, and you equate it with reason. I'm telling you it hasn't worked. It's supposed to instil devotion to the good of mankind. But apart from a high-calibre few, it doesn't. On the one-hand we live in dread of technological horrors . . . On the other hand there's a powerlessness to do much about it. A failure of will – because of this feeling that a darkness of soul is closing in and death is the end and science has made everything hollow and pointless. Now if that's so (and I can give you evidence, clinical scientific evidence, that it is), then I wouldn't call it a flight from reason to look elsewhere for rescue. It's thoroughly rational. At least, it can be.'

To propose to step into this territory is still to invite the comment that it is too absurd to be worth stepping into. At the outset I will merely suggest, in keeping with the foregoing paragraphs, that those who frequent it have a case in principle and are not necessarily insane. I will now venture a further suggestion. At least one piece of their offbeat mental equipment, one idea which a great many of them hold, has a solid interest for the reflective public at large. However peculiarly, however obliquely, it impinges on areas of orthodox study, and it does so with a challenge which cannot be dismissed out of hand.

What it challenges is the doctrine of progress, as

generally favoured by scientists and humanists. It opposes this, not in a spirit of romantic nostalgia, but with an alternative concept often worked out in detail. While admitting that progress has occurred, here and there and at various times, occultists maintain that progress is not the norm. Today they are joined by many others who have reached a similar state of mind. It is argued that the mental and spiritual history of mankind has never been a movement forward in any broad, unqualified sense. The typical pattern has been degeneration, countered by partial, piecemeal recovery – rather as if a clock were always running down and being wound up again.

The theme has several variations. Usually, however, there is said far back in the past to have been an Ancient Wisdom. It has existed for untold ages. At various periods, in various places, large portions of it have been widely known and applied. But it never lasts. In the historical phase most familiar to us, the past few thousand years, we can see both our science and our religions originating as parts of this greater whole. They distil out, so to speak; they develop along their own lines; but the development has loss in it as well as gain, and, in the deepest sense, more of the former. The Ancient Wisdom in its fullness has passed into eclipse. Science and religion have gone astray, giving narrow, distorted, often false views of the universe. Great truths have been perverted into dogmas and myths, their inner meaning no longer understood.

Occultists add a second major assertion. The Ancient Wisdom, though broken up and obscured, has never vanished beyond recall. Its survival, however, is no longer open to view, and a great deal of it takes the form of esoteric or magical doctrines which official orthodoxies despise because they do not understand. In such disguises it has been preserved by secret schools of initiates, and occasionally restored to the world in small doses. Parts of it have been handed down by continuous tradition, and released at suitable moments. Other parts, though entirely lost for millennia, have been reinstated among an elect few by higher beings who befriend humanity.

These higher beings are the Ancient Wisdom's custodians, and they taught it in the first place. They are sometimes described as 'Masters', perhaps incarnate as human beings, perhaps not. Many of the gods of legend were really Masters, who have since been ignorantly worshipped. Such was Krishna in India. Such, for tha matter, was Christ. The right-thinking occultist is in on the secret. Professedly he is helping to restore human knowledge and powers to what they ought to be, and what they actually were (at any rate for a much larger number) when the Wisdom flourished intact. The occult revival of the 1960s and 1970s has given this claim an optimistic, expansive turn. Mankind is alleged to be passing into an Aquarian Age which will be marked by increased openness. Restriction of enlightenment to small circles will no longer be necessary. The process of restoration will be speeded up – presumably by the will of the hidden Masters, and with their aid.

Whatever the prospect for the future may be, this higher Wisdom in the past is not purely a fantasy of modern eccentrics. It has antecedents. There is a link with many deep-rooted myths of a Golden Age. Among Hindus, indeed, the supposed Golden Age has an 'Ancient Wisdom' bias which partly explains the high value placed on Hinduism in occult quarters. That Age is pictured as an earlier, superior world-epoch when humanity was illumined by semi-divine Rishis or sages. Ever since then, darkness has been gradually closing in, though Krishna and other exalted beings have partly rekindled the light at intervals.

In the West, where mythology has been rather different, the occultists' conception of man's mental career can nevertheless be traced in respected circles. During the Renaissance something very like it (rather than progress) was even the norm of advanced thinking. When western Europe rediscovered classical literature, much more was read into it than was actually there. Special stress was laid on certain Greek books, the 'Hermetic' series, which pretended to record a lofty philosophy taught long before by the gods themselves. Openly or implicitly, some sort of Hermetic Wisdom theory – often with a strong element of magic – underlies the thought of several major figures of the sixteenth century: Paracelsus, for instance, one of the

4

founders of modern medicine; Giordano Bruno, apostle of the new astronomy of Copernicus; John Dee, mathematician, geographer, philosopher of religion and general polymath.[1]

A hundred years later, we find the greatest scientist of the age – one of the greatest in any age – still holding much the same convictions. Isaac Newton was mentally a Renaissance man and a believer in the ancient Hermetic revelation. In his own eyes he was only rediscovering what the sages of antiquity knew, but wrapped up in myths. According to Newton, Greek mystics who spoke of the music of the spheres were hinting at gravitation. The strings of Apollo's lyre corresponded to the planets. Their relative lengths corresponded to the planets' distances from the sun. The planets' names symbolize the Copernican system, if we read the cipher correctly. It was all there, all known, ages ago.[2]

So when occultists and their fellow-travellers talk of Ancient Wisdom, they can claim major supporters and an intellectual pedigree. After Newton the theory went into abeyance, but it was kept alive in other forms – notably by one man of sovereign genius, William Blake – and it returned with a flourish in 1875 with the foundation of the Theosophical Society. Most modern occultism derives from this. It derives, to be precise, from Theosophy's remarkable foundress, Helena Petrovna Blavatsky, 'HPB' as her followers call her.

Madame Blavatsky will be concerning us again. For the present it is enough to note that she drew on both the Indian and the Renaissance traditions; that she popularized (though she did not invent) the secret and semi-divine Masters, who taught, and perpetuate, the Ancient Wisdom; that she offered an array of alleged proofs, archaeological, mythological and otherwise, that this Wisdom lies in the background of all civilizations. We may also note that several of the sensational modern theories, without being strictly occult, are Madame Blavatsky's in science-fiction garb. One such is the notion that flying saucers are vehicles of higher beings, sky-people, who have been watching mankind for many centuries and have plans for it. Another is the notion of Erich von Däniken (and many

5

more) that the gods and heroes of legend are astronauts from outer space, who visited earth a long time ago bringing with them a superior culture, are responsible for most of the major works of antiquity, and may perhaps be expected to resume contact or even to return. The sky-people, the astronauts, are HPB's Masters of Ancient Wisdom in sci-fi disguise, setting civilization in motion and keeping an eye on it through its later declines and recoveries.[3]

2

Is there any evidence for an Ancient Wisdom?

That inquiry is the primary theme of this book. If a positive answer should emerge, we may go on to ask whether there is anything in the second part of the theory: that the sources of Ancient Wisdom are still active, so that human knowledge or powers may presently be heightened by fresh infusions. Some would say, by the re-opening of communication with the Masters; others, by renewal of contact with alien astronauts or advanced sky-people, who once landed on earth and taught its primitive tribes, and still have plenty to impart.

We are venturing, of course, into fringe country. Today the judgement of almost all orthodox scholars would be that Ancient Wisdom is not merely a conjecture but a useless one. History has no real problems which it would help to solve. There is no point in looking for it. Moreover, the idea of Ancient Wisdom defies the accepted pattern. Human societies, it is assumed, do progress. Their progress may be erratic, they may attain civilization and then crumble into barbarism, but they never start from a high point. The notion of a superior Something at the beginning is chimerical.

However, the Wisdom theory is subtler, or at least it can be put more subtly. It need not imply that there was ever a complete higher civilization, coming more or less from nowhere, which then declined. Ancient Wisdom could have spread from some centre through a kind of missionary activity – a teaching of certain myths, doctrines, or scientific concepts. These, we might suppose, were planted in nascent societies which afterwards applied them in varying degrees, but did not alway make any progress from them, and sometimes forgot or debased them.

Views along this line have been proposed in the past by scholars of repute. In Germany, for instance, a Pan-Babylonian theory was once popular. It averred that Babylon, thousands of years ago, had a sophisticated religious system based on astronomy, which embodied a good deal of genuine knowledge. Greek mythology was based on it, and so was the religion of Israel, but both lost touch with their origins and sank into unscientific fantasy. When Pan-Babylonism was found to be unconvincing, an English school of thought devised a Pan-Egyptianism of much the same type. These systems are no longer in favour, but they were never purely ridiculous. A modern author, Joseph Campbell, has tried to trace most of the basics of civilization the world over – writing, for example, and decimal counting, and time measurement, and the wheel – to a single highly inventive Sumerian priesthood about 3200 B.C.[4]

If the notion of Ancient Wisdom is put like this, it becomes more arguable. Until lately, of course, all prehistorians would still have insisted that it went against the fact of progress. Ancient societies always started in virtual savagery. Systems of thought such as astronomy or mathematics had to evolve in settings where a degree of civilization had already been reached. We never find them dropped from an unidentifiable Otherwhere into the midst of an undeveloped culture, and then helping to develop it. That was the assumption, but it is no longer as secure as it seemed to be. Professor Thom, for instance, has managed to convince archaeologists that ancient circles of standing stones were lunar observatories, implying exact observation and calculation. Megalithic Britain is beginning to afford glimpses of a phenomenon that is out of line with progressive dogma. Here was a prehistoric society with a strange, unfamiliar pattern, barbaric in some ways yet advanced in others, with crude technology and no known writing, yet also with solid intellectual attainments which it is hard to picture evolving in such a setting.

Anomalies like this are slowly coming to light in prehistory, and they pose genuine problems. If anything could point to an imported Wisdom, such an anomaly might be it. Do the megaliths themselves furnish a clue? Probably not yet. Despite Professor Thom, and others, they are still too inscrutable to have a clear message. But might we identify a clue somewhere else, in an early society that is better understood, or in several? Gazing back through the millennia, can we detect any peculiarity in the mental or imaginative handling of life which seems not to fit, not to explain itself; which could suggest the planting of a seed from outside – whether by missionaries, aliens, or theosophical Masters?

Occultists and their kin have made many such claims. Most of what they say is unhelpful. Snatching at all sorts of historical problems and non-problems, they have 'solved' them by postulating influence from whatever mysterious source they wish to believe in. Several early civilizations, it is often asserted, appear suddenly with no trace of a prior gradual development . . . ergo, they didn't develop; they were founded ready-made, by colonists from the lost Atlantis of myth, where the higher Wisdom was once enthroned. Geology indicates that no large tract of the Atlantic sea-bed has been above water for millions of years. Occult enlightenment, however, has its ways of getting around such obstacles. Atlantis had to exist, therefore it existed. Theosophists and others have proclaimed not only lost Atlantis but lost Lemuria, a similar continent sunk beneath the Pacific. Some have also alleged a sort of world spiritual headquarters in, or under, the Gobi Desert, founded by higher beings from Venus eighteen million years ago.

The very weirdness of such theories, and their incompatibility with non-occult data, seem to count in their favour rather than against them. Even when an occultist veers towards a recognized view, something nearly always turns out to be different. The Russian magus Gurdjieff said Christianity was taken from Egypt, a statement which might suggest that he agreed with the Pan-Egyptian school. But no: Christianity, he hastened to explain, was not taken

8

from the Egypt of history, but from a 'far older Egypt' which is unrecorded.[5]

When we turn to occult-derivative writers like von Däniken, who have given Ancient Wisdom a sci-fi dress, we find them thinking in the same style with a different emphasis. Their classic clues are mysterious ancient arte-facts, structures, pictures, legends. These, it is alleged, cannot be accounted for except by supposing that civilized aliens from another world left their mark on this one. A Saharan cave-painting is said to portray a man in a space helmet. A relief on a Maya tomb is said to portray a man in a rocket. And so on. The barrage of pseudo-scientific data looks more impressive than the occultists' 'proofs' of, say, Atlantis, which tend to appeal to dubious traditions or revelations. But with most authors who argue in this manner, the case fails at the other end. Its Atlantis never surfaces. It fails to lead back to any single locale that can be pinned down, any specific place where the wise visitors may be thought to have landed. The argument is simply a blur spreading out all over the world. Anything may have happened anywhere. We get no hypothesis that can be tested. And if we take a closer look at the evidence itself, it dwindles to a point where even the vague feeling that 'there must be something in it' hardly survives.[6]

3

Apparently, then, the advocates of Ancient Wisdom do little to help others to run it to earth and bear them out. This at least is the broad impression. We may still ask (and will shortly do so) whether there is any exception; whether, somewhere in the jungle, there is a trail after all, an occult clue to Ancient Wisdom which is what it purports to be and does lead back to a possible reality. However, if we are to pursue this question, a certain authority will need to be borne in mind and recalled at intervals. The first reason for this is that he is the only modern man of his stature who has taken occultism seriously, and discussed it in such a way as to aid anyone else who explores it. The second reason is that he is the author of a theory which seems, on the face of it, to block any argument we might hit on, and must therefore be taken carefully into account.

I am speaking of Dr Carl Gustav Jung. Famous during his lifetime as the great disciple of Freud who broke with him and became the great heretic; as the founder of the Zurich school of psychiatry; as the guru of a swarm of clinicians calling themselves 'analytical psychologists' instead of 'psychoanalysts' – Jung has since blossomed into a patron saint of the whole revival of occultism, magic and myth. Over the past half-century or so, his schema of the human psyche has been one of the strongest factors in the rebirth of such interests. More influential than any of his ideas has been his attitude. Jung was willing – in defiance of other scientists, including his own mentor Freud – to treat occultism and myth with sincere respect. He investigated alchemy and astrology, numerology and geometrical symbols, even flying saucers, not as superstitious or morbid symptoms but as valid clues to human nature and human experience.

However, although he built up a general and well-known concept which conferred status on such things, the same concept condemns the explanation of them which we are now considering. Jung had no use for an underlying Ancient Wisdom, because he had another way of handling such facts as might seem to favour it – or at least, the majority of them. The main feature of his psychology, as distinct from Freud's, is the Collective Unconscious. Eleven thousand dreams reported to him by his patients led him towards it. Below the conscious threshold, he said, we all possess not only a personal unconscious but a much vaster psychic inheritance which is not personal. It is the same in everybody – a system of patterns or 'archetypes' built into the brain. Working to the surface through each person's individual equipment, the Collective Unconscious has a profound effect on dreams. But it is behind many other things as well – seemingly preternatural happenings, feats of imagination and intuition, myths. These last are not mere fantasy. They are the wisdom of the Collective Unconscious breaking through in symbolic forms, which whole human societies can adopt as their common property and organize their world with. The same

10

is true, in a more restricted way, of magic, and that is why magical notions should never be brushed aside. They may not be literally true, but they can give us illuminating insights into the deeper recesses of human nature.

If we are to attempt any inferences backward in time to an Ancient Wisdom, this Collective Unconscious is a potential obstacle. Suppose, for example, that we were to find several early nations all attaching mystic importance to a diagram of a cross in a circle. It turns up in various myths and works of art, which cannot have influenced each other. We might feel inclined to say, Aha! they must all have got it from an earlier common source, an ancient system which used that diagram as a symbol, and was carried far and wide by wandering teachers. We are certainly on the track of something here. Jung would reply: Not so. There is no need for a common source, and you can't draw any conclusions about historical happenings. If you look at drawings made by my patients, and at records of their dreams, you'll see that that diagram is just an archetypal pattern, which the Collective Unconscious throws up. Any number of people may have hit on it independently and felt that it came to them like an inspiration, because the Collective Unconscious is the same everywhere, and has been the same for millennia.

Many arguments for an Ancient Wisdom will be similar to the one above, if not quite so naive. Hence, the Jungian method of explaining-away, of dismissing phenomena as 'all in the mind', is a barrier. Whatever we may think of Jung, we must at least remember him as we go along, and see not only whether his occult studies shed light but whether any evidence that may emerge can rebut his type of criticism. In a broader sense this is not confined to Jung. Freud himself did the same kind of explaining-away after a cruder fashion, making out almost everything to be sexual imagery. Others have tried to explain all mythology as, for example, sun-myths or vegetation-myths, from which it would follow that mythology is imagination and nothing more, has nothing to do with history, and can never disclose anything that actually happened or existed – such as Ancient Wisdom.

From the fate of these latter thinkers, however, we can

draw comfort and fortify our hearts to some extent against Jung himself. With mythology at least, the 'all-in-the-mind' view has been tested and found wanting. It has been proved wrong many times, chiefly by archaeologists. A factual, historical element very often does exist. You do not dispose of a legend merely by saying that it reflects the Oedipus complex, or something similarly of the mind or the imagination. It may indeed reflect the Oedipus complex, but it may also be a clue to historical fact, none the less.

Long before psychologists came on the scene at all, classical scholars proved that Troy was a literary figment. Then Heinrich Schliemann dug it up. Biblical scholars torpedoed Noah's Ark by finding parallels to the story of the Flood in Mesopotamia, so that it had to be just a story and nothing more. Then Leonard Woolley discovered traces of an immense flood in that very area. The same sort of upset has happened in Crete, Palestine, Mexico and elsewhere – dismissal of mythology by scholars as pure fiction, and then proof by archaeologists that there is some truth in it.

Of course the romanticist is wrong too when he infers from these results that the tale of Troy, or the tale of Noah, is factually true in detail. That is not the point. The point is that mythology can and should be taken seriously, and not merely in an inward, mental or psychological sense. It is an amalgam which often has a historical content too substantial to ignore. The occultists, the astronaut-seekers, and all their kind, who use mythology to reconstruct a remote past and an Ancient Wisdom embedded in it, have at least the right to claim that their method *can* be valid, *need* not be completely irrational.

We shall be trying it ourselves, if with a shade more caution. At the same time we shall keep the great figure of Jung in view, and test our findings by seeing whether his 'archetypes' can explain away whatever data we come upon. If not, we can be all the more confident about pressing onward to trace the outline of a reality behind the data: an Ancient Wisdom far back in history, or prehistory, scattering seeds of mental growth in early societies we already know.

12

Not necessarily all the early societies. We are not required to be as ambitious and world-embracing as most modern theorists. We are under no obligation to find a single Wisdom branching out over the whole earth and underlying every culture. There may have been several, with different spheres of influence. Or there may have been only one that did not reach everywhere. It will be ample if we can detect even one.

CHAPTER TWO

Secret Doctrine?

1

In all the fantasy which occultists have deployed, can we isolate a single clue that really does lead somewhere, really does point to an arguable Wisdom (or whatever we care to call it) that is prior to known cultures? I believe we can. I do not defend the way it has been presented, or the inferences that have been drawn. All the same it exists, and survives scrutiny. If followed resolutely for long enough, it does lead in a certain direction. It enables us to delimit a certain part of the earth's surface, and say: 'Something happened here. If Masters of Ancient Wisdom ever lived, this is a likely place for them to have been. If superior aliens from another planet ever landed and instructed mankind, this is a likely place for them to have done it. And perhaps we can go on to test the possibility further.' Even to get as far as that modest claim, the path is long and roundabout. But the path is there, and the sights along the way are unfamiliar and interesting.

To find the clue we must go to the originator of modern occultism, Madame Blavatsky, HPB. As has been observed, a number of theorists like von Däniken owe a debt (usually unacknowledged) to her account of the human species and its career. She founded the Theosophical Society in 1875. Within a few years it was beginning to exert a powerful and widely diffused influence, not only in itself but through people affected by it who rose to prominence in ways of their own. Indirectly it inspired other esoteric revivals such as the Order of the Golden Dawn, which included W. B. Yeats among its members, as well as the fantasy-writers Algernon Blackwood and Arthur Machen, and the notorious neo-magician Aleister Crowley. Theosophy spawned the breakaway Rudolf Steiner movement and its work in education. Partly through Annie Besant – who was converted by reading one of HPB's books, and afterwards threw herself into the politics of India – it had its impact on Gandhi, the Nehrus, and other leaders of Indian nationalism. It moulded best-selling fiction; Conan Doyle's story *The Maracot Deep*, Edgar Rice Burroughs's romances of Mars, even the bizarre mythology of H. P. Lovecraft, all have theosophical antecedents. It also influenced modish pseudo-science, notably the strange account of the solar system and earthly prehistory devised by Hans Hörbiger in the 1920s, which played a part in Nazism and carried over into the speculations of H. S. Bellamy and Immanuel Velikovsky.

Theosophy, which set all these things in motion, can hardly be dismissed out of hand as altogether vapid and unsubstantial. It may be completely false. It may be – in fact it probably is – largely false. But the mind behind it, however untrustworthy, was active, acquisitive, formidable. What concerns us here is not to appraise HPB's teaching as a whole, but to ask whether any specific ingredient stands out from the rest; whether, woven somewhere into the complex fabric, there is an idea which an impartial mind must admit to being in favour of Ancient Wisdom. It will appear, I think, that this is so.[1]

Madame Blavatsky's chief works are *Isis Unveiled* (1877) and *The Secret Doctrine* (1888). The second of these is more important. The theosophical Ancient Wisdom is built into a colossal scheme of world history, which makes out the human species to be much older than palaeontologists suppose even today. HPB sought to rescue a more or less religious world-view from the onslaughts of Darwin and his followers, not by contradicting them as Christians foolishly did, but by outdoing them. In her scheme humanity has existed for countless millions of years, evolving through cycles and mutations in which almost anything affirmed by any religion or mythology can be held, in some sense, to have happened. For instance, legends of cities in lost continents can be squared with geology. If the face of the earth takes interminable epochs

15

to change, that does not matter: there were always human being around. Stories of dragons can be grounded on a tradition of dinosaurs. And so on.

Humanity, we are told, is passing through seven evolutionary forms called root-races, each divided into seven sub-races. The first root-race was purely astral. One of its sub-races grew into the second root-race, the Hyperboreans, who were a little more solid but still not strictly physical; they lived in a continent of which Greenland, Spitzbergen and northern Asia are remnants. The third root-race lived in Lemuria, now mostly under the Pacific. Some of their sub-races resembled humanity as we know it, and were instructed in useful arts by visitors from Venus. The fourth root-race was made up of the highly civilized inhabitants of Atlantis. Several peoples known to history, such as the Toltecs in Mexico, began as Atlantean sub-races, at a far earlier date than is normally assigned to them. The fifth root-race comprised the Aryans, and we are still living under the Aryan dispensation, though many descendants of the previous races are still extant. Two more root-races are yet to come.

Central to Theosophy is the saga of the semi-divine Masters or 'Mahatmas', who have guided mankind through many triumphs and failures, and who, at sundry times, have taught the eternal Wisdom. This Wisdom is a vast system of truths about cosmic law, the nature of man, reincarnation, and other matters. In the past few millennia it has gone through a phase of disintegration and perversion. But all religions and mythologies are based on it, and transmit pieces of it. Hinduism and Buddhism, one gathers, are closest to it, and India and Tibet are the countries with most to teach. The Ancient Wisdom can be reconstituted – to some extent – by comparing religions and mythologies, extracting what they have in common, and applying 'keys' that unlock the symbolism behind their gods and heroes. The keys involve numbers and geometrical symbols.

According to Madame Blavatsky, Paracelsus and the other magus-scientists were initiates who knew at least some of the keys, and kept esoteric truth alive. Reaching back further into the past, she cites various archaeological enigmas to support what she says about the earlier races, the mentors who guided them, their status and powers. She discusses Stonehenge, Carnac in Brittany, and Easter Island. Thus she blazes a trail which many subsequent speculators have followed. More recent apostles of Ancient Wisdom have carried on in her style, and taken up her hints. Like her, they introduce us to lost continents and civilizations. Like her, they reconstruct the past out of myths and legends and dubious archaeology, and appeal to unsolved problems, real and alleged. Like her, some of them suggest that adepts and occult traditions have handed on secrets. Also like her, several offer numerical and geometrical keys. One such is 'Fulcanelli', putative author of a book called *The Mystery of the Cathedrals*, which purports to show that a kind of super-science derived from antiquity is concealed in Gothic architecture. Another, with a more interesting case, is John Michell, who also makes much of sacred measurements, and has advanced the theory of 'ley lines' – straight lines joining ancient sacred sites – as preserving clues to the magical arts of pre-Christian Britain.

When HPB worked out her own, parent system she maintained that she was not working it out at all. It had been dictated to her by Masters or Mahatmas, still living in remote fastnesses and influencing world events. She was in telepathic touch with them, or, at least, with one or two who took a special interest in her. Furthermore she had read ancient texts, unknown to anybody else, such as the 'Book of Dzyan'. She could also recover the past intuitively by a sort of astral tuning-in. *The Secret Doctrine* was the book that converted Annie Besant and thereby secured the theosophical succession. In it, HPB does not pretend to be restoring the complete Ancient Wisdom, for which mankind is not ready. Indeed she does not pretend to have all the keys herself. The book is *about* Ancient Wisdom rather than a full exposition, sketching its nature as a synthesis of science, religion and philosophy. Religion and philosophy as we know them are corrupted bits of it, in so far as they are true; while science is either rediscovering its grand insights or (more frequently) mistaken. The sum of present knowledge is less than the lost whole. Occultism alone preserves techniques for working back from what we possess to what we have lost. These techniques include getting in touch with the Masters. Luckily they also include methods of argument which can be pinned down and tested.

The Secret Doctrine is a huge, shapeless, amateurish book, often obscure. A good deal of it is plagiarized, yet it has features which inspire respect. For instance, when HPB discusses comparative religion and mythology, she points to recurrent themes, images and so forth, such as dragons in unconnected contexts, which may be held to imply a common source of ideas. Parallels of this kind are a mainstay of the Jungian type of thinking mentioned in the previous chapter – the thinking which rejects any historical inference from mythology on the ground that it is all in the imagination, archetypal or whatever, and tells us nothing of events that actually happened. People in different countries think of dragons because the Collective Unconscious makes them do so, not because all dragon traditions have a common source, much less because dragons ever existed. I have said that archaeology has undermined such opinions, at least where the subject-matter is more human and less exotic. Although it seldom proves legends to be true, it does often prove that they have something solid behind them – Troy, for instance. When Madame Blavatsky was writing, the study of mythology was dominated by a school of thought which explained everything as sun-myths. In defiance of professional scholarship, HPB did know better. She was ahead of her time.

> [The present writer] is one of those who feel convinced that no mythological story, no traditional event in the folk-lore of a people has ever been, at any time, pure fiction, but that every one of such narratives has an actual, historical lining to it. In this the writer disagrees with those mythologists, however great their reputation, who find in every myth nothing save additional proofs of the superstitious bent of mind of the ancients, and believe that all mythologies sprung from and are built upon *solar myths*.
>
> (*The Secret Doctrine*, Vol. I, p. 303)

While this utterer of Ancient Wisdom is wrong, very wrong indeed, as an exact scholar, she shows here an intuitive rightness which scholars have repeatedly lacked.

In her view, all the themes of mythology are 'exoteric' fragments of the single great system, expounded millions of years ago and elaborated since. It includes much history, including the history of its own development. When translated 'esoterically' with the aid of her keys, all myths and legends and religious motifs can be seen as parts of the great system, linking up and harmonizing because that is what they are. The Ancient Wisdom of the Masters must have existed, because this could not happen by chance, any more than a cipher key applied to a jumble of letters could produce a message unless the message was there to start with.

Fair enough in theory. In practice, most of the Blavatsky keys are of doubtful value. Even when she applies them it is hard to see what enlightenment they bring. But she has one theme that stands out and compels attention. Her series of human races and sub-races will already have indicated its nature. It is *the magical and sacred character of the number seven*.

In *The Secret Doctrine* she presents seven as the supreme number of the higher mysteries. This is not entirely original. She draws on an earlier work by Gerald Massey, a Victorian poet and critic who built up a highly original Egyptology. But she goes much further than he does. Besides her seven races she emphasizes the seven 'planets' of Western astrology, and, in explaining why the Wisdom has been confined for so long to a few initiates, says that this number is a key to dangerous forces.

> Doctrines such as the planetary chain, or the seven races, at once give a clue to the seven-fold nature of man, for each principle is correlated to a plane, a planet, and a race; and the human principles are, on every plane, correlated to seven-fold occult forces – those of the higher planes being of tremendous power. So that any septenary division at once gives a clue to tremendous occult powers, the abuse of which would cause incalculable evil to humanity.
>
> (Vol. I, p. xxxv)

She draws attention to numerous biblical and Christian sevens – seven days of creation, seven archangels, and so forth – claiming, of course, that these are mere superficial images of deeper realities. She speaks of the Wisdom as having been taught by seven sages. She stresses the fact that there are seven recognized vowel sounds. In these ways and in others she reverts to the number, time and again. It is 'the special representative, or *Factor* number' of this present life-cycle.[2]

Significant heptads – some real like the seven-day week, some probably invented by HPB – are sprinkled through the packed pages of *The Secret Doctrine*. On the whole, this septenary dogma is a special Blavatsky theme. It is not developed very much by her successors, though another well-known occultist, Gurdjieff, has some sevens of his own (seven human types, seven cosmoses, a 'law of seven' interpreting vibrations).[3] More notice should have been taken of it. However wild *The Secret Doctrine* may be in general, its stress on this number is acute. If we consider seven impartially, certain facts about it become plain, and all of them suggest that perhaps – just perhaps – Madame Blavatsky has got hold of a thread that is worth following.

2

To begin with, if there are indeed any such things as occult clues to Ancient Wisdom, the number seven looks as if it could qualify. Two major sciences did emerge from magical systems which, in their Western forms, were grounded on seven. Astronomy emerged from astrology, chemistry from alchemy; and astrology and alchemy were mystically linked by this number, which was supposed to be fundamental to both, and to relate them together in a greater whole.

A word of explanation is needed. Newspaper astrology today (fortunately there is no newspaper alchemy) conveys the impression that horoscopes depend on twelve rather than seven. Your sign of the Zodiac is the sign the sun was in at your birth, and there are twelve of these, sky-sectors

A medieval alchemists' diagram showing the symbols of the Seven Metals within their corresponding planets

named from constellations. But newspaper astrology is a debased version. The sun is only one of the seven so-called planets or wandering bodies which, in the Western world, astrology has relied on. The Zodiac has little specific meaning apart from their movements through it.

For more than two thousand years astrologers worked not only with the sun, but with the moon and the five true planets known as such, Mercury, Venus, Mars, Jupiter and Saturn. Their modern heirs have tried to add the three planets discovered since, Uranus, Neptune and Pluto, but the results have seldom carried conviction. For all vital purposes, Western astrology has always been a septenary system, based on the 'planets' wandering through the signs, the Seven interpreting and channelling the Twelve, and exerting influences of their own. (Madame Blavatsky makes the point in her own inimitable manner. Her all-wise ancients knew that there are more planets, but they picked out the seven that really count as influences, and revealed only these to the wider public.)

The planets have their alchemic counterparts. Western alchemy may well have begun with the realization – perhaps about 200 B.C. – that just as seven planets were known, so, at that time, seven metals were known. A spiritual lore of metals, with gold as chief, spawned a fertile system from which chemistry was presently to disentangle itself. Each metal was matched to a ruling planet. The sun, naturally, had gold; the moon, silver; Saturn, lead; Jupiter, tin; Mars, iron; Venus, copper; and Mercury, the metal formerly called liquid silver or quick-silver, which owes its present name 'mercury' to this astral scheme. Right through to the Renaissance it was believed that metals grew in the earth, and that the growth of each was nourished by its governing planet. Mines were shut down at intervals to allow the planet to renew the supply.[4]

Whether or not this branch of occult science gave Madame Blavatsky her idea, it shows that she did not spin it out of her own fancies. Many of her mystic sevens are highly suspect, but she lays her finger on a genuine problem, a human quirk that has no obvious motive. In itself the pairing-off of metals with planets might seem trivial, a mere chance exploited by superstition, implying nothing about the number as such. But the frequency of seven in other contexts (the Bible, for instance) proves that we are confronted here with a deep-seated mental reality which deserves attention.

Moreover – this is a second outstanding fact – the spell

of seven is not of purely esoteric or antiquarian interest. Whether or not because of any Wisdom enciphered in it, it really does seem to underlie much of the shaping of Western culture. It has bitten into our mental conditioning.

We will schedule our work and leisure by the seven-day week. Its stubborn survival has no logic or convenience. A different week with a non-prime number of days could be made divisible into halves, thirds, quarters. Or if divisibility does not matter, our week has the undoubted awkwardness of not fitting into the year an exact number of times: which is why Christmas, for example, falls on a different day each year. A five-day week would fit. Or we could keep fifty-two weeks of seven days, making 364, with the odd one over as a holiday by itself, giving an unvarying calendar; but no, the cycle of seven is too sacrosanct to allow even that exemption. Every single day has to belong to it. In spite of the results it has triumphed and endured, supplanting handier time-schemes, and defying reformers' efforts to break its hold. It is not 'natural'; it never appeared spontaneously in the Orient, or Africa, or America; it was imposed by what was, for a time, the world's ascendant culture, the nominally Christian culture of Europe. But where did Europe get it from, and how did Europe come to be so firmly committed to it? In what essential package was it an item?

That is only the beginning. Most human beings who have lived by the seven-day week, as a native inheritance, have also attuned their ears to a seven-note scale and made their music with this for many centuries. A physical fact does underlie its length. If you start from C, the next C, an octave higher, has twice the vibration-rate. But the seven steps on the way, CDEFGAB, are a product of conditioning. The Chinese do not have them. Their scale consists of five notes, CDEGA.

So likewise with optics. We insist on regarding the spectrum as having seven colours, violet, indigo, blue, green, yellow, orange, red. A panel of innocent-eyed observers, looking at a rainbow, would be unlikely to agree. Does anybody truly distinguish indigo from the colours on either side of it? The Chinese, to cite them

23

again, count differently. A Chinese myth tells how a primordial giant shattered the heavens, and the world's divine ruler searched for someone who would restore them, till at last he succeeded: 'From the eastern sea arose the ruleress, the heavenly Ny-uka, shining in her armour of flames. She forged the *five* colours of the rainbow in her magic forge and restored the heavens.[5]

With our chemistry born from an alchemy of seven metals, and our astronomy born from an astrology of seven planets, the same is true. Far back in time is a powerful pressure which has not yet been explained. Westerners (or their cultural forbears in the nearer part of Asia) felt obliged to have seven metals, to match the planets. They felt obliged to have seven planets, because ... well, because of what? The number was vital, and that, for the moment, is all we can safely say. The list of planets was made up by the Babylonians' decision – an odd one, if you compare the bodies concerned – to give the sun and moon the same status as Mercury, Venus, Mars, Jupiter and Saturn, the five true planets that could be seen before telescopes. Here, again, the heptad had nothing natural or inevitable about it. Early Iranian astrology had nine planets. So did the Hindu astrology that was derived from it. The Chinese, as in other cases, settled on five, the correct list without the sun and moon.[6]

Behind Western man's organization of his world, of time and sound and colour and matter and the heavens, the septenary hovers. To that extent at any rate, Madame Blavatsky is right. To that extent she succeeds in establishing a truth. So, when she asserts that this truth is a key to Ancient Wisdom, we are justified in asking whether any meaning can be attached to her statement, and in studying it with more respect than most such claims deserve.

That justification is stronger in the light of a third outstanding fact. The dominance of seven has thus far defeated all explainers-away. It does not yield to any known technique of psychological analysis. The reason for it seems to lie in some other direction. Here is our first test for Jung's ideas, and they fail; indeed Jung most curiously evades the problem. He goes on at great length about other numbers he deems important, seeking to show how they express his archetypes, and how they produce various myths and numerical obsessions. Three and four are his favourites. As for seven, it escapes him.

Yet he knows it to be important. In one of his most copious case-histories the patient dreamed about his father 'calling out anxiously, "That is the seventh!"' Jung comments that 'in the language of initiation, "seven" stands for the highest stage of illumination and would therefore be the coveted goal of all desire'. To judge from this and from the rest of the passage, seven ought to be a master-number in his own therapeutic scheme. His writings, however, dodge the issue, as if he could not see how to handle seven, could not work out a psychological interpretation. Another of his patients drew a design with a line spiralling inwards to a centre, making seven circuits. Jung's note reacts to this drawing with an out-of-character brusqueness as 'poor in form, poor in ideas', and goes into other aspects of the diagram without once mentioning its septenary formation.[7]

His forays into myth and the occult turned up a fair assortment of manifestly mystical sevens. But they never yielded to his analysis. He cited the Seven Sleepers of Ephesus as symbolizing rebirth, and was then left with the burden of explaining why there were seven of them. (Compare, in lighter vein, *Three Men in a Boat*: 'We shouted back loud enough to wake the Seven Sleepers – I never could understand myself why it should take more noise to waken seven sleepers than one.') He met with groupings of seven gods, initiations in seven grades, even what he himself called the 'hidden magical Septenary' in alchemy, yet no reason for them ever presented itself. The nearest he came to probing below the surface was to pause briefly on the notion of a prototype-seven which might account for all the rest, and for the number's apparent fascination. The prototype, he thought, was the astrologers' set of planets with their presiding deities. He brought them in to illustrate the 'that is the seventh' dream, and also to cope with the Seven Sleepers, who, he says, 'indicate by their sacred number that they are gods', that is, 'the planetary gods of the ancients'. The suggestion

25

about the planets had been put forward by Franz Cumont, an authority on the Mithraic cult, and it is echoed by others besides Jung.

It does not work. Western astrology began with the astral lore of Babylon, and the list of seven planets was not fixed even there till long after the mystic seven had planted itself in Mesopotamian, Hebrew and Greek religion, as we shall shortly see. Astrology did not reach the Greeks till the fourth century before Christ, and did not come to maturity there till later still, when they assigned gods of their own to the planets and exploited the implications. Jung's 'planetary gods of the ancients' are not known as such till the last two centuries B.C. A glance at a Bible concordance (to go no further) will show that seven carried a special weight long before that. It looks, in fact, as if the Babylonians chose to have seven planets because of a pre-existing mystique of the heptad.[8]

Thus far, then, the clue comes through safely. Its mystery is intact. Perhaps it actually is a key. Further progress requires that we study seven's behaviour in more detail.

CHAPTER THREE

The Prevalence of the Heptad

1

An interesting qualification has already emerged. It would not suit Madame Blavatsky, but it holds out hope for less prejudiced inquirers. The seven-mystique seems to have geographic limits. Thus far it seems to belong to Europe, and at an earlier stage to the countries of nearer Asia, where much of Europe's civilization is rooted. Elsewhere it is absent, or, at any rate, less obtrusive. If it is a clue at all, it is a clue with a shape. The problem is in no danger of spreading out in a Dänikenesque blur all over the world. Geographic limits, of course, restrict the scope of any Ancient Wisdom that may lie in the background. No matter. There could have been several Wisdoms, active in different regions of the earth. Enough, for the present, if the mystical quality of seven puts us on the track of one of them.

Perhaps we can be more exact still. Take the European seven-day week. This is biblical. It is based on a Jewish religious custom which was adopted by Christianity, and then propagated by Christian nations. Is that by any chance the whole secret? Can we trace the origin of the seven-mystique to the religion of Israel, as set forth in the Old Testament, with no need of any other source? If so, this particular quest for Ancient Wisdom is at an end – a dead end. The religion of Israel cannot qualify. It was neither ancient enough nor influential enough. Greek philosophy, to look no further, was not derived from Moses. Nevertheless the Israelite tradition looks as if it can help somehow in defining our clue and making it more precise, even if the way it can help is not instantly apparent.

27

Scripture offers a great deal more besides the seven-day week. It has a whole medley of plainly significant sevens in other contexts.

The number is linked with wisdom in the Bible itself, as Madame Blavatsky, in one of her more felicitous moments, pointed out. Here is the passage which she cites:

> Wisdom has built her house,
>> she has set up her seven pillars.
> She has slaughtered her beasts, she has mixed her wine,
>> she has also set her table.
> She has sent out her maids to call
>> from the highest places in the town . . .
> 'Come, eat of my bread
>> and drink of the wine I have mixed . . .
> Live, and walk in the way of insight.'

This comes from the ninth chapter of Proverbs. It occurs in one of those scriptural backwaters which few readers explore, yet which are apt to harbour amazing things. The Lady Wisdom is more than a poetic abstraction, she is a demi-goddess whose place in the Jewish scheme of things is frankly anomalous. In the previous chapter she has made her entrance, calmly asserting that she was born before the world; even hinting that she helped God to bring order out of primal chaos.

> 'The Lord created me at the beginning of his work,
>> the first of his acts of old . . .
> When he established the heavens, I was there,
>> when he drew a circle on the face of the deep . . .
> When he marked out the foundations of the earth,
>> then I was beside him, like a master workman;
> And I was daily his delight,
>> rejoicing before him always,
> rejoicing in his inhabited world
>> and delighting in the sons of men.'

Wisdom's presence beside the male and single Lord Yahweh is an awkward crux for orthodoxy, suggestive of something breaking in from outside. Unperturbed by the trouble she is causing, she descends to earth, installs herself in that seven-pillared house, takes on domestic staff, and invites the public to a symposium. Though pious Jewish commentators tried to reduce her to an allegory, she is more than that. She reappears in the Apocrypha, notably the book of Ben-Sira or Ecclesiasticus, chapter 24, where she is so exuberantly a person rather than a symbol that the Catholic church annexed the description of her to Mary. Who Wisdom is, what flaw in Jewish monotheism let her through, are riddles that remain unsolved by frontal attack. There are grounds for thinking that she is based partly on the Canaanite goddess Anath – and Anath opens a door on a much higher antiquity than any book of the Bible.[1]

At this stage, however, it is Wisdom's seven-pillared house that demands attention. This is a strange number of pillars for a house to have. Where would they be? If they were lined up at the front in a colonnade, the middle one would block the centre, and push the doorway unsymmetrically aside. If arranged at the corners they would make the house heptagonal, a clumsy, unsettling shape. If arranged along an aisle, three on the left, four on the right, they would obtrusively not balance. Some other layout seems to be implied, an unusual layout with a preordained reason. Wisdom has to have *seven* pillars. With that number, as rabbinic exegesis accepts, her nature is bound up.

Why? Snap answers, such as 'Wisdom has seven pillars because the lampstand in the Jewish Temple had seven branches', merely alter the form of the question. However phrased, it looms large in the Old Testament. Proverbs, though placed before the Prophets in the biblical order, is one of the latest written books. But earlier ones offer enough sets of seven, in enough variety, to prove this a number of ancestral as well as polyhedral virtue in Israel.

Right at the beginning there are seven days of Creation. Noah is given seven days to load the Ark, and told to take seven pairs of all 'clean' animals. Abraham gives Abimelech seven lambs in token of an oath. Jacob serves Laban seven years for each of his wives. Pharaoh dreams about seven cows, seven ears of grain. The Law of Moses spells out the seven-day week, with its prototype in the days of

Creation. It also dictates a long-term economic cycle based on seven years and seven-times-seven, the Jubilee. Bezalel makes a lampstand for the Tabernacle with seven lamps. Balak sacrifices seven bulls and seven rams on seven altars. The Israelites conquer the Promised Land by defeating seven nations. Solomon celebrates the opening of his Temple with a festival that lasts seven days (or according to some readings, twice seven). Elijah sends a servant seven times to look at the weather. Naaman is cured of leprosy by washing seven times in the Jordan. Zechariah sees visions of a seven-faceted stone in front of the High Priest, and of another lampstand with seven lamps, said to be 'the eyes of God which range through the whole earth'. The extreme instance, excluding all possibility of chance, is the fall of Jericho. Joshua's army marches round it on seven successive days with seven priests blowing trumpets, and on the seventh day they march round seven times and shout, and the walls collapse and the city is taken.[2]

Seven, therefore, has a sacred and special power, of very long standing, yet not for any obvious reason. The Old Testament identifies no single holy heptad which all the rest are reflecting. Other texts complicate matters further by revealing a colloquial use, rather like 'half-a-dozen' in English. Israel's vanquished enemies are to scatter in seven directions. Naomi's daughter-in-law Ruth is more to her than seven sons. The Lord's blessing enables the barren woman to bear seven children. In a shortage of male population, seven women, it is foretold, will be pursuing one man.[3]

Though not to be explained from within the Old Testament; the septenary of ancient Israel is so potent that it branches out into three religious systems following on from it: Judaism, Christianity and Islam.

According to the Jews' apocryphal lore, seven supreme angels stand in the Lord's presence. Rabbis divided the earth into seven continents, the celestial regions into seven heavens. They recognized seven chief names of God, and the pronunciation of the holiest of these, YHVH, is said to have been taught by sages to their disciples once in seven years. The human body, they maintained, is composed of seven ingredients.[4]

Christianity inherited Jewish sevens with Jewish scripture, and added many more of its own. Christ taught a prayer in seven petitions:

Our Father who art in heaven, hallowed be thy
name,
Thy kingdom come,
Thy will be done in earth, as it is in heaven.
Give us this day our daily bread.
And forgive us our trespasses, as we forgive them
that trespass against us.
And lead us not into temptation,
But deliver us from evil.

In the Gospels, Christ speaks seven times on the cross. The Fourth Gospel describes seven miracles worked by him. The New Testament's final book, the Apocalypse or Revelation, introduces the number no less than fifty-four times in a long and varied series of groupings: seven churches, seven candlesticks, seven stars, seven spirits before God's throne, seven seals, a seven-horned and seven-eyed lamb, seven angels, seven trumpets, seven thunders, a seven-headed dragon, a seven-headed beast, seven vials of wrath, seven hills.

The Church carries on the theme. Almost the first recorded step in Christian organization is the appointment of seven 'men of good repute' to be deacons (Acts 2: 2–6). Catholic teaching includes seven sacraments, seven virtues, seven deadly sins, seven gifts of the Holy Spirit, seven works of mercy, seven sorrows and joys of the Virgin. There are seven archangels. An early Christian chronological scheme divides the world's history into seven ages.

As for Islam, Mohammed professed to be restoring the true faith of Abraham, and he drew on the Old Testament as Christians did, if less accurately and persistently. Islam, like Judaism, has seven heavens. It also has seven hells, and, in the teachings of some exponents, a sevenfold purgatory. The basic text is in the Koran: 'Seven are the astronomical heavens and seven the earths, as are seven the seas, the gates of hell and the mansions of paradise.'

On which an Arab writer comments: 'Of almost all things there are seven – seven are the heavens, the earths, the mountains, the seas . . . the days of the week, the planets . . . the gates and floors of hell . . .' Islamic legend relates that Adam was synthesized from seven different kinds of earth, and had seven sons. Pilgrims at Mecca walk round the Kaaba seven times.[5]

2

Clearly the Israelite seven was charged with power. But, once again, the Bible itself never discloses why, and it is quite possible that none of the authors knew. Madame Blavatsky is correct in implying that we cannot understand the septenary, even in its Old Testament setting, without ranging outside the Old Testament. A very little research proves it to be more than Hebraic. Behind its biblical behaviour, older factors are at work which the authors of the Bible have censored, as they are known to have censored other material from heathen sources. Whatever the Lady Wisdom means by her 'pillars', it is not absurd to take a hint from their number – a hint that we can attain to some sort of wisdom by penetrating its secret. The secret, however, is pre-scriptural. If we try to work back to origins, they are beyond the Old Testament horizon. Although Israel's religion gave a tremendous impulse to the seven-mystique, the notion that it was the sole and ultimate source can safely be dismissed.

Even in strictly religious terms the seven-mystique of Israel is anticipated outside it. The number occurs in Canaanite and Mesopotamian mythologies underlying its own. A Canaanite hymn of about 2000 B.C., long before any of the Bible was written, salutes a deity as conquering a seven-headed primeval serpent. (This monster, by the way, turns out to be hard to kill. He reappears in Egypt as the serpent Apep, who also – in some versions – has seven heads; and he reappears again, more surprisingly, in Christian scripture two millennia later.) Canaanites had a theory about seven-year spells of famine and drought, caused by the periodic exile of their god of vegetation.

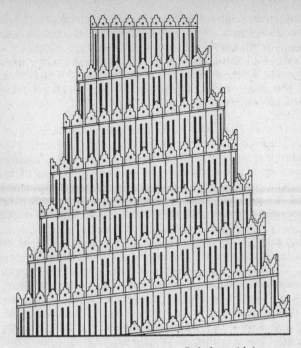

A reconstruction of the ziggurat in Babylon with its seven tiers

There is some evidence that their kings were ritually replaced at seven-year intervals, or, at any rate, that their reigns were held to pass through septennial phases.[6]

When we turn to Babylonia, we find that the great temple in its capital city had seven tiers, and that the Epic of Creation, one of its principal sacred writings, was divided into seven sections on seven tablets. Many such motifs in the cults and myths of Babylon were derived from the Sumerian civilization, extending back in time well into the third millennium B.C.; and Sumeria had the seven–mystique too, not merely as an embryonic fancy to be developed later by Israel, but as a thing already planted and potent. The Sumerians, for instance, told stories about Ereshkigal, goddess of the underworld. In her realm lived

33

seven divine judges. Her sister Inanna, wishing to go there, protected herself with seven divine laws inscribed on tablets, and entered by passing through seven gates. Or, to cite the history of religion as well as its myths: a Sumerian king, about 2500 B.C., built a temple for the goddess Nintu in the city of Adab with seven gates and seven doors, and dedicated it with seven times seven sacrifices.

Texts translated by S. N. Kramer also yield the following, related to the Sumerian religion in varying degrees: seven mountains; seven fate-decreeing gods; seven halting-points on a god's journey; seven days of flood (in the Sumerian version of the Deluge); seven weather-demons; seven trees felled by the hero Gilgamesh; seven other heroes associated with him; his axe weighing seven talents and seven minas; and seven heavenly lights.[7]

So, does the explanation lie in religious motifs of the Fertile Crescent, of Canaan and Mesopotamia? It does not. There are many other sevens in ancient religion for which an inspiration from that area is not easily credible.

In an immemorial past, long before Mohammed, the most solemn oath of the Arabs was taken on seven blood-smeared stones. Greek religion has its sevens as well. Before Zeus the ruling gods were seven Titans, headed by Zeus' father Cronus, and paired with seven Titanesses. When these deities dismembered the infant god Dionysus they tore him into seven pieces. The Cretan bull-cult demanded seven Athenian youths and maidens as regular offerings to the Minotaur. Hesiod, in the eighth century B.C., says there are three holy days in each month, the first, fourth and seventh, and the seventh is holiest because Apollo was born on a seventh day. All Apollo's main festivals, in fact, were held on the seventh day of the month in which they occurred. Greek religion of the later, Hellenistic era became obsessed with astrology, and laid ever-growing stress on the seven planets and their influences.[8]

That stress carried over into non-Greek cults such as Mithraism. But Mithraism, or rather its background, is worth a glance in its own right. It was a late offshoot of the religion of Persia, founded by Zoroaster. A survey of that religion as it was in its homeland shows that the septenary had status east of the Fertile Crescent as well as west; and it is worth remarking that there, at any rate, the seven planets can have had nothing to do with it, because astrology in the lands beyond Babylon reckoned nine. Nevertheless Zoroaster's Supreme God, Ahura Mazdah, had a court of seven divine beings called the Bounteous Immortals. The Bible tells a tale in a Persian setting which preserves what may have been corresponding sevens in Persian protocol: the King of Persia has seven chamberlains, there are seven princes who 'see the King's face', a feast lasts for seven days (Esther 1:5, 10, 14). Zoroastrian myth recognizes the seven metals of alchemy, and asserts that they flowed into the earth from the body of Gayomart, the Primordial Man. More familiar, thanks to Omar Khayyam, is the magic cup of the legendary king Jamshyd:

*Iram indeed is gone with all its Rose
And Jamshyd's Sev'n-ringed Cup where no one
    knows.*

The cup was made of gold and held the elixir of life. It was hidden by spirits under Jamshyd's command, though, despite Omar, some say it was dug up again when Persepolis was founded.[9]

Seven makes its mark also, and more strongly, at the early levels of Hinduism. It is here that influence from the Fertile Crescent is hardest to credit – not only because of geography, not only because the sets of seven are nearly all unlike each other, but above all because there is no trace of influence from that quarter in any other respect. The first Hindu sacred book is the *Rig Veda*. Basically it is a collection of hymns, three of four thousand years old, composed in the Indus Valley region which is now Pakistan. Some were translated into English by the philologist Max Müller. In his edition, which appeared in 1891, Müller instances various sets of seven – seven sons of the dawn-goddess, seven rivers, seven flames of the fire-god Agni, and so forth. He insists that although seven is sacred in the *Rig Veda*, is it not more so than several other numbers, such as three, five, or ten. If, however, we examine a fuller version by Ralph Griffith, published in 1896, it becomes

35

clear that Müller's statement is highly dubious. However its sacredness may be assessed, seven is the dominant number in the *Rig Veda*. Griffith indexes a total of 154 occurrences of phrases involving it. The runner-up is three, with 137 index entries. Five has 54, ten has 32. Obviously other numbers besides seven are significant, especially three, and we shall consider their significance later, but there is no doubt which is ahead.

The groups of seven indexed by Griffith begin with the seven Adityas, who are the dawn-goddess's sons noted by Müller. The list continues with seven castles, celestial streams, communities, cows, fiends, flames of Agni, forts, 'germs', glories, guards, heroes, horses, 'hotars' (a kind of priest), lights of sacrifice, metres, mothers, mouths (of a river), oblations, priests, regions of the earth, reins, ridges, rishis (semi-divine teachers), rivers, sages, singers, sisters, spears, splendours, stations of sacrifice, sunbeams, threads of sacrifice, tones, treasures, and troops. There are also allusions to seven-headed beings, a seven-wheeled vehicle, a sevenfold human race. Many of the heptads occur several times.[10]

These early Vedic hymns lead us indirectly to a further discovery. Hinduism evolved as a major system, not in the place where they were composed, but eastward and southward in the Indian subcontinent. The *Rig Veda* went on being revered as a sacred text. But in developed Hinduism, with its vast epics, its complex cults, its subtle philosophies, the septenary fades out. Seven is no longer prominent. It is swamped by other numbers. On the whole, as we explore eastward and southward beyond the Indus, we are moving into lands where it has no distinctive magic. A boundary, therefore, can be drawn.

There are apparent exceptions. The Indian mystical systems known as Tantric are based on a theory that the human organism has seven centres or chakras, one above another. Tantra, however, is a specialized doctrine aloof from mainstream Hinduism; its origins are obscure and may themselves lie in the same Indus Valley country that cradled the *Rig Veda*. In another direction the traces are ambiguous. The septenary persists mutedly in the Buddhism of Tibet and Central Asia, which has a Tantric

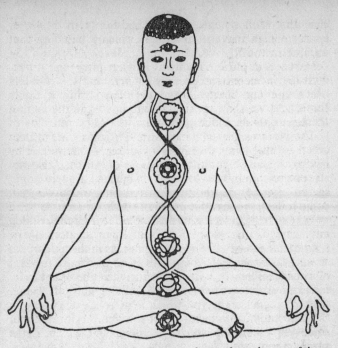

The seven chakras of the Tantric scheme, from the top of the head downwards

substratum – though that may not be the whole reason. Lamas explain (or did, before the Chinese Communist conquest) how to awaken the seven chakras. They analyse human life as an evolution through seven cycles, on each of seven planes of experience – forty-nine in all. They compose verses in a metre with seven syllables to a line, as the most suitable rhythm for religious teaching. The same number is dotted about in their mythology. According to Tibetan legend, for instance, when the Buddha was born he stood up and walked seven paces towards each point of the compass. But in this part of Asia the seven-mystique has remained less conspicuous than it is in Sumeria and biblical Israel. Influences from China have left their imprint too. Esoterically seven may be important; but the

37

Tibetan cosmic scheme has an imposing myth of world-epochs and their presiding powers which is based on five, a Chinese motif.[11]

Hence, while the data from religion prove the seven-mystique to be extensive, they confirm that the problem has shape and limits. Large negations bring it under control. Seven is *not* special, and never was, in the mature Hinduism of the Indian peninsula, or in the religions of China. Nor was it special in the pre-Christian cults of Italy and the Celtic lands. Nor does it ever seem to have carried any particular weight in the religions of Africa, Australasia, or pre-Columbian America (subject to a query about sevens in the Hopi traditions of Arizona, which we shall come to later, pages 147, 215, note 13).

Very striking indeed is its near-absence from the religion and religious mythology of ancient Egypt. It does occur, but not notably often, and sometimes, as in the case of the seven-headed serpent Apep, with an air of being a product of outside influence.[12] The greatest civilization of antiquity failed to evolve the septenary. Surely we are not dealing with a Jungian archetype which is present everywhere in the Unconscious, but with a factor which was infused into some early cultures and not others, and which Egypt simply never received?

During two or three pre-Christian millennia, the history of religion shows the mystique coming gradually into view in an area stretching from Greece to the Indus Valley. It varies in prominence from country to country, but is clearly present most of the way between these extremities. Beyond, it quickly becomes shadowy, at least in advanced and documented societies, till we reach areas where there is no clear trace of it. Its later world-wide spread, in such institutions as the seven-day week, is due mainly to the imperial exploits of biblically conditioned people.

3

Thus Madame Blavatsky's vindication, though interesting enough to pursue further, is partial only. Seven is a clue to something, but it is not a universal clue, at any rate in religion. What if we look outside religion? Do we get the same impression of a specific area of origin, with definite boundaries?

What, for instance, about the seven-note musical scale? Here the history can be sketched in. The scale has been traced back through Greece to Canaan and (probably) Sumeria. A Canaanite tune from Ugarit, dated about 1800 B.C., has been deciphered and played on a replica of a Sumerian lyre which dates back to 2600 B.C. Music puts us inside the same territory and date-range as before.[13] In ancient Asia, however, such a clear-cut distinction between 'religious' and 'non-religious' is seldom easy. Some of the Sumerian heptads – the mountains, trees and so on – could be counted as either, since the objects are physical, yet figure in myths about divine beings or the world's divinely ordained structure. The same is true of the heptads in Vedic hymns.

But the literature of Greece opens up another field. A good deal of Greek mythology may be said to look in a secular direction. It is closer to known realities, which it often professes to account for. It shades into heroic saga, which, in turn, shades into history as at Troy and Mycenae. There is in addition – as there is not (for example) in the Bible – a wealth of material that is not religious in any sense. And Greek literature yields another crop of sevens, in a variety of contexts. They are not Hebraically profuse, but they suggest at least a bias, a receptivity, ruling out chance.

The musical scale itself illustrates this. The Greek instrument that embodied it was a seven-stringed lyre. A myth traceable as far back as 600 B.C. tells how the young god Hermes made the first. His choice of the number seven is given a prior reason: his mother Maia was one of a group of seven nymphs called Atlantides. Afterwards Hermes handed over the lyre to Apollo, whose instrument it became, and who is sometimes portrayed with it, as is his disciple Orpheus. Septenary myth is here made to explain septenary fact.[14]

Musical magic underlies the saga of Thebes, in the heroic age before Homer. Its king Amphion raised walls around the city, not with hands but by the power of his lyre, another one made by Hermes and presented to him. Amphion had seven daughters, and he built a gate in his magical city walls for each one, named accordingly. Tiresias, the seer who figures in the disaster that struck Thebes through King Oedipus, was sentenced by Zeus to live through seven lives. after Oedipus' death, seven-gated Thebes was besieged by seven champions in an attempt to enthrone Oedipus' banished heir. Each champion drew up his forces facing one of the gates. The siege failed, but afterwards the seven sons of the champions avenged their fathers by besieging Thebes again, and took it.[15]

After the wars of Thebes came the war of Troy, Homer's theme in the *Iliad*. Homer himself does not seem attached to seven, but legend makes his hero Achilles a seventh son, and exceptional for that reason. When Greek towns competed as the birthplace of Homer himself, the list was always quoted as seven:

> *Seven cities warred for Homer being dead,*
> *Who, living, had no roof to shroud his head.*

The cities were Smyrna, Rhodes, Colophon, Salamis, Chios, Argos and Athens.

Greek myth-makers were slow to develop stories about the stars, but they very early picked out a group of seven and gave special importance to it as the Great Bear, Ursa Major – surely for some compelling reason, because, pictorially, this meant giving the Bear a long tail such as no bear has. They also insisted that the Pleiades cluster had seven members. A telescope shows more, while the naked eye gives doubtful results. In this matter of the Pleiades a numerical preconception can almost be proved. For calendric reasons the cluster is important in star-lore the world over, even among primitive peoples. With some tribes, such as the Ugi of Melanesia, it is the only star-group to be recognized and named. But it is seldom enumerated, and hardly any, unprompted, declare it to consist of seven. Outside Greece the Blackfoot Indians are perhaps alone in doing so. The Dyaks of Sarawak go so far as to concede that there were formerly seven, but now, they say, there are only six. The Greeks themselves, unsure of being able to see the number they wanted,

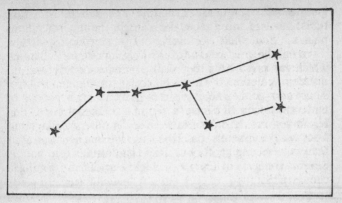

The Great Bear, Ursa Major

resorted to a legend on the same lines only more so. They alleged a 'lost' Pleiad. It vanished at the fall of Troy and is now invisible; however, it is still there, even though you cannot see it. The tally of seven is still made up.[16]

From this dogmatic reckoning came a new meaning of the word Pleiad, as a group of seven outstanding persons, 'stars' in some activity. Greek philosophy was said to have been founded by Seven Wise Men, Solon and Thales – who flourished around 600 B.C. – being the most famous, and these were the Philosophical Pleiad (perhaps related to seven sages of Babylonian lore). In the third century B.C. the Greeks of Alexandria claimed a Poetic Pleiad, inflated to the required number by ranking minor poets such as Philiscus with major ones such as Theocritus.[17]

It may have been merely accidental that the Greek alphabet had seven vowels (A, long and short E, I, long and short O, U). But the occult lore of decadent paganism treated this feature with solemn reverence, matching the vowels to the planets, and to the strings of Apollo's lyre. Demetrius, an Alexandrian author of the first century B.C., wrote: 'In Egypt the priests sing hymns to the gods by uttering the seven vowels in succession, the sound of which produces as strong a musical effect on their hearers as if flute and lyre were used.'[18]

Some Greek minds hovered around notions of septenary

41

architecture, septenary structures and groups of structures. Seven-gated Thebes, far back in the second millennian B.C., supplied a prototype. But Herodotus gives a more flamboyant account of the Median city of Ecbatana, which he says had seven walls, one inside another, all different colours – white, black, scarlet, blue, orange, silver and gold. The basis may have been a report of Nineveh, which did have a septuple crenellation in different colours. Near Sparta were seven pillars arranged in what was cryptically described as 'the ancient pattern'. From the second century B.C. the Hellenistic world had its Seven Wonders, a heptad of mighty artefacts forming a canonical list:

> The Pyramids of Egypt
> The Hanging Gardens of Babylon
> The Tomb of Mausolus
> The Temple of Diana at Ephesus
> The Colossus of Rhodes
> The Statue of Zeus by Phidias
> The Pharos of Alexandria

Rome, incidentally, was built on seven hills – a fact proverbially attested by a series of Romans steeped in Greek culture (Cicero, Virgil, Ovid and others), and taken up by the Christian author of Revelation (17:9) to weave into his septenary web.[19]

Medieval and post-medieval Europe succeeded to Graeco-Roman civilization, and to Christianity. Much was lost, much was altered. The Bible and the Church spread their hallowed forms of the seven-mystique throughout Christendom. Besides that, however, it is worth noting how strong seven's spell continued to be in other ways. Heptads persisted from the pagan classical age. Europe adapted them and invented many more of its own. Sometimes the pagan ones were, so to speak, baptized. In a curious extension of the Pleiad motif, Pope Gregory the Great wrote that Christ 'coming in the flesh, joined the Pleiades, for he had within himself, at once and for ever, the works of the sevenfold Holy Spirit'. New Pleiads were named, in the Greek sense: a group of scholars at Charlemagne's court headed by Alcuin; a French school of neoclassical poets headed by Ronsard; and a second school under Louis XIII – all numerically correct. A new list of Wonders of the World ran as follows:

> The Colosseum of Rome
> The Catacombs of Alexandria
> The Great Wall of China
> Stonehenge
> The Leaning Tower of Pisa
> The Porcelain Tower of Nanking
> The Mosque of St Sophia

Stonehenge is an intruder. It is older than most of the ancient ones, let alone their proposed successors. But the obligatory total had to be reached.[20]

Medieval education was grounded on the Seven Liberal Arts – grammar, logic, rhetoric, music, arithmetic, geometry and astronomy. Legend averred that the elements of all these had been inscribed on seven tablets of stone, which were fashioned by Adam after his expulsion from Paradise, and found in the vale of Hebron by the deified sage Hermes Trismegistus. Medieval imagination devised further heptadic legends. Fascinated, for instance, by folk-tales of enchanted heroes asleep in caves, it planted the miracle of the Seven Sleepers of Ephesus in the lore of Christendom. They were said to have hidden in a cave in the year A.D. 250, when the Emperor Decius was persecuting the Church, and to have wakened and emerged alive more than two centuries later. Afterwards the mystic seven transferred itself to other such tales of mortals spellbound in the recesses of the earth or in some land of faerie. Frederick Barbarossa, the German Emperor asleep in a cavern in the Kyffhäuser, turns over every seven years. At the same interval Ogier the Dane, an undying paladin of Charlemagne, hammers on the floor of his hall in Avalon with an iron mace. Thomas the Rhymer and, according to some versions, Tannhäuser spend that period of time in the Otherworld.[21]

Saints were not exempt from such pattern-making. Several very diverse national patrons were collectively transformed into heroes of romance as the Seven Champions of Christendom. St George of England, in real life a fourth-century Levantine martyr; St Andrew of Scotland, an apostle; St Patrick of Ireland, a fifth-century British missionary; St David of Wales, a sixth-century monastic founder; St James of Spain, another apostle; St Denis of France, a third-century martyr in Gaul; and St Anthony of Italy, a thirteenth-century Franciscan – all became knightly adventurers living at the same time, a chivalric Pleiad.

Out over the Atlantic, meanwhile, a Christian colony was reputed to be flourishing in the Island of the Seven Cities. These cities had been founded by seven Portuguese bishops leading parties of refugees from Moorish conquest. Their island haven was sometimes called Antillia. Reports of it influenced Columbus, and explorers sailed out from Bristol to search for it.

Besides Shakespeare's set-piece 'seven ages of man' in *As You Like It*, he also has 'the seven stars', as a phrase needing no gloss, in *King Lear*:

> *Fool.* The reason why the seven stars are no more than
>   seven is a pretty reason.
> *Lear.* Because they are not eight?
> *Fool.* Yes, indeed; thou wouldst make a good fool.

Alas, the reason is insufficient. These 'seven stars' are probably the ones that compose the Great Bear. Unlike other constellations it has always been familiar to people in general, without literary background. They have attached fancies of their own to it, making it the Dipper, or, with more dignity, a sky-chariot for national heroes – Charles's Wain (i.e. Charlemagne's), and in Cornwall, Arthur's.

Sevens abound in popular balladry and folklore. Even apart from subject-matter, the standard English ballad metre has a septenary rhythm, with seven stresses leading up to the first rhyming word, and likewise on from that to the second.

> *God prósper lóng our nóble kíng,*
>   *Our líves and sáfeties áll;*
> *A wóeful húnting ónce there díd*
>   *In Chévy Cháse befáll.*

A seventh child, it is said, may be clairvoyant. A seventh

son of a seventh son has second-sight and a healing touch. Swift travelling can be done magically in seven-league boots. The substance of the human body renews itself every seven years.

In more recent times we still get instances of this number being forced on unruly facts. The Seven Bishops who defied James II at least actually were seven. But the Seven Seas revealed by the age of discovery are artificial. A proper list of the world's major seas would be: the Mediterranean, the Atlantic, the Pacific, the Indian Ocean, and the Arctic and Antarctic Oceans. Six. You can only get seven by leaving out the Mediterranean, and splitting the Atlantic and the Pacific (which does not lend itself to such treatment) into northern and southern sections.

Another contrived seven with dogged vitality is the Heptarchy, the group of Anglo-Saxon kingdoms into which England is supposed to have been divided before unification. These are given as Kent, Sussex, Wessex, Essex, East Anglia, Mercia and Northumbria. In historical fact a full dozen are recorded, their number and relationships fluctuated, and the term 'heptarchy' is virtually without meaning. Yet it still heads an article in an encyclopedia published during the 1960s. The writer admits that 'the term is employed in a general sense, and does not imply the existence of seven separate and independent kingdoms throughout the period'. That is putting it mildly. The notion that there must have been seven, a royal and constitutional Pleiad in the land of Albion, is too potent to drop.

In so far, therefore, as we can disengage the seven-mystique from religion and religious mythology, its behaviour confirms what appeared before. While the magic number flourishes widely in European civilization, it only does so because that civilization inherited Christianity and classical culture. There is little to suggest that it amounted to anything in Europe earlier, among the barbaric Celts and Teutons. When we go back to the sources they lie within the same ground that has already been sketched out. The musical scale is Sumerian, Canaanite and Greek. Greece also produced its medley of miscellaneous heptads which (as with the Pleiad count) show signs of an underlying septenary pressure. But nothing takes us outside. Heptads in Egypt, such as the Alexandrian vowel-magic, were due to Alexander's conquests and the adoption of Greek language and ideas by educated Egyptians. At primary levels the first results are borne out. When all are taken together, it is still true that the seven-mystique can be traced back to the dawn of history in Greece, the Fertile Crescent, Iran probably, the Indus Valley certainly – and nowhere else.

Its strength and persistence vary. In Iran, for example, an astrological scheme of seven planets was not imposed. Within the defined boundaries, however, it is clearly present and widespread many centuries before Christ. Outside, it fades. No other contemporary culture shows any plain trace of it. The significance of the Buddhist sevens in Central Asia is open to debate. Scattered instances of magical and ritual sevens exist further afield – among the Shilluk of the Sudan, the Navahos, and other peoples. But in most cases they are isolated. The number, where it occurs, may be due to chance. Inference back to a remote past is out of the question.

In China the spell definitely snaps, because, so far as the Chinese have ever had a significant number, it is five. Their traditional cosmic scheme acknowledges five planets (Mercury, Venus, Mars, Jupiter, Saturn) paralleling five elements (water, metal, fire, wood, earth), five directions (north, west, south, east and centre), the five-note scale (CDEGA), five colours of the rainbow and five social duties. Chinese astrology considers a person under five headings (life, body, power, fortune, intelligence). Nor is the pentad confined to China. In the composite Buddhism of Tibet the Supreme Being or Adi Buddha is differentiated into five Dhyani Buddhas. From each dhyani Buddha emanates one of the five colours, five elements, five senses, and five vowels; and the world passes through five epochs, with one of the Dhyani Buddhas governing each. Further south, Hindus also recognize five elements – ether, air, fire, water, earth – and match them to the five senses, hearing, touch, sight, taste and smell. In these Eastern lands, the trail of seven peters out. Nor can we pick it up again by going further east still. The film *The Seven Samurai* was made in Japan, but it was a Westernized Japan.[22]

CHAPTER FOUR

Numerologists and Psychologists

1

Again, therefore, it must be said: facts fail to support Madame Blavatsky's thesis as taught by her. The seven-mystique is not universal. Yet she has a point, if an overstated one. A case does exist for a tradition coming down from a single source, and proselytizing ancient peoples from Greece to the Indus with some sort of proto-philosophy, in which the number seven had cosmic status. Whether or not anything survives of the proto-philosophy, its septenary conditioning (arguably) does. But it would be premature to ask at once whether the inquiry can be pushed further along that line, whether the source can be identified. Precisely here we confront the challenge – Jungian or otherwise – to all such theories. Can the seven-mystique be explained psychologically? Has the number perhaps a special quality in itself, a special relevance to the human body or psyche? Are sets of seven 'natural', so that they tend to occur spontaneously without the need for any diffused influence?

The obvious comment is that if seven were 'natural' it would carry the same significance for all nations. Still, cultural factors might have encouraged a stress on it in some places and not in others. The real question is whether a special quality can be detected in it at all. On the face of it, the answer is 'no'.

Even numerologists have found this number's attraction a stumbling-block. If it were six that had the mystique, they could point out that six is a 'perfect' number, the sum of its divisors, $1 + 2 + 3$. Eight might have possibilities as the primary cube, two each way, an emblem of solidity.

But why all the heptads? Why seven? Being a prime, it has no inner relationships, no factors to play with and fantasize about. Far from being ubiquitous, it is elusive. Multiply it by any digit apart from 1, and it vanishes. You get 14, 21, 28, 35, 42, 49, 56, 63. Not a single 7, everything else but. If you add the digits in these products you still never get 7 back: 1 and 4 add up to 5; 2 and 1 add up to 3; and so on.

Seven is uncooperative, and it plays tricks. There is no snap test for divisibility by it. Any number can be divided by two if its last digit can, and by three if the sum of its digits can. Similar tests cover divisibility by every other number from four to ten – except seven. The only way to find out whether a large number is divisible by seven is to try doing it. When you divide seven into the other digits you keep getting the same recurring decimal, 142857, starting at different places. You are shut up in the septenary and never break away into anything else.

If, as a quantity, seven looks difficult and aloof, does it come close to us through some human characteristic? Not so as to convince. In physical terms, the numbers based on the fingers are far more 'natural'. Hence perhaps the mystique of five in China, and hence certainly the practice of counting in tens. The best that numerologists can do here is to cite the seven main features of the head (eyes, ears, nostrils, mouth) and what they choose to describe as the seven orifices of the body. But the first set is contrived, because in practice you think of one nose rather than two nostrils, and the second is dubious to say the least.

Nor does a set of seven have any fitness based on perception. It is just a shade too complex to be instantly seen as what it is. Two, three, four or five objects can be taken in at a glance without counting. Six is a borderline case. When you go beyond six you must count the objects to be sure how many there are, unless they are in a known layout like pips on a card. Thinking visually, we might expect people to make as many as five a standard set. Seven is the first number we would definitely not expect in that role. Yet there it is.

As with perception, so with memory, and mental handling in general. Seven is just too many for comfort. Its awkwardness appears in surprising contexts. Thus according to classic management theory, a department head's span of control is six people. Except with the most routine type of work, that is as many direct subordinates as he can supervise properly. A seventh is liable to over-extend him. Another and more frivolous example comes from Walt Disney. He made *Snow White and the Seven Dwarfs* in 1937, and despite massive publicity, box-office success, and countless re-screenings since, it has always been a notoriously hard job to call to mind the names of all seven dwarfs. Even in the film's heyday, many who had seen it could get as far as six, but few could complete the list.

Faced, in spite of everything, with the undoubted image of seven as complete, right and somehow sacred – an image hallowed by the Bible even in periods when the majority read no other book – numerologists have done their best to expound it. They call it inscrutable. They interpret it in human terms as the ruling number of mystics, recluses, scholars, introverts. It is rounded and self-contained, intensely individual, but on the whole good rather then merely mean or stand-offish. Septenary people (those whose ruling number is seven) may be reserved, and appear colder than they are. At their best they are also richly reflective, attuned to the deeper rhythms of the world and its life.[1]

Such fancies amount to very little. They do not convey a hint, as occult doctrine sometimes does, of genuine insight disguised by jargon. Even if they were true, they would shed no light on the facts. They carry no implication that the septenary person is an ideal or dominant figure, whose number tends to have an advantage.

2

Far more important than numerology is psychology. Enthusiasts for Jung's Collective Unconscious would of course claim that the widespread sevens do not in the least require a shared influence or a common source. They simply reflect an archetype in the minds of human beings in general. True, as we have seen, Jung himself is uneasy with seven and shows signs of evasion. Yet although nobody has yet managed a Jungian explaining-away, that does not rule it out. Such images as the seven-pillared house of Wisdom look as if they ought to be quite at home in the populous landscape of the Zurich psyche. But if we try to locate them there, what happens?

To begin with, we enter a region which is notoriously ill-defined. Jung claims to guide us through levels of our being where such words as 'magical' and 'religious', 'mystical' and 'sacred', are more or less interchangeable in a numinous haze. He claims to offer clues to alien, elusive states of mind, in societies dead for thousands of years. His further claim that his clues are universal would appear to be weak in this case, because of the geographical limits. Still, it does not take much acquaintance with his works to see what might be an explanation staring us in the face. Jung may shy away from seven itself, but he has plenty to say about three and four, which he maintains are the key numbers of the psyche. If they are, then surely seven has the value it has because it is three and four added together?

This apparently simple question is in fact a tough one. It can be answered, but not quickly. The justification for going into it at some length is that the quest, if persevered in, leads to a conclusion that is surprising and fruitful: our first serious hint that the denial of progress which the Ancient Wisdom doctrine implies may, in some respects, be well grounded.

Since Jung found seven such a problem, and preferred not to discuss it, why was his attitude to these other numbers so different? Why should three and four be key numbers of the psyche? Much of his theorizing is based on mandala symbolism. 'Mandala' is a Sanskrit word for a circle: not merely as a shape, but as a sacred diagram, such as the Buddhist Wheel of Life familiar to readers of Kipling's *Kim*. As a therapeutic technique Jung used to invite his patients to draw, freely and spontaneously. The result might be a picture or a design or a hybrid of both; but he noticed a tendency to draw something with a perimeter, a centre, and a symmetrical pattern. Some of the patients' dreams had the same bias as the drawings. They would dream of people in enclosures making circling movements. Or they would dream of a central point – a hill, an island in a lake, a fountain in a garden – which they might or might not reach in the dream, but felt to be the heart of it.

Freudian explaining-away via the womb and sexual organs did not seem helpful. Jung interpreted the circle as symbolizing the psyche as a whole, and the centre as what he called the 'self', meaning not its conscious ego-aspect but its true innermost nature. He found, moreover, that some of the drawings were like formalized mandalas in eastern religion, especially Tibetan Buddhism. Since there had been no copying or influence, the likeness told in favour of his world-wide immutable Collective Unconscious.[2]

Mandalas, it appears, show numerical norms which are often the basis of their symmetry. Having projected a circle, the Unconscious may well go on to project a cross or a square inside it, or at all events a four-way pattern of some sort. To draw such a pattern is the most natural thing to do. A sceptic might murmur that squares and crosses are easy to draw, but the truth, according to Jung, is that the ground-plan of the Unconscious is a quaternity.

There is more to come. Mandalic diagrams vary, and the quaternity is not always stable, because the conscious ego (especially, one gathers, the male ego) has a trick of imposing a three-motif in place of the four-motif. Other numbers occur too, but, says Jung, the predominant numbers are these: three and four. 'Primitive patterns of order are mostly triads or tetrads', and mandalas, even when drawn by highly civilized people, reveal the substratum of that fact. They further prove that three and four, being on different levels of the psyche, are apt to come into conflict or set up a tension. A set of three may seek a fourth, a set of four may dispose itself as three-plus-one, with an odd or uncertain member.[3]

These numerical tendencies are alleged to be built into the brain. The whole theory may sound very abstract. However, a few examples will convey the idea.

Consider three, the favourite number of the conscious ego. It appeals to the mind as neat, complete, logical. It conjures up a triangle, the simplest enclosure. It evokes the whole of space (length, breadth, height) and the whole of time (past, present, future). Therefore, it tends to mould behaviour in that spirit. We think of it as summing up the whole history of a thing or event (beginning, middle, end), and – with less reason – the whole range of possibilities ('I'll give you three guesses', 'third time lucky'). Triadic rhythm is so strong that it can falsify. Though Churchill said 'I have nothing to offer but blood, toil, tears and sweat', the phrase is remembered as 'blood, sweat and tears'.

For many centuries Europeans saw three as the principle of reason itself. The standard logic invented by Aristotle was based on the syllogism. This could take several forms, but always had three steps:

> All men are mortal.
> Socrates is a man.
> Therefore Socrates is mortal.

And so on through the permutations of 'all' and 'some' and 'none', but never with more or less than three parts. Among later philosophers, Hegel and Marx worked out the entire history of mankind in terms of a three-stage dialectic, with the clash of opposing forces constantly being resolved in a third thing, a synthesis, containing the seeds of the next conflict. The successes of Marxist movements might be held to attest the spell of the triad, its power to carry a conviction of truth. Sets of three in myth and folklore have the same air of rightness and completeness. There were three Fates, three Furies, three Graces. Fairy-tale fathers have three sons. Heroes have three wishes. Heroines have three suitors.

Four, by contrast, seems – according to Jung – to go less with conscious fitness and more with a deep-down intuitive response to the world, a 'that's-the-way-it's-planned' feeling. Hence the crosses and squares inscribed in mandalas. Human beings tend to see impersonal nature as quaternary. Consciousness, as a rule, fails to impose its abstract three on the world of empirical experience. Instead there are four cardinal points, north, south, east and west; there are four winds; there are four seasons. Ancient Greek science, the pre-experimental science of thoughtful guesswork, explained the living body by the interaction of four

53

'humours' (phlegm, blood, choler and black bile), and matter in general by the minglings of four 'elements' (earth, air, fire and water) and four 'qualities' (hot, cold, moist and dry).

Three and four – we are still with Jung – are psychologically related but not in harmony. The three-biased conscious mind tries to assert itself against the four-biased Unconscious, and the Unconscious presses its own claims with varying success, so that in the debatable ground of imagination we have odd ambiguities. One of Jung's patients dreamed of going up in a lift to 'the third or fourth floor'. I myself have been told of a dream about a box with three billiard-balls in it, the correct number, yet with room for a fourth and even an empty piece of wrapping-paper. Early alchemists taught that their Great Work of gold-making had four main stages, which were marked by the materials turning black, white, yellow and red; later alchemists of a more intellectual temper dropped yellow and reduced it to three.[4]

Sets of four certainly do have a habit of not being precisely equal, as if three were somehow breaking in and affecting them. Four tends to be three-plus-one. This seems to happen especially in the mind's more ambitious flights, in philosophy and religion. Plato, planning his ideal Republic grounded on four cardinal virtues, imagines three social classes corresponding to three of the virtues, prudence, fortitude, temperance. When he comes to the fourth virtue, justice, he does not make it correspond to a body of people (the judiciary, for example), but sees it as an abstract regulator among the three. In Ezekiel's vision of the Divine Chariot, the 'living creatures' have four faces of which three are animal and one is human (Ezekiel 1:10, and see also Revelation 4:7). In the set of four Gospels accepted by the Church as authentic, those of Matthew, Mark and Luke – the 'Synoptic' Gospels – go together, while John's is different. In the legend of the Holy Grail, the Grail is kept with three other hallowed objects, the Lance, Sword and Dish, but in this quartet the three are subsidiary and the Grail alone is the arch-mystery and goal of the quest.

Jung may also be right in arguing the same point in

reverse. Three, despite its assurance, is sometimes uneasy and feels that there is need for a fourth to be added. Occult fantasy about a 'fourth dimension' owes more to this feeling than to science. The same may be thought to apply to the Christian Trinity, Father, Son and Holy Spirit. This is an attempt by male minds at a diagram of the fullness of perfection. It is nobly conceived, but in Jung's view not stable, being at odds with the psyche. It rejects vital portions of the human make-up, which reach out from the Unconscious and change the three into a four. Such a change has been effected in two different ways. One part of the Unconscious may conjure up an overblown Devil, a projection of all evil rivalling God himself. Or instead another part may appear as a dizzily exalted Virgin, Mother of God and Queen of Heaven, the idol of Mariolatry. And even then, adding the fourth fails to resolve the tension entirely. Four remains three-plus-one, the Trinity is still not a true Quaternity. Satan, however terrific, is the enemy of the three Persons and not their partner. Mary, however ardently adored, keeps her femininity and her lowlier rank as a created being.[5]

Because some of these statements are so plausible, a word of caution is in order. We should not be overawed by Jung's claim that his patterns are literally part of the organism, that they are built into the brain. He never says anything to prove it, and when he does try to connect the Unconscious with material facts, the results are so grotesque that the absence of any real evidence is plain to see. For instance:

It would seem, therefore, that there is normally a clear insistence on four . . . Now it is – as I can hardly refrain from remarking – a curious 'sport of nature' that the chief chemical constituent of the physical organism is carbon, which is characterized by four valencies; also that it is well known that the diamond is a carbon crystal. Carbon is black – coal, graphite – but the diamond is 'purest water'. To draw such an analogy would be a lamentable piece of intellectual bad taste were the phenomenon of four merely a

55

poetic conceit on the part of the conscious mind and not a spontaneous product of the objective psyche.[6]

We hardly need bother much about the valencies of the carbon atom. Only the facts matter. Still, the facts do offer a Jungian explanation of the seven-mystique: that seven not only combines three and four, but resolves their tension in a unity containing both.

Another aspect of number-lore seems favourable to this idea. Three, four and seven can be viewed as members of a related quartet. While the sum of three and four is seven, their product is twelve; and though twelve has never had seven's multiple spell or anything like it, there are some weighty instances showing that the number has commanded respect. There are twelve months, twelve signs of the Zodiac, twelve hours of the day; twelve Olympian gods, twelve labours of Hercules, twelve tables of Roman law; twelve tribes of Israel, twelve apostles, twelve articles in the Apostles' Creed, and twelve days of Christmas. True, some of these dodecads are derived from others. Christ appoints twelve apostles to show that his flock will be the Chosen of God in succession to the twelve tribes (see, for example, Matthew 19:28). But whatever the extent of such pairings, twelve undoubtedly has a certain power, and has it, furthermore, in an obscure but definite linkage with seven. It tends to be important in contexts where seven is important also, and they sometimes appear together.

The calendar that has the year of twelve months has the week of seven days. The astrology that has twelve signs of the Zodiac has seven planets moving through them. The Jewish Temple had twelve loaves of shewbread standing for the tribes, alongside a great lampstand with seven lamps, the Menorah. In Acts 6:2–6 the twelve apostles appoint the seven deacons. Occasionally twelve is a variant or doublet of seven. This is so in Greece with the Titans, the gods who reigned before Zeus. In what is probably the earliest form of the myth there are seven chief Titans, each matched with a Titaness, and the number is emphasized. Hesiod's poem *Theogony*, however, lists male and female together mentioning no number, and if you count them,

3   5   7

2   4   6

there are twelve. The Minotaur's tribute of youths and maidens has a similar variant. Many centuries later, European alchemists subdivided the main stages of their work into either seven or twelve sub-stages.[7]

A psychological answer, then, might explain the magic of seven and the related, lesser magic of twelve by simple arithmetic. Three and four were potent at deeper levels, as witness Jung's mandalas and other evidence, and they transmitted some of their power through addition and multiplication: $3 + 4 = 7$ and $3 \times 4 = 12$. In default of further data, this is a view likely to appeal to a modern mind. It is evolutionary. It is 'reductionist'. It implies a progress from simple to complex. Three and four are small tidy numbers that can be taken in at a glance. Each has that sense of inbuilt neatness: the logical neatness of beginning-middle-and-end, of length-breadth-and-height, of past-present-and-future; the aesthetic neatness of the cross and the square, of the compass-points and seasons. In Jungian language, their sum and product would both suggest integration of the psyche and therefore fulfilment.

Moreover, if we introduce three we can get back behind the schism of the analysts and cite Freud as well. Freud too noticed that three had an allure. As might be expected, he argued that it had its prototype in the male genitals. Though Jung's threes have more to them than this, they do sometimes suggest masculine thinking, while his fours are more feminine. Nor is this merely modern theorizing. Numerologists were treating odd numbers as male and evens as female thousands of years ago, and for a Freudian

57

reason. If the numbers are portrayed as patterns of dots, it is plain that in words used by the Greek philosopher Plutarch, the odd ones have a 'generative middle part' and the evens 'a certain receptive opening and internal space'.

So three added to four, male plus female, could give the heptad an aura of sexual union, while three multiplied by four would combine the sexes more subtly.[8] Which sounds hopeful. On the face of it, the mystery about seven is a mare's-nest. Freud and Jung, in their different ways, supply the materials needed to account for its magic, and for the related magic of twelve as well. There is no need to look for ancestral sources. There is seemingly no clue here to Ancient Wisdom.

3

Psychological pattern-makers, however, show a distinct unwillingness to face history, and test their theories by asking such vulgar questions as 'When?' and 'How?'. If we are to suppose that certain Asians and Greeks began, several thousand years ago, to put three and four together making a magical heptad, we must at least try to catch them doing it. We may also have to ask (however idiotic the question sounds) whether they could have done it.

In Roman times it undoubtedly happened. By then the mystic divinity of numbers was firmly enthroned, and the fact that three-plus-four-equals-seven was a hallowed identity. So far, so good – but it is not very far. This classical numerology goes back to Pythagoras, about 530 B.C. We can trace it to him and still feel that the ground is fairly safe. His disciples did think in terms of three-and-four-together. They swore oaths on a symbolic three-sided pattern with four dots to a side:

The diagram was known as the Holy Tetraktys and showed that $1 + 2 + 3 + 4 = 10$ – hence, that these small numbers were the root of all larger ones, since the Greeks counted in tens. Pythagoreans called it 'eternal Nature's fountain-spring'. Whether or not Pythagoras himself made anything of the three-plus-four sum, it is a wholly plausible operation in the context of such ideas.[9]

Now, however, the real problem begins. Seven was magical in Sumeria as early as the third millennium B.C. That is a long time before Pythagoras. Can we go back so far beyond him and still find such a mental process occurring or likely to have occurred? Indeed, can we prove that three and four were special *in themselves* so early? As magical numbers, are they senior to the heptad at all or even equally old? Would anybody have thought of concocting a stronger magic by putting them together?

Sumeria, taken by itself, gives the answer 'no' at all points. Its myths and poems do not show either three or four as having the same sort of weight as seven, let alone as combining to make it up. In that setting the heptad appears to be senior and to have priority. But perhaps we are being misled by selective Sumerian borrowing from some other quarter. The wise course it to reserve judgement and look outside, surveying significant threes and fours – the triads and tetrads which Jung says are the standard 'primitive patterns of order' – and asking how old they really are, what they are like, and how they behave.

Three, at any rate, has a numinous air with some ancient peoples if not with all. Its roots may well be deep. In the *Rig Veda* it is the commonest number after seven itself. Built into several languages it suggests the superlative, the fullest possible, as in the Greek *trismegistos*, 'thrice-greatest', and the Latin *ter felix*, 'thrice happy'. Major religions had divine or semi-divine triads long before the Trinity, with ritual and art answering to them: the gods Anu, Enlil and Ea in Babylon; Osiris, Isis and Horus in Egypt; the Three Fates, Three Furies, Three Graces, Three Gorgons; the Triple Goddess in her classic guises including Diana, and her Celtic guises including Brigit,

59

the three-formed deity of the Irish, whose cult a Christian namesake annexed.[10]

The case for the antiquity of a sacred three looks promising. However, it falls short. The effect of the Sumerian absence is not cancelled by a wider search. Where the sacred seven appears early, we cannot trace the sacred three any further back, and in most places we cannot even trace it equally far. When we can, as in the *Rig Veda*, it still does not look as if it had priority or could have been a 'cause' of seven.

The Old Testament supplies documentation. Its holy seven-day week is in the Commandments (Exodus 20:8–11), written before 800 B.C. The stories of Abraham's gift of seven lambs, Jacob's seven-year service for his wives, Balak's sacrifice of victims in sevens on seven altars, are – in part at least – older still (Genesis 21: 25–31, 29: 16–30; Numbers 23: 1–4, 14, 29–30). No three-motifs as clear as these seven-motifs occur in such ancient passages, except perhaps in the incident of the trio who visit Abraham at Mamre, and seem to be disguises of the Lord and two angels (Genesis 18 and 19); even here the actual number is not stressed. The books of the Old Testament written later add remarkably little. Throughout the canon, although three occurs often (about as often as seven itself), it seldom carries a special impact – certainly nothing to compare with the pounding reiteration of sevens in the Jericho story (Joshua 6: 1–21). It occurs for rhetorical effect, as four also does, in Amos 1 and 2, but few texts press it any further.

One that does has a curious twist. This is II Samuel 24: 12–13. It is paralleled in I Chronicles 21: 11–12, where the same events are retold. King David is offered a choice of three divine punishments, and each of them is triple – three years of famine, three months of defeat, three days of plague. Samuel was written in the sixth century B.C., Chronicles in the fifth, so they are far from having priority in any case over the 'seven' texts from the Pentateuch. But the intriguing point is in Samuel. A Hebrew manuscript giving the probable original reading, and followed in the King James version, says seven years of famine! The impression is not that three preceded seven, but that seven

60

preceded three. In the later copies of Samuel, and in Chronicles, we catch a subsequent generation of scribes trying to tidy the sentence up.

Most of the hints at an ancient magic of three – admittedly, not all – are outside the Fertile Crescent. They occur among Indo-European peoples, Celts and Greeks and Vedic Hindus. Not only are they unhelpful with the seven-mystique, as and where it appears earliest, they place a query over the whole notion of its having resulted from arithmetic. Scrutiny of Greek myth and ritual suggests that sets of three were never pictured in a way that would have lent itself to number-magic through the addition of four.

The distinction is subtle, but worth making. Numerological jugglery as we know it is not only an invention of Pythagoras, but an utter anachronism if we project it into a setting much before him, the context of the first sacred sevens. Far in primeval shadows we have to reckon with a state of society (it still persists in remote places) where counting scarcely existed. It was confined to 'one, two, many'. Even in far more advanced epochs, the number-after-two tended to refer vaguely to multiplicity or abundance rather than to literal three-ness. In the Greek setting where documentation is good, a triad's emphasis was not exactly on the number as such, but on a unity having several facets or members, or a divine power having several aspects. Such was the Triple Goddess. Cerberus' three heads belonged to one dog. The three Fates were different masks of Fate, together making up the complete image. Aeschylus calls them 'triune', like the Trinity, and the Trinity itself transplants the theme to the Christian realm: three Persons are one God.

This interpretation of three agrees with Jung, but it holds out no hope for the proposed Jungian elucidation of seven. Three might be sacred in itself, but not as an element that could enter into calculation. A Greek triad would never have combined with another number to make a larger set. It would have resisted such tacking-on of alien matter. When three Furies made up the complement, fully expressing the Fury-nature, what would have been the point of producing four further demons to reinforce them?

New recruits could not be fitted in. It is doubtful whether Celtic or Hindu triads would have been more amenable.

There is no reason, then, to think that the mystic heptad arose from adding four to a prior three; no reason to think that it even could have. And quite apart from the actual cases considered, we should be cautious about the general claim that three is a 'natural' number which consciousness everywhere gravitates towards. Take the threefold division of time into past, present, future. Surely, if you think about time at all, there is no other way of thinking about it? But there is. The triplicity of the Western way is not universal. In the chief languages of the Hindus, the same word does duty for 'yesterday' and 'tomorrow'. Or take the syllogism. It looks like a form which an argument, if set out in full, simply has to take. Yet in the chief Hindu system of logic it has five steps instead of three. Our three-step type appears first in Aristotle (384–322 B.C.) and has nothing perfect or necessary about it even when stated. Frege and Bertrand Russell showed Aristotle's logic to be open to grave criticism.[11]

If we cannot find ancient sevens being built up by starting from three, can we do any better by working the other way round? Could the basis be four, with three added to it?

Since four is alleged to be closer to the Collective Unconscious, it ought to be more primitive. Some of Jung's oriental mandalas, with their four-way patterns, might be held to show that it is. So might some of the sacred diagrams of native America. The trouble is that such evidence is remote from the homelands of the seven-mystique. Within that area the early traces of four are much less distinct. Before 3000 B.C., pottery in the Middle East has crosses and swastikas as decorative motifs, but they are not the only motifs and there is no proof that they possess any special meaning.[12]

Better instances do exist. The disc-emblem of Shamash, the Babylonian Sun God, has a cross on it with four intermediate arms. But on the whole, the early territory of seven fails to support Jung. Four has little importance in the *Rig Veda* (and twelve, by the way, is insignificant). Over the Middle East and the Hellenic world, far from being rooted in a primordial instinctive past, groupings of four mostly belong to the era of dawning science, literary art, reflective theology.

Once again the Bible sheds light. Its account of the four rivers of Eden (Genesis 2: 10–14) is indeed very old. But although commentators have invested the number with profound meanings, none are apparent in the text. Behind the Hebrew myth is a Canaanite one about a paradisal place 'at the source of the streams', that is, of all earthly welfare – water being symbolic of this. The Genesis author who adapts the theme simply names four great rivers (with some very wild geography) which are probably all the ones he has heard of.[13] The oldest thing in Hebrew scripture with a strong quaternary stress is the Chariot in the first chapter of Ezekiel. This dates from the middle sixth century B.C., no earlier, and is a highly wrought piece of symbolism far removed from the free outpourings of Ezekiel's forerunners in prophecy. Even here, Ezekiel's reaction to his bizarre experience is to sit dumbfounded for *seven* days (3: 15). That stretch of time is proper for digesting a divine vision. Seven is in his mind already.

Jewish awe of the Tetragrammaton – the Name of God in four letters, YHVH – is well known. However, that awe did not reach its height till after the Babylonian Exile, and by then the rebuilt Temple was functioning in Jerusalem with its seven-branched Menorah, already present and revered. This was in the last centuries before Christ. Symbolism added by the New Testament, based on the four arms of the cross and the four Gospels, cannot have influenced anything before Christ.

As for the Greek tetrads, which are the most important, they are not only wrong in date but subversive of the whole Jungian position. They do not at all suggest a welling-up from the depths of an immemorial Unconscious. They are products of thought, and of fairly sophisticated thought, with nothing instinctive or natural about it. The Holy Tetraktys was not a restatement of any older magic. It was an invention of the school of Pythagoras – in other words, a coterie of mathematicians. Significant fours arose in Greece appreciably later than significant sevens. They arose from direction-finding, from refinement of the calendar, from theorizing on the structure of matter. At least two can be ascribed to historical persons.

Take the cardinal points, north, south, east, west. Their present precision is a legacy of Greek geographers. It was attained little by little, through experience at sea and prolonged star-gazing, not through any instant inevitability. In the northern hemisphere there is a close enough true south, marked by the sun's position at noon when the shadows are shortest. Nevertheless, the classical Greek for 'south' is not derived from 'noon' but from the name of the wind-god Notus, whose wind blew only approximately from that direction. In Latin, 'south' is *meridies*, mid-day, showing a more precise awareness. The other points are at first very indefinite indeed. During the millennia before Christ, owing to the precession of the equinoxes, there was no Pole Star to give a true north. In Greek, 'north' is *arktos*, referring to the Great Bear, and in Latin it is *septentrio*, referring to the same constellation. The Bear moves in a large circle and gives only a rough direction. East and west are not originally exact either. The Greek terms for them mean 'sunrise' and 'evening', and the Latin are *oriens* and *occidens*, 'rising' and 'setting'. As sunrise and sunset vary in position throughout the year, the resultant east and west are broad sectors of the horizon only.

Two fixed points on the 'orient' horizon – sunrise at the midsummer and midwinter solstices – mark the ends of the sector. Two sunset points correspond. These could perfectly well have produced a double east and west with a total of six directions, and in Britain, to judge from alignments at Stonehenge, they may have done so.

Since this alternative was open, should we see the dominance of four as confirming Jung and the four-way bias of the Unconscious? No, because as the Greek and Latin terms betray, the process was gradual. There is no evidence that human minds imposed a neat right-angled cross on the world, a cross which was mystically necessary or compulsive. They slowly tightened up the handling of a few useful celestial phenomena, and arrived – Greeks and Romans, if perhaps not Britons – at the best method of doing it. In the nearer portions of Asia likewise, we have no early traces of four precise and unvarying directions branching out at right angles. A plan which has survived of the Sumerian city of Nippur is not oriented by compass-points. In Numbers 2, the Lord tells Moses and Aaron how the tribes of Israel are to camp in the wilderness. The Tabernacle is to go in the centre. Three tribes are to pitch their tents 'on the east side toward the sunrise', which the Tabernacle faces (3: 38). Three are to go on the south, three on the west, three on the north. The arrangement here is by the sun, from religious motives, and would vary with the seasons.

Fixed cardinal points, at right angles, emerge in Greece about the fifth century B.C. It is hard to see anything in the process but a conscious refinement of technique. Quaternary pressure from Jungian psychic depths is superfluous. Furthermore it is doubtful – as other Jungian motifs are doubtful – on comparative grounds. In other places where the four compass-bearings have become more or less established, the number of directions has not always been thought of as four in spite of this. In ancient Ireland and India it was thought of as five – north, south, east, west, and 'here'. In China it was usually thought of as five, sometimes as six. In parts of Polynesia it is thought of as seven – north, south, east, west, and 'here', plus up and down as well. Four has no magic.[14]

Are the four winds primitive, in Greece or anywhere else? Homer recounts Odysseus' visit to their master Aeolus (*Odyssey*, Book X). Yet while the poet is interested enough in numbers to tell us that Aeolus had twelve children, he still fails to tell us how many winds he was in charge of, saying only that he was warden of all of them. In another passage (V: 331ff.) Homer briefly mentions four great winds in contention. These are the Boreas, Notus, Eurus and Zephyrus assigned by later Greeks to north, south, east and west. But in Homeric times their directions were not really considered to be part of their character. Boreas was simply a strong cold wind which, in Greece, did happen to blow from the portion of the sky marked by the Bear. Notus was a warm wind which blew from Africa. The linkage of compass-bearings with winds, and the consequent precision and pre-eminence of the four used in this way, came with the definition of the compass-bearings themselves about the fifth century B.C. At the period further back when the four enter our field of vision, they do not enter alone. As Homer's Aeolus myth implies, they have colleagues, an ill-defined, dangerous gang headed by Typhoeus.

Obviously no number-mystique is at work here, quaternary or otherwise; many winds exist in the Greek scheme because many winds *do* exist, blowing from every direction. Hesiod mentions three winds by name – Boreas, Notus, Zephyrus – plus the anonymous Typhoean winds, which seem to be in rivalry with them. Latin gives names to a group intermediate between the main four, and not all of them simply at 45-degree angles. They include Thrascias, a maverick who blows from the north, but not precisely from the north.

The standard 'four winds', in fact, show every sign of having resulted from the same tidying-up that fixed the cardinal points. They are not a primitive quartet, they are rationalized survivors of a larger and vaguer brood. In the Bible they do not appear till Jeremiah 49: 36 ('I will bring upon Elam the four winds from the four quarters of heaven'), and Jeremiah wrote when his people had come under Gentile influence, long after several of the biblical passages that emphasize seven. The literature of Babylon includes the Creation Epic, which is well over a thousand years older. It does mention Four Winds – but it also mentions Seven Winds. That is the utmost which can be done for the priority of four over seven, and it is still inadequate.[15]

Next, the four seasons. These can be fixed objectively by four points in the year, the two equinoxes and the two solstices. Yet even with that advantage, the four-season scheme is found neither early in Greece nor generally elsewhere. Again no unconscious compulsion can be discerned favouring it. Natives of tropical South America count only two seasons, a dry and a wet. Some Polynesians likewise have only two. Other Polynesians have three, as do the Burmese and many African tribes, though the Shilluk have as many as nine. The aboriginal North American peoples have three, four or five. Ancient Egypt

66

had three (Nile flooding, seed-time, harvest), and so did ancient India (warm, rainy, cold), but in India two more were added, making five. The early Indo-Europeans from whom the Greeks were descended seem to have had three. These were winter, spring and summer; the Indo-European languages have no common root for 'autumn'. The Greeks themselves began with three only.

We can catch the present four taking shape among them. In Homer, 'fruit-harvest' is recognized as a time of year. In the seventh century B.C. the poet Alcman refers both to three year-divisions and to four. This is the phase of transition. Afterwards, four seasons is the calendric norm. Classical Greek, however, continues to be a three-season language, its word for 'autumn' meaning only 'the after-summer'. The change from three to four is not psychological, it is due to the shift from a lunar calendar to a more exact solar one, in which the solstices and equinoxes come to be employed as markers. Even then Theophrastus, a scientific writer of the fourth century B.C., divides the years into five seasons.[16]

Lastly, the four 'humours' and four 'elements'. These were not quaternary concepts handed down in unreasoning awe from remote medicine-men. The humours were proposed by the Greek physician Hippocrates (c. 460–377 B.C.), one of the most lucidly unsuperstitious thinkers of antiquity, to account for variations in body function and character. The elements also were a product of attempts to explain facts, not to force a numerical pattern on them. Actual portions of matter – a stick of wood, a gallon of wine, a cloud – were not visibly compounded of earth, air, fire and water; these were read into them by pioneer scientists, beginning with Empedocles about 440 B.C. His ideas were backed in due course by the four 'qualities' and by an atomic theory. Not only was the scheme an outcome of deliberate thought, fairly civilized thought at that, it was objective and practical in its bias. It contained no implication that there had to be four, and the proof is that it was soon modified by further speculation about a fifth element, the quintessence. China, as we have seen, had five elements all along, and so had India. These physical theories show no more sign of a controlling 'four' archetype than the progress of direction-finding or year-division.[17]

Of course it need not be contested that sets of four affected each other, and eventually gave the number a special character. When one quartet had been defined, it may have encouraged further quartets. The four cardinal points may have slightly predisposed Greek minds to favour four elements, four humours. A Christian author, Irenaeus, shows this mode of thinking at a more advanced stage: he argues that four is the correct number of canonical Gospels, because they correspond to the four winds from the world's four quarters. But the difficulty is not removed. Throughout those areas where the seven-mystique flourished in ancient times, any demonstrable importance of four as such comes later, and is of no help in accounting for it. Further, when four does begin to loom large as it does in classical Greece, the reasons seem to be practical and rational, or at any rate would-be-rational. Ancestral unconscious patterning is at best not proved, nor is any quaternary magic.

So the insistent seven cannot be the sum of three and four. Timing is fatal if nothing else. Even after Pythagoras, when numerologists do give mystical meanings to the two smaller numbers, combining them to make the larger one, they do it in a context of other fancies so far-fetched as to kill any interest the operation may have. Throughout the enormous range of heptads it is hard to find more than a couple that were made up by combining a triad with a tetrad. These are the seven Christian virtues and the seven liberal arts. The seven virtues are the four cardinal virtues of the natural man – prudence, justice, temperance, fortitude – plus the three theological virtues of the good Christian, faith, hope and charity. Plato supplied the four and St Paul the three. The seven liberal arts of medieval schools comprised the *Trivium* of grammar, logic and rhetoric, plus the *Quadrivium* of music, arithmetic, geometry and astronomy. That is as far as the search takes us. Both instances belong to an era many centuries after seven was first hallowed.

In any case the things combined are of the same type, and go together. Virtues can be added to virtues, arts to arts. Further back in time such mergers would very seldom have worked. The older triads and tetrads are unlike in kind. Even apart from the query over the meaning of three-ness, they can scarcely ever be pictured fusing into groups of seven. Nobody in the myth-making era would have added three heads of Cerberus to four winds. The thinking that can make up an abstract seven out of an abstract three and four presupposes a mathematical habit of mind which is not found early enough in the right places.

4

A word, lastly, about twelve. Though it nowhere had the multifarious magic of seven, it reinforces the point. The notion that it became sacred as three-*times*-four is open to the same objections as the notion that seven became so as three-*plus*-four. Some of the objections are less forceful than they are with seven, but the last one, about the mathematical habit of mind is more so.

You can add things together after a fashion by juxtaposing them, even if they are unlike. You cannot multiply things together at all. 'Three Graces multiplied by four seasons' is meaningless. What would the answer be? Even 'three months multiplied by four months" is meaningless, strictly speaking. Multiplication is repeated addition. 3×4 is $4 + 4 + 4$ ('three fours') or $3 + 3 + 3 + 3$ ('four threes'). One of the figures must stand for 'times' and cannot cover anything else.

Such abstract reasoning was slow to develop. It occurred fitfully in early ages – witness the seven-times-seven sacrifices to Nintu (page 34 above) – and it made progress in Babylon, but it cannot be traced in Palestine or Greece as far back as the sacred twelve can. When God tells Adam and Eve to be fruitful and multiply, he has another activity in mind. When Homer says the Trojans had a thousand camp-fires with fifty men at each, he does not add 'so their army was fifty thousand strong'. Numbers were multiplied in classical Greece and Rome. However, the clumsy pre-Arabic numerals made it heavy work, and it remained somewhat esoteric. It had so little to do with anything which habitually happened in the mind that the multiplication sign × was not invented till very much later, by William Oughtred (1574–1660). Even then the idea seemed almost supernatural; he declared that it 'came into his head, as if infused by a Divine Genius'.

As eventually with seven, and more often, we do come across cases of twelve being thought of as three-with-four. But the way in which this occurs is eloquent. It is analytic, not synthetic. A group of twelve exists first, and its breakdown into three fours or four threes is later.

Over the centuries, for instance, astrologers have come to make a practice of treating the Zodiac as a 3×4 pattern. The twelve signs are given by the annual track of the sun. For finer readings astrology splits them up into four sets of three, or three sets of four. They are made to correspond in threes to the four seasons, and also, more reconditely, to the four elements. They are also grouped into 'quadruplicities': there are four Cardinal signs, four Fixed and four Mutable. Always, however, the list of twelve signs is the starting-point. The three-by-four schemes merely express their supposed meanings. It is never suggested that the Zodiac was built up by putting such sets together.[18]

Likewise with the twelve Olympian gods, Zeus, Hera, Poseidon, Demeter, Apollo, Artemis, Hermes, Athene, Hephaestus, Aphrodite, Ares and Hestia. 'The Twelve' were worshipped together as such in the seventh century B.C., and probably before. Athens had a collective altar for them. When a new god, Dionysus, became popular, Hestia stepped down to make room for him. It was out of the question that the total should deviate from the round dozen. Nobody speaks of any sub-grouping within it till the very last age of classical paganism. In the fourth century A.D. an author named Sallustius wrote a treatise, *On the Gods and the World*, in aid of the Emperor Julian's rearguard action against Christianity. This tries to make philosophic sense of the Olympians by arranging them in four groups of three according to their imagined functions. The exercise is painfully artificial, an afterthought. The set of twelve came first.[19]

Christianity offers at least two parallels. In Revelation 21: 12–13 the New Jerusalem has three gates in four walls. This image goes back to an account in Ezekiel (48: 30–4) of a Utopian earthly Jerusalem, and thence to the story already mentioned of the encampment of the twelve tribes of Israel, in Numbers 2. The number of tribes is the explicit reason for the arrangement. The 3×4 design is simply a symmetrical way of handling a given twelve, and in Revelation this number is stamped on the apocalyptic city in other forms. Outside the Bible, Christian writers have indulged the fancy that the number of Christ's apostles was twelve because they were to spread knowledge of the Triune God to the four quarters of the world.[20] It was not. The company of apostles was also planned to match the tribes of Israel (Matthew 19: 28), and, in fact, the New Jerusalem description mentions the apostles as well as the gates. Again the dodecad is the thing that comes first. The 3×4 breakdown follows it, a far-fetched meditation on a number that is prescribed already, and senior in its origins.

CHAPTER FIVE

The Mandalic Universe

1

A conclusion follows which is hard to adjust to, and strange in its implications. Jung's findings (with partial support from Freud) may show well enough that three and four are significant today. But they cannot be traced – not with the right sort of attributes – as far back as the significant seven, or the less significant but still august twelve. In some early contexts, the *Rig Veda* for instance, seven is already present and powerful when three is less so and four is negligible.

In this matter of numbers, then, we are faced with several ancient societies whose mental movement runs counter to evolution, very much as the occultists maintain. Reductionism fails. The complex was not built up from the simple. The bigger numbers which could not be taken in at a glance were not synthesized out of smaller ones which could. On the contrary, seven was *given* as magical or sacred; so, probably, was twelve; and if three and four were ever related to them, they emerged through fission. The mental processes were not '3 + 4 = 7' and '3 × 4 = 12'. Seven and twelve stood up for centuries in their own right. Afterwards – perhaps – came the mental processes '7 = 3 + 4' and '12 = 3 × 4'.

This last process can be seen happening, step by step, in the series of scriptural passages we have just been looking at. When Numbers tells how the tribes of Israel camped in a four-sided formation, this obviously gives three tribes to a side, but the numbers three, four and twelve are not specified. Ezekiel's account of gates for the tribes in the walls of a square city does use the word 'three'. The

Christian development in Revelation spells out the twelve, the three and the four in plain terms (21: 12–16).

Seven, however, remains supreme – aloof, intractable, hard-to-handle seven, which has no inner logic, no psychological basis, no human aptitude, no physical relation to man, and no prior evolution behind it, yet, over a large portion of the earth, is the most venerable sacred number of all. Which, though it agrees with neither Jung's scheme of things nor Madame Blavatsky's, is closer to hers than to his. Seven has no Jungian explanation. With its geographic and cultural limits, it does not work as a universal archetype. But it could, on the evidence, have been the key number in some senior Wisdom of unknown provenance, which left its imprint on peoples from Greece to the Indus Valley.

In view of this mysterious charge which the number carries, and in view, also, of the way twelve was sometimes taken apart, the notion of fission is by no means insanely fanciful. It could quite well be that after the heptad was stamped on human minds over that area, the eventual importance of three and four (whatever it amounted to) was due in part to a cleavage within it, a separation of seven into the two smaller numbers, each with a share of its pre-existent magic. This might have been possible where the reverse process, the synthesis of a magical seven by adding them together, was not.

Jung himself reports a case which relates his mandalic four to seven in such a way as to give seven priority. As with some other cases, he stops short of discussing it in full. A woman patient with a gift for conjuring up visions described this experience:

'I climbed the mountain and came to a place where I saw seven red stones in front of me, seven on either side, and seven behind me. I stood in the middle of this quadrangle. The stones were flat like steps. I tried to lift the four stones nearest me. In doing so I discovered that these stones were the pedestals of four statues of gods buried upside down in the earth. I dug them up and arranged them about me so that I was standing in the middle of them. Suddenly they

73

leaned towards one another until their heads touched, forming something like a tent over me. I myself fell to the ground and said, "Fall upon me if you must! I am tired." Then I saw that beyond, encircling the four gods, a ring of flame had formed. After a time I got up from the ground and overthrew the statues of the gods. Where they fell, four trees shot up. At that blue flames leapt up from the ring of fire and began to burn the foliage of the trees. Seeing this I said, "This must stop. I must go into the fire myself so that the leaves shall not be burned." Then I stepped into the fire. The trees vanished and the fiery ring drew together to one immense blue flame that carried me up from the earth.'[1]

Jung comments on the patient's climbing, the square-in-circle formation, the four directions, the four gods . . . but on the prior, reiterated seven, from which the square is formed and the mandalic imagining unfolds, he says nothing; not a word.

2

At last a question is inescapable. Can we trace the seven-mystique to a source; to a specific area; to a specific culture? In other words, to a possible seed-bed of Ancient Wisdom? A line of advance may still be open. The heptad in itself leads nowhere. We cannot connect it with other numbers, or with anything in the human make-up. But can we connect it with anything else at all; with a theme or myth, say, which appears in its company and points in some definite direction? Here, despite Jung's evasions, his mandalic theory offers a hint. In one field of early thought, it does fit a known and recurrent image of cosmic reality. That image is much better defined in the territory of the seven-mystique than it is anywhere else. A connection, therefore, may exist.

From Greece to Mesopotamia, and perhaps among the Vedic Hindus as well, an idea of *circularity* governed early conjectures about the universe. It agreed with what was seen, and extended itself to what was not. The starry heavens could be watched circling, the ring of the horizon met the eye on all sides. At an early period the earth came to be pictured as a disc. Above and about it was the azure Ocean; the word 'Ocean' probably means 'that which surrounds'. The Heavenly Ocean was of sky-stuff, *aither* in Greek. The Earthly Ocean below was a ring of water – the Bitter River, Babylonians called it – incessantly flowing round, sometimes personified as a giant serpent. Inside it was the circular land-mass on which humanity lives, with dark waters of chaos (according to some) underneath.[2]

With local variants, this mandalic scheme was so firmly fixed that new geographical data continued to be slotted into it as a matter of course, until the fifth century B.C. or later. Greeks divided the land-mass into Europe, Asia, and Libya (meaning North Africa). Most of its rivers, they believed, flowed into the Mediterranean, the Mediterranean flowed into the Ocean at the Straits of Gibraltar, and Ocean was the greatest river of all, continually on the move around the world-island.

This girdled disc of land was admitted by the better informed to be ragged at the edges, but a disc it remained. In Hebrew it was called the *tebel*, in Greek it was the *oecumene* or inhabited world, in Latin it became the *orbis terrarum*, the circle-of-lands. The biblical passage on Wisdom already quoted, Proverbs 8: 27–31, depicts her as at God's side 'when he drew a circle on the face of the deep', and as afterwards 'rejoicing in his inhabited world', a rendering of *oecumene*. Proverbs was composed in the third century B.C. when Hellenic influence was biting into Jewish minds, but the images of the cosmic circle and *tebel* are far older and not solely Hellenic.

A Babylonian map, or diagram, shows the circular world. Pieces are missing, but the inscriptions and general design leave no doubt as to what was in them. Jung's follower Erich Neumann claimed the map as a cosmic mandala. It is not so very ancient itself – fifth century B.C. or thereabouts – but it does preserve ancient ideas. Around the disc-shaped land-mass is the ring of the Earthly Ocean. Outside that is the larger and vaguer ring of the Heavenly Ocean, with zodiacal gods. And in the Earthly Ocean, spaced around the disc like rays of a star, are seven triangular islands. Each has a description, and it is plain that the islands are vital parts of the diagram. In the one at the north-west, 'semi-obscurity reigns'; in the northern, 'the sun is not seen'; in the eastern, 'the sun rises'.[3]

The seven islands, as such, do no more than suggest a linkage between the cosmic pattern and the magical number. In itself the hint is not very fruitful, and vagueness as to age is a drawback. There may be echoes of an old septenary geography in the rabbinic division of the world's land into seven continents, and also in Hindu legend, though the Hindu scheme is too heavily overlaid with embellishments to be safely compared.[4] But the Babylonian map has a further feature. Like Jung's mandalas it is laid out around a centre, and the centre is Babylon, the holy capital of the people who drew it.

They were not alone in this attitude to their city, and enough is known of it to confirm the essential antiquity of the whole concept. Sumerians, Greeks and Israelites also gave their earth an exact centre – like the mandalic 'self' point – and revered it as focal to the life of the whole. With each nation the centre was the site of a temple or temple-complex. The great ziggurat in Babylon was called the Etemenanki, 'Temple of the Foundation of Heaven and Earth'.

On the centre's whereabouts there could obviously be no agreement. As Babylonians claimed the honour for Babylon, so Sumerians before them had claimed it for Nippur, and Greeks afterwards claimed it for Delphi, Israelites for Jerusalem. The Israelites were firmest, and managed in the end to convince others. In Ezekiel's words (5: 5): 'Thus says the Lord God: This is Jerusalem; I have set her in the centre of the nations, with countries round about her.' In 38: 12 he repeats that the Chosen People dwell 'at the centre of the earth'. His phrase gives precision to a more primitive idea of the Lord's home on the hill of Zion as the heart of his creation and the abode of his blessing. Jewish tradition takes up Ezekiel's text, declaring that the first piece of solid matter which God made was the rock destined to be the base of the Temple. 'From Zion', the rabbis taught, 'was the world founded.' God built Palestine round the rock, working outward from the centre, and then the less holy remainder of the *tebel* round Palestine. Furthermore he created Adam at the centre and wafted him to Eden from there.

As medieval maps show, the disc-world with Jerusalem more or less at its hub became a public mandala in its own right, for Christians as well as Jews. The Christians improved on the Jewish legend of Adam, saying that he had come back to Jerusalem to die and been buried under Golgotha. The latent symbolism did not escape Jung, who translated it into his own terms, writing of 'the self, enthroned in the place of the middle, and referred to in Revelation as the beloved city (Jerusalem, the centre of the earth)'.[5]

The Temple on its central rock was the special dwelling-place of the God of Israel, he who had made the world in seven days. There the holy heptad was given visible form in the Menorah, the huge lampstand with seven branches, its design familiar today in candlesticks and ornaments. A mere chance juxtaposition of seven with the centre? Let us look a little more closely at the ideas involved, and see whether we have hit on a motif which the septenary goes with and which may therefore shed light on it.

What has been called the 'hierocentric' concept of the universe had ramifications elsewhere as it had in Israel. The place of the centre, of the central precinct, was regarded in Mesopotamia as the bond of cosmic unity. It was a triple bond – between earth and heaven; between the different districts of the land; and between surface and underworld. Several temples had names conveying this 'bond' idea in some form. They were not all in the same area. That may be because the concept dates from an era of small communities, before even the earliest consensus as to where the earth's centre was; or perhaps there was one original centre, and rivals challenged it. In the Sumerian heyday, however, Nippur's predominance was accepted. The city was said to have been peopled by gods before human beings existed. Its sanctuary was 'the bond of heaven and earth', the mystical meeting-point or hub which held the visible cosmos together. The same

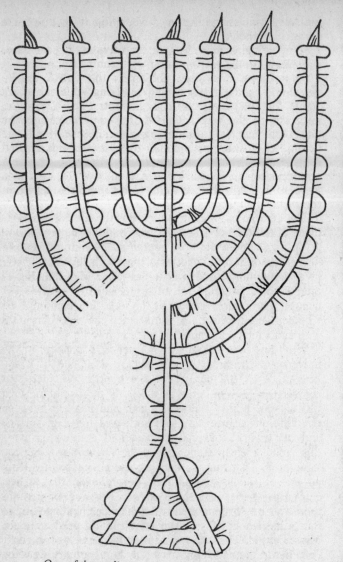

One of the earliest representations of the Menorah

function was assumed later by Babylon in its role as a sacred metropolis.

Some temples, including apparently the Nippur one, were described by the term *dimgal*, meaning quite literally a binding-post. The binding-post in that sense usually meant the 'bond of the land', the towering landmark which all men looked towards over level country. In Babylon the same notion was attached to the royal palace, since by then, with advancing state organization, the bond was political as well as visual and mystical. *Dimgal* was applied in another sense too. The temple might be held to have a relationship with the powers of the underworld. Libations were poured to them, possibly down actual drainpipes. Hence, the temple was the binding-post of the underworld. The numen extended into the depths like an unseen pillar. It was a vertical bond.[6]

The special character of Jerusalem was due in part to the Israelites adapting this concept to their own centre, the hill of Zion. Their ancestors were migrants from Ur, a Mesopotamian city, and they annexed the Mesopotamian notion in a competitive spirit. Their tale of the tower of Babel, which was to reach up to heaven and did not, is a gibe at Babylon's claims about its lofty ziggurat, the alleged means to ascent to encounters with the gods. Manifestly their own Temple was the true centre! Lacking a mythological underworld, they adapted that part of the concept by asserting that the Temple rock was a kind of stopper, sealing up the place where the 'waters under the earth' were nearest the surface. They are even supposed to have poured libations down fissures in it, like their heathen forbears, but as a rain-making ritual.[7]

As for the principal holy place of the Greeks, Delphi, that too was regarded by its devotees as the centre of the earth. Its most sacred feature was the *omphalos* or navel-stone, so called by analogy with the navel as centre of the body. 'Navel' is the word used for the centre by Ezekiel also, when he speaks of the centrality of Jerusalem; in Greece as in Zion, the world's mid-point was a rock. Delphi was said to have been the home of a dragon or snake, the Python. Apollo arrived and slew it, took over the place as a sanctuary for himself, and installed priestesses through whom he spoke. The establishment of his cult probably occurred between 1500 and 1000 B.C. Delphi thus became the 'bond of heaven and earth', in the sense that its famous oracle was the voice of deity.

While Apollo reigned it was not so clearly linked with the underworld, though the snake, an underworld creature, might suggest that such a link existed before his advent. But it did become the 'bond of the land,' in the sense that it was the only thing which united Hellas. Envoys from all the city-states came to consult the oracle. They looked to Apollo not only for decisions in special cases, but for guidance on policy. Sparta claimed that he had dictated its constitution. Athens did not go so far, but its legislators habitually made use of the god's counsel. In several cities Delphi had spokesmen called exegetes, who were attached to the government and interpreted the divine messages. Plato, in his *Republic*, seeks to found a social system on pure philosophic reason; yet even he says that 'the greatest and finest and most important of legislative acts' – those determining the republic's religion – should be entrusted to Apollo. 'For he is the national expositor who explains these things to all men from his seat at the navel of the earth.'[8]

What has all this to do with seven? The answer is simple. Just as the God of Israel, who made the world in seven days, dwelt in Zion with the seven-branched lampstand as his symbol, so the three other ancient centres all had prominent septenary features. To judge from an early map, the city of Nippur had seven gates. The top of the Etemenanki in Babylon was reached by a spiral path climbing through seven tiers. And as we saw, Apollo of Delphi, alone among the Olympian gods, was a septenary being. He was born on the seventh day of a month. Each of his chief festivals was held on the seventh day of whichever month it belonged to. The lyre which was his emblem as god of music had seven strings, and a vase painting shows him sitting on the Delphic navel-stone with the instrument in his hand. Over the entrance to his temple were inscribed the maxims of the Seven Wise Men. The eminent scholar M. P. Nilsson was so impressed by Apollo's sevens that he thought the god's cult must, at least in part, have been imported into Greece from Mesopotamia.[9]

Seven, therefore, appeared in every case at the sacred centre, the hub or heart of the world. True, all these occurrences – at Nippur, Babylon, Jerusalem, Delphi – look as if they could quite well have been accidental. They are all different and have no obvious logic. Yet the very fact that they are different, with only the number itself in common, could also be read as hinting at some subtle association between the number and the centre.

3

In at least two cases we can add more. Not only is a septenary motif linked with a centre, a further notion is interwoven with both.

Babylon's Etemenanki was a round temple 250 feet high. Its path, circling round seven times, corkscrewed up in a narrowing coil to a holy-of-holies on the top, where a ritual of divine marriage was solemnized by the King. What we observe here is more than the simple numinosity of the world's centre. It is also a delayed and difficult access, a gradual, indirect approach. The centre was there, but nobody could merely walk into it.

The Sumerians had nothing like this in physical fact, but they did in myth. Their own sacred centre extended down as the 'binding-post' of the region below, and their notions about that region are revealed in a poem called 'Inanna's Descent to the Nether World'. Inanna, a powerful goddess, decides to visit the underground temple-palace of her sister Ereshkigal, and assert her own authority there. She dresses herself alluringly in a splendid robe, with a crown, a golden ring, a breastplate and jewellery. She protects herself as well by girding on seven divine laws inscribed on tablets as charms.

Her sister's subterranean home, however, presents obstacles. The visitor finds that she has to pass through seven gates. At each gate, by Ereshkigal's order, a custodian removes part of Inanna's costume, telling her that this is a rite of the nether world. She arrives in the presence chamber naked, and confronts not only her sister but seven Annunaki, divine judges. They treat her as dead. To free herself she must offer a substitute. Escorted by demons, she returns above and appoints her own husband, the shepherd-god Dumuzi, to take her place. (This is the earliest known version of the renowned *Golden Bough* myth about the young god who regularly dies and rises again, embodying the cycle of seasons. The name Dumuzi becomes the biblical Tammuz.)[10]

Here too the heptad is combined with a theme of difficult access. The dark centre below the sunshine of the upper world is approached gradually, painfully. It is tempting to take a mental leap back to the Palaeolithic cave-paintings of western Europe. In such subterranean galleries as that of Trois Frères in the Pyrenees, the marvellous figures of animals, and perhaps deities, may or may not be provably magical on the internal evidence. What clinches their character is that they are not painted in caverns where people lived, or even close to them. They are not simply art. They are far down in darkness through tortuous and hazardous passages, in shrines only to be reached by way of natural mazes antedating even legend by tens of millennia.[11]

Practices handed down from ancestors in a geologically different land – not, of course, the Pyrenean cave-people themselves, but others like them – may have influenced Sumerian myth-makers. When wandering tribes settled in caveless Middle Eastern country, they still pictured hollows beneath their feet; and when they thought of this underworld, and imagined the dwelling of its inhabitants, a remembered subterranean complexity may have suggested a sanctum laboriously and circuitously approached. Indeed the same notion may in time have been extended to the architecture of real temples uniting surface and underworld at the sacred centre.

But the word which the cave galleries bring to mind, 'maze', evokes the theme of centrality in another form. A true maze path is, precisely, an approach to a centre by a difficult and gradual route. The idea of the labyrinth was in fact part of the Mesopotamian world-scheme. Furthermore it was connected with the underworld. Babylonian

A septenary spiral maze pattern on a Cretan coin

writings associate mazes with the 'bowels of the earth' and the coiled intestines of animals killed by augurers. It was also connected with – or at any rate, present at – the cosmic centre itself. The hidden heart of a maze had something in common with the heart of the world. The spiral path up the Etemenanki, though not strictly laby-rinthine, was a circuitous approach to a goal.

Ancient mazes, therefore, are worth a moment's study. They too imply an association of 'charged' centrality with hard or roundabout access. Do they show the heptad figuring in this mental pattern?

Even in its earliest forms, the maze has several variants. Sometimes it is a plain spiral, which winds in to the centre without deviating or dividing, and simply takes a long time to get there. The ascent of the Etemenanki was such a maze. Sometimes it is a complex sprial that winds back and forth, inwards and outwards, before finally reaching the same goal. Sometimes it is a puzzle – a maze in the modern sense – with false turns and a choice of routes. But always it leads towards its own heart, and its convolutions have a magical quality.

Egyptian seals have designs on them which at least approximate to mazes. These are thought to be symbols of royal tombs, or settings for stylized figures which are placed in the middle. They are formed by straight lines. Some are crude, some elaborate. Their degree of symmetry varies. Several of the pharaohs' tombs were actually constructed with winding approach passages and confusing multiple entries. In the nineteenth century B.C. Amenemhet III built a real labyrinth, a vast temple complex in the Fayyum. Its nucleus was a royal tomb, but the surroundings were maze-like in the modern sense of planned bafflement.

Middle Eastern coins and plaques show spiral designs around the heads of gods. These may express superhuman life. In Babylonia as in Egypt, the maze, if embodied in a structure, had as its nucleus a holy-of-holies, a sacrosanct enclosed centre which the tortuous route made it laborious to reach. The sacred enclosure might, in Egypt, be a tomb; but both here and in Babylonia it seems to have been a setting for religious acts such as fertility rites, symbolic combats, ceremonies of the death and rebirth of deified kings.

The maze entered the Greek world – at least as an idea – by way of Minoan Crete, in the second millennium B.C. Coins of Cnossus, once the capital of Minos, have swastika-like designs adapted from Egyptian seals, and also spiral patterns which are more truly mazes, and interesting for two reasons. First, some are non-Egyptian in style – of which more in a moment. Second, though far later than the Minoan age, they recall the labyrinth of the Minotaur legend, and the bull-cult which it reflects. Apart from the design itself, some of the Cretan coins have a bull's head inside the maze-pattern, or a Minotaur figure on the reverse.

*A graffito scratched on a pillar in Pompeii 2000 years ago –
a sevenfold maze pattern*

According to legend the Minotaur's temple-dwelling was planned by Daedalus, the prototype of master craftsmen. Ariadne's thread guided Theseus when he groped his way in to slay the monster. The word 'labyrinth' means 'house of the double axe', the weapon of sacrifice. Although the palace of Cnossus had a temple it does not seem to have been very labyrinthine. What is significant is that myth-making imagination should have given it such a form. It had to be pictured as a fully-fledged maze with a centre that was hard to reach, because the concept of such a concealed enclosure where a ritual took place (in this case a ritual slaying) was planted in tradition. Classical authors such as Pliny, describing Amenemhet's labyrinth in the Fayyum, took it for granted that Daedalus built a real Cretan counterpart with the Egyptian maze as his model. They were right to look in that direction, but the character of Aegean myth in general would suggest Asian influence as well.

The idea survived into later ages, though the complexity varied. Gaza in Palestine had a round temple with concentric colonnades. Lemnos, in the Aegean, had a temple reputed to be modelled on that of Daedalus. The motif spread to Italy and beyond. Porsena, King of Etruria, was entombed in a pretentious labyrinth-sepulchre reminis-

*A maze pattern on an Etruscan vase of the 7th century B.C.,
showing a labyrinth ritual, the Trojan Game (or maze dance)*

cent of Egypt, and a similar royal burial custom existed
among the Celts. A spiral maze pattern like those on the
Cretan coins is painted on a Etruscan vase, and another is
on a pillar in Pompeii, with a scrawl saying 'the Minotaur
lives here', a rude reference to the owner of the house. As
far off as Scandinavia, rows of stones are arranged in
magical patterns similar to those of Crete. The Cretan
spiral appears in Britain also, carved on a rock at Tintagel,
and preserved in rustic turf mazes in Wales and elsewhere.
In the Middle Ages, some churches had mazes on their
floors. It is said (though without contemporary proof) that
penitents crawled along the single path to a centre known
as 'the Heavenly Jerusalem'.[12]

With the original sacred mazes, we are certainly in the
presence of something august and awe-inspiring. To quote
C. N. Deedes:

> Such facts as are known about the Labyrinth reveal
> much of great interest; but the mystery which sur-
> rounds it is by no means dispelled. Research into the
> ancient history of myth and ritual will doubtless give
> us further knowledge about the great centres of
> religious belief – those places which contained lab-
> yrinths. There the king-gods performed magical acts
> and spoke magical words for the welfare of their
> people; and the psychological state created thereby
> in their subjects doubtless produced certain material
> results. Such conditions are difficult for us now to
> realize.

Above all, the Labyrinth was the centre of activities concerned with those greatest of mysteries, Life and Death. There men tried by every means known to them to overcome death and to renew life . . . The Labyrinth was the centre of all the strongest emotions of the people – joy, fear and grief were there given the most intense forms of expression. These emotions were directed into certain channels, producing ritual and the earliest forms of art – not only music and dancing, but also sculpture and painting. The Labyrinth, as tomb and temple, fostered the development of all art and literature, activities which in those days possessed a semi-religious and life-giving significance . . .

Now, the life-giving magic of the labyrinth is lost, and however many clues we may yet discover, it is doubtful whether we shall ever know its mystery.[13]

One plausible conjecture is that the rites enacted in the maze shrines had been enacted before, in simpler societies, by dancers circling round an image or tomb. Mazes may well mark the track of forgotten companies filing along in sinuous imitation of serpent gods, or spiralling in and reversing out, first towards a symbolic death and then towards a new life. This is not mere guesswork, or, as it might appear, a retroactive projection of the maypole. Greek authors associate the dance with the most famous maze of all, the Cretan Labyrinth itself. Homer preserves what may be the fundamental truth when he describes the pictures worked by Hephaestus on the shield of Achilles (*Iliad*, XVIII: 590ff.):

The god depicted a dancing-floor like the one that Daedalus designed in the spacious town of Cnossus for Ariadne of the lovely locks. Youths and marriageable maidens were dancing on it with their hands on one another's wrists . . . Here they ran lightly round, circling as smoothly on their accomplished feet as the wheel of a potter . . . and there they ran in lines to meet each other.

In some versions of the Daedalus legend he devises a

dance himself which gives the plan of his labyrinth. Either he or Ariadne teaches it to Theseus, who later institutes it on the island of Delos as a regular ritual. Whatever the historical facts, the satirist Lucian in the second century A.D. in a treatise *On Dancing* mentions dances called 'The Labyrinth', 'Ariadne' and 'Daedalus', and people in Crete and Delos were still dancing them.

Before Lucian's time a similar maze dance had spread to Italy, where it was a male parade-ground manoeuvre that included men on horseback. Virgil brings it into the *Aeneid* and compares its movements to threading the Cretan Labyrinth. It was called, however, not the Game of Crete but the Game of Troy. The reason may lie in a Trojan cult of Hippolytus, who was Theseus' son and whose semi-divine honours may have involved a 'labyrinthine' ritual. At any rate the connection of mazes with Troy is strangely durable. The Etruscan vase with the spiral has TRUIA painted on it. The design which Welsh shepherds were still cutting in turf in the eighteenth century was called Caerdroia, the Citadel of Troy, and the name 'Troy Town' has been popularly given to earthworks in England. Some of the Scandinavian stone spirals have names like 'Trogin', also derived from 'Troy'.[14]

The maze, then, gives us a well-attested tradition of magical centres and devious access to them. Its imagery intersects with the larger theme of the world's centre, in the plan of the Etemenanki for instance. But does the maze show a bias towards seven, or indeed towards any number? Since we are on quasi-mandalic ground, it is worth recalling that a design produced by one of Jung's patients in the same manner unquestionably did. This was the drawing with a line coiling in towards the centre, which he criticized as 'poor in form, poor in ideas,' and discussed for a whole page without mentioning its outstanding feature – that the line made seven circuits. Was this patient unconsciously recreating a habit of past generations?

It appears that she was. Ancient mazes do indeed show a heptadic motif, and it is in harmony with the data on the heptad's geography. The Egyptian ones, coming from a country outside the main field of the seven-mystique, give a square or cruciform effect with no numerical norm. But in Mesopotamia, where the sacred seven flourished, they had maze-structures to correspond: not only the Etemenanki with its seven-tiered spiral, but another ziggurat at Borsippa which also had seven stages (though the method of ascent is less certain) and was named the Temple of the Seven Rulers of Heaven and Earth – these possibly being seven 'fate-decreeing gods' annexed from the Sumerian pantheon. With the Cretan coin designs there is an eloquent contrast. Those which are Egyptian-inspired are cruciform and not strictly mazes. Those which break free from Egypt have continuous paths winding in to the centre of a square or circle. These are complex, backtracking spirals that advance and retreat in a prescribed manner. Counting from the circumference to the centre we find that the path goes round seven times. If a person threading the maze planted a flag on its periphery before going in, he would pass it seven times on his way to the centre.

As we have seen, this Cretan pattern is the prototype of quite a number of mazes, and they all have the same design and numerical keynote. The spiral on the Etruscan vase makes the same seven circuits, in and out and in again; so does the Pompeian graffito; so does the carving on the Tintagel rock; and so did the Troy-Town turf cuttings of Welsh shepherds – with them because Troy, allegedly, had seven walls. A modern theory of a maze on Glastonbury Tor, in Somerset, professes to trace remnants of an ancient track going round the hill in the same way, with the same number of circuits – an ascending spiral as on the ziggurat, only more complicated.[15]

Once this heptadic maze is recognized as a well-marked convention, originating in Crete and spreading through Europe, it suggests speculations as to where various other sevens might have come from. Thus the human tribute for the Minotaur, in the Cretan Labyrinth, comprised seven youths and seven maidens. Cretan frescoes indicate that these victims were ritual dancers. The stylized septenary design on the coins may thus go back to an original 'labyrinth' dance by seven couples. Again, a riddling medieval Welsh poem entitled *The Spoils of Annwn* tells how some of Arthur's men entered an enchanted fortress, Caer Sidi, the Spiral or Revolving Castle. Only seven returned; the number is reiterated and stressed. Some Celtic ritual at a maze shrine could underlie this poem.

The setting of Arthur's Annwn adventure is a Welsh underworld. The maze had such associations in Babylon also. Since the Sumerian underworld visited by Inanna is so plainly septenary, with its seven gates and seven judges, we might wonder whether the heptad is subterranean in origin, and came to be connected with magical centres (and thence doubtless with many other things) because mazes carried underworld characteristics with them. That suspicion is seemingly reinforced by facts of the same kind in other places. The Greek shrine of the oracular god Trophonius (the architect, incidentally, of the temple of Delphi) was in a cave with a maze-like arrangement of spikes and railings, and the pilgrim who threaded it was supposed to pass into the infernal regions. When Virgil's hero Aeneas comes to Cumae in Italy to venture below and consult the shades, he finds a temple with sculptured scenes of Daedalus, the Labyrinth and the Minotaur. The Cumaean Sibyl then guides him down through a cave entrance, quite in the style of Ariadne.[16]

It is undoubtedly easy to imagine the maze motif beginning its career underground in prehistoric cave-sanctuaries, from the age of the Palaeolithic artists onwards. The maze's likely antecedents in dancing are not inconsistent with such a view. Early ritual dances are thought to have imitated the track of snakes in motion, chthonic gods in serpentine form; and snakes come out of holes in the ground – thus, perhaps, out of the underworld. According to one theory, all primordial serpents of myth are derived from a Sumerian Arch-Serpent in subterranean waters, whose name was Zu. Apollo took possession of Delphi itself by killing a serpent already there, at the earth's navel.[17]

Yet however potent the underworld factor, the seven-mystique itself does not appear to have begun as part of a maze 'package' originating below. Mazes may have been suggested by caves, but the recurrent Cretan-type spiral is not seven-circuited *because* of this. At the oldest of the public world-centres, Nippur, the seven gates show no trace of such inspiration. They were not even labyrinthine, or set up as an obstacle course like the seven encountered by Inanna in the world below. A traveller entering the town did not have to thread an indirect route or pass through more than one of them. They were simply utilitarian breaks in the city walls – three on the south-east, three on the south-west, one on the north-west. The fourth side of the city was taken up with its main temple complex.

We have got as far as this: that there are signs of the heptad being connected with a mystic centrality, and, in particular, with the sacred centre of the world above and below ground level. In some recondite sense the place of the cosmic 'bond' was septenary. Anything on that spot, or closely related to it, or conceived with it in mind, was apt to have seven in it. In Sumeria the city built at the centre had seven gates, and the underworld which was the centre's downward extension had seven gates also, though differently arranged. In Babylon the main temple on the surface, housing the city's sovereign numen, had seven tiers. The Lord of the Jewish Temple on Zion had a septenary emblem. The resident god of Delphi was septenary in his own emblem and his ritual calendar. Mazes with magical centres, and complexities perhaps imitating the underworld, had a sevenfold path.

We may now have at least a part of the reason for the seven-mystique as such. Power flowed to the number from its central, therefore holy, associations. So the Sumerian king who built the temple of Nintu at Adab – less than a day's journey from Nippur – gave it seven gates, seven doors. Several of the earliest Greek sevens are connected with the god of Delphi, through the mythology of the lyre, and through such stories as Apollo's massacre of the seven sons of Amphion, king of seven-gated Thebes. The earthly land-mass itself seems to have acquired a septenary character radiating from its centre. Hence that map with Babylon in the middle and seven islands spaced round the rim. Hence, ultimately, the seven continents of the Zion-oriented rabbis. The Jewish cosmos had a further feature of interest which can now be better interpreted. This rabbinic earth not only had seven continents. It was sustained beneath, according to one school of thought, by seven pillars. The sage who propounded that idea cited the text from Proverbs about the Seven Pillars of Wisdom.[18]

But why the association in the first place? It is no use looking to Nippur, Babylon, Zion or Delphi for the clue, because the form taken by the septenary was different in each. Nippur had seven gates, Babylon a seven-tiered temple, Zion a seven-branched lampstand, Delphi a septenary god. No one of these could have suggested the other three. The clue is elsewhere.

CHAPTER SIX

The High Place

1

Here, if anywhere, a Jungian explanation should offer itself. Jung's numbers may have failed, but his diagrams, surely, are apposite. He did see that the ancient image of the disc-earth was mandalic. He also saw that it could be construed in his own manner, as projecting the human psyche with the 'self' at the centre. Yet the mandalas drawn by his patients, and those he collected from symbolic art, are no help. They hardly ever have a pattern which suggests seven, or implies that the Unconscious tends to project it. Whatever the antecedents, he is quite correct in saying that most of them favour three or four, in plain terms or in multiples. Confronted, very rarely indeed, by a motif of seven, he seems unable to fit in it. The stylized Cretan-type mazes, with a spiral path going round seven times, are mandalic figures, yet I do not think he mentions them. One of his followers, Dr C. A. Meier, has done so, but without taking the numerical problem further.[1] The heptad was surely already established when these mazes were drawn, *and for non-psychological reasons*. It is futile to invoke archetypes to explain them, in defiance of virtually all evidence as to the way mandalic imagination does function when it works freely.

Since psychology has no answer here either, we may be excused for trying the Ancient Wisdom theory instead; or rather, the mode of approach which it implies, without any sensational assumptions. We can search for a prototype, a prior world-centre which the rest imitated or reflected. This centre, if it existed, caused those following to be septenary because it was so itself, and for some clear reason which was inherent in its nature or whereabouts. If such a prototype does turn out to have existed, we shall have our first glimpse of what at least could be a sort of Ancient Wisdom in action: if only because the prototype would supply an ancestry for the seven-mystique, and therefore for many aspects of our mental organization of the world to this day – colour, music, the calendar, and so forth.

In this case, the likeliest place to pick up the trail is Jerusalem. Its massive scriptural documentation cannot be equalled anywhere else. And in fact it has a very odd feature. Israel's holy hill Zion, where the Temple stood, was the heart of the city and often identified with it. The name originally applied to the ridge of Ophel, David's site for his infant capital. Approached by the uphill road from Jericho, Jerusalem is silhouetted against the sky. Topography, however, would scarcely prepare us for a Jewish belief, attested by rabbinic tradition in the Talmud, that the Temple rock is not only earth's centre but its highest point.[2]

This certainly introduces a fresh idea, and a bizarre one. Zion is plainly no Everest. Part of the explanation may be that the earth-disc or *tebel* was conceived as dome-shaped rather than flat. Its centre was nearest heaven even though mountains at the rim might be taller. But that is not enough. After all, Zion is topped by the neighbouring Mount of Olives, as anybody can see now, and could have seen in the past. Zion's exaltation shows traces of a much stranger influence. Psalm 48, verse 2, has the astounding phrase 'Mount Zion in the far north'. Commentators have struggled to tone it down, but without carrying conviction. The holy mountain seems to have acquired stature through being mystically identified with another, much higher one, which was not in Palestine at all. The same northern mountain figures in related myths of the Canaanites. They called it 'Safon' and said it had an earthly paradise on it. 'Safon' occurs in the Bible as a synonym for Zion, and Ezekiel (28: 11–16) places 'Eden, the garden of God' on a 'holy mountain of God' which cannot possibly be the mundane hill of Jerusalem.[3]

Nor does the mystery end there. To judge from another

prophetic text, Isaiah 14: 13, some such belief existed among the Babylonians too. Isaiah, denouncing the King of Babylon, uses these words: 'You said in your heart, "I will ascend to heaven; above the stars of God I will set my throne on high; I will sit on the mount of assembly in the far north." ' The 'assembly' is the assembly of gods with whom the impious monarch aspired to equal himself. The 'far north' phrase is the same applied to Mount Zion in the psalm. Ezekiel, himself in Babylonia, saw a vision of the Lord's chariot careering towards him. It did not come from the direction of the Palestinian Zion, where the Lord supposedly had his home. It came from the north on a storm-wind (1: 4).

Where then was this other mountain, paradisal, proto-typal (at least to Zion), and supreme over all? We might guess that it was a Semitic version of a 'world-mountain' which is familiar in independent legend over much of Asia. Its best-known guise is the Mount Meru of Hinduism. The ancient Hindus, who were a migrant Indo-European stock with ancestry in what is now the Soviet Union, pictured the world as having a centre much as other peoples did. But they did not locate it in the countries they occupied. They were not yet deeply enough rooted, and they had no great single capital city. Meru was far away to the north, and it was the centre of the sky as well as the earth, of the entire universe in fact. The Hindu epic *Mahabharata* puts it beyond the Himalayas, and, describing a journey to it, says the travellers passed 'a vast desert of sand', suggesting a location north of the Gobi region. The same epic declares that it 'stands carrying the worlds above, below and transversely'.

Meru contained a paradise, like the Canaanite Safon, and an abode of gods. Above its peak was the celestial pole, and the heavens rotated round it as a pivot. Iranian and other legends portray the same mountain. Among Buddhists it is usually called Sumeru. Sometimes it is said to have a temple on its summit – the hierocentric concept again. In some accounts the temple has a golden spire which we see as the Pole Star.

Furthermore – a reason to consider it carefully – the world-mountain tends to have septenary attributes. Meru in early versions has seven sides, facing the seven divisions of the earth. Other descriptions speak of seven tiers rather than sides. More interesting still, it is regularly frequented by the Seven Rishis. These are the celestial sages of Hinduism, and they are closer than any other characters in recognized myth to being Masters of Ancient Wisdom in the Blavatsky style. These mighty seers are human yet more than human. They are associated with the beginnings of man and knowledge, and they appear whenever a fresh revelation is required. Their names vary from cycle to cycle of creation, but there are always seven of them. They may be remote prototypes of other groups, such as a heptad of Babylonian sages in the Epic of Gilgamesh, and the Seven Wise Men of Greece. Incidentally the Iranians' world-mountain is inhabited by seven gods.[4]

If (as seems to have been the case) some rumour of such a northern world-centre, real or fictitious, was current in the Middle East at least as early as Old Testament times, how might Zion or Babylon have been brought into relationship with it? How should we construe the mystical identity implied in Psalm 48? In that psalm, Ronald Knox translates the 'far north' phrase as 'true pole of earth'. Which is ingenious. Behind the startling image of a northern Zion is a crux which hierocentric minds had to resolve. The binding-post of earth and heaven ought to go straight up to the zenith. But up there, the zenith was not the centre. The stars did not revolve around it but around the celestial north pole, the 'navel of the sky', marked today (very nearly) by the Pole Star, but before about 500 B.C. by part of the constellation Draco.

A literal and local Zion could not be a Meru. The binding-post of earth and heaven could not go straight up from it, because the celestial pole was not overhead. So the solution was a mystical bilocation. Zion 'became' the world-mountain dimly recalled from Canaanite and other pre-biblical myth, and was thereby joined to the pole regardless. Israelites did not spell this out, at least in any writing that has survived. Others have done so in a more primitive form. Ceylon has Buddhist topes or shrines symbolizing the world, with a square stone in the centre which explicitly means Meru.

Mesopotamia had no high country. But even its earliest temple mounds may have been magical models of the gods' mountain, on the principle of the witch's image of a person which 'is' that person. Sumerians of the civilized era did believe in a far-off 'mountain of heaven and earth', though they were vague about its direction; the sun emerged from behind it each day. Nippur's main temple was sometimes called the House of the Mountain. Babylon had similar temple names, including 'Mount of the Mountains of All Lands', showing that the temple itself was assimilated to the cosmic mountain. Babylon's giant ziggurat, with its seven tiers and summit-shrine, was a more sophisticated essay in the magical style. By such devices, it seems, the earthly centre was made to be at one with the heavenly.[5]

Whatever the traditions were that stamped the world-mountain on Middle Eastern minds, they were certainly stronger than these sketchy hints attest. Centuries afterwards, despite many conquests and upheavals, the mountain reappears in Islamic legend. Transmitted via Iran, it has become slightly blurred, and its attributes have been split up, but it remains in origin the same mountain. One Moslem story still places it at the earth's centre, with a bridge leading from its summit to heaven; the ascent is a kind of purgatory. Other stories shift emphasis to the Earthly Paradise said to be on top, and transfer the mountain to Syria, Persia or India. Adam's Peak in Ceylon is a favoured candidate. In other versions again, the mountain is more vaguely located but definitely the highest. However confused, however fragmented, the tradition comes through and must therefore have been strong in the first place.

Islamic sources account, partly at least, for a remarkable rebirth of the mountain in fourteenth-century Christendom from the mind of Dante. He not only adopts it, he draws it together into a unity again. The Mount of Purgatory in the *Divine Comedy* is a colossal Christian Meru. Dante seems determined to make it central, yet geography forbids him to do so in the ancient ways. He accepts the Christian map which puts Jerusalem at the centre of all lands, and he rejects the notion of the heavens being crudely pivoted on a physical peak. However, he also knows that the earth is spherical. That knowledge enables him to attain his object. Jerusalem is still the centre of the inhabited world, but the Mount of Purgatory is on an island at its antipodes, in the corresponding centre of the opposite hemisphere, which is otherwise all ocean.

Furthermore it is a kind of ziggurat. Under the tutelage of angels, souls of the dead are purged and prepared for blessedness on a series of horizontal paths that encircle it, one above another, with connecting stairways. The number of these paths (we might almost predict it) is seven, with a sin allotted to each. At the top (we might almost predict this too) is the Earthly Paradise. Though the summit is not in physical contact with the heavens, it gives access to them. From here Dante is led by Beatrice upward through the planets and stars, to the presence of God.[6]

Obviously, neither Moslem legends nor a medieval Christian poem are evidence for pre-Christian myth. What they do suggest is a profound inherent stubbornness in a complex motif. Thrust down and disintegrated for hundreds of years, the world-mountain – central and septenary, with a surmounting paradise, more-than-mortal inhabitants, and contact with the heavens – can still surface again as a unified conception. If we revert to the Asian centres, Nippur, Babylon and Zion, the assembled facts do suggest mystical affiliation to a prototype on that pattern. It was a towering Something supposed to exist in the remote recesses of the continent, probably in a northern latitude. It had divine and paradisal associations. In some sense or other it was septenary. And it was central to the revolving sky, while the three earthly cities paired to it were held, each by its own patriots, to be central to the earth.

2

What about the Greeks? Was their earthly 'navel', Delphi, affiliated to anything of the same sort?

The Hellenic invaders of Greece in the second millennium B.C. were distant cousins of the Iranians and proto-

98

Hindus. Among these migrants from the north, who knew mountain ranges at first hand, it was natural to think of mountain tops as divine dwellings. Hence the special dignity of Olympus, where the sky-god Zeus planted himself. Yet Olympus was not made out to be the world's centre. Delphi was; and the background of Delphi's cult was more curious.

It was the home of Apollo, and Apollo, in origin, did not belong to the Olympian group of gods, though the Greeks rewrote his life so as to fit him in. He was a latecomer, with an established legend of his Delphic advent and dragon-slaying. Partly because of this legend, partly because of his septenary ritual calendar, it is today accepted that he entered Greece from outside and not in the company of Hellenic Zeus. Inscriptions in Asia Minor show that his cult flourished there in the second millennium B.C. and moved west across the Aegean. An attempt has been made to prove that he began his career as Apulunas, a Hittite god of gates. This, however, is open to serious doubt, and there are grounds for thinking that he was born beyond Asia Minor and earlier still.

Greek myth gives him a cryptic northern connection. Despite his adoption by Hellenes who had themselves come from the north, it does not seem to relate to them or their wanderings. Apollo's northern milieu is utterly alien. He was a special friend of a nation called the Hyperboreans, dwellers-at-the-back-of-the-north-wind (or at any rate, 'beyond Boreas'), who were not Hellenic. He left Delphi for three months every year to live among them, riding through the sky in a chariot drawn by swans. Straw-wrapped offerings delivered annually to another of his temples, on the island of Delos, were alleged to come from his Hyperborean worshippers. They lived in a carefree country, a secret Elysium, with inhabitants a thousand years old.

Had they any earthly reality? Herodotus says their country extended to a sea which, in his context, might be the Arctic Ocean or Baltic. Other Greeks locate them anywhere from Britain to the borders of China, with, on the whole, a north-east rather than a north-west bias. Hercules goes among them on his third labour to chase a 'golden-horned hind' which is apparently a reindeer (see page 132). Most likely there was an actual nation behind the story, or an amalgam of several. But the semi-deified members of it whom Apollo visited were not at ground level. The poet Pindar wrote: 'Neither by ship nor foot couldst thou find the wondrous way to the assembly of the Hyperboreans.' That assembly is inferred to have been in the sky, and the road to it which Apollo travelled, going neither by sea nor by land, was perhaps the Milky Way. His chariot-drawing swans recall a 'road of birds' that leads to the celestial realms in northern folklore – that of Lithuania, for instance.[7]

The blessed assembly was not the only thing in that high place at the back of the north wind. The polar axle on which the heavens turned was there also. These are mythological fragments which no single story brings together. It looks, however, as if the Hyperborean paradise could have been the same one which other myths placed on top of the northern mountain, sky-supporting Meru, and as if its semi-divine inhabitants were the beings imagined elsewhere as Rishis or gods. By his annual stay among them Apollo kept the earthly centre at Delphi in contact with the celestial centre, the axle, the heavenly pole. He was a bond of heaven and earth in his own person. Like Meru he was septenary.

We might venture to wonder about a real outflow of myth and cult from a real northern centre, a literal Siberian or Mongolian Meru, with disjointed ideas drifting down to various peoples, from Greece to India. An odd verbal coincidence has emerged already. Pindar speaks of the Hyperborean 'assembly', and Isaiah calls the northern mountain the 'mount of assembly'. The coincidence may be odder. According to one etymology Apollo's name means 'god of the assembly'. If that is too fragile to support even speculation, it is still worth noting how strange it is that Apollo should have been credited with a cult in the far north, unless he actually came from there.

W. K. C. Guthrie has maintained that he did. Guthrie argues that the key to Apollo lies in the Delphic priestesses' prophesying and oracular frenzies, and in 'ecstatic' conduct ascribed to Apollo's devotees, who claimed powers of shape-shifting, astral travelling, and thauma-turgy of other kinds. He draws parallels with Siberian shamans or medicine-men, and suggests that Siberian tribes were the real Hyperboreans and that Apollo began his long career in that part of Asia. His cult spread south-westwards to Asia Minor and entered the Hellenic world by that route, bringing female prophetesses with it. The Greeks adopted him and he became, in time, the most quintessentially Greek of deities. But he never shed a tradition of eerie worshippers 'beyond the north wind'. Nor, it may be added, did his cult shake off shamanistic influence, which flowed into it in a second instalment when the Greeks colonized the Black Sea region and made direct contact with the shamans of Scythia, now Russia.[8]

This theory, of course, derives the lord of Delphi from a territory so ill-defined that it does not lead (in itself) to any identifiable Meru. Still, so far as the world-mountain has a location at all, the clues are consistent with its being somewhere in Siberia, the homeland of shamanism; and one literary outgrowth of Apollo's cult can be read as narrowing down the field in a manner which is quite startling. This is the tantalizing story of Aristeas of Proconnesus. He seems to have lived in the seventh century B.C. and to have been a priest of Apollo. The accounts of his patron's Hyperborean home inspired him to go in search of it. Returning safely, he described his adventures in a poem entitled *Arimaspea*. No copy of it survives, but fragments, quotations and paraphrases in other authors reveal a knowledge of Asian peoples and folklore suggesting that he did actually make the journey and that he travelled north and east.

To judge from what can be reconstructed of the poem, he admitted that he never reached the goal of his quest. However, he made contact with a people called Issedoni-ans who told him of other nations beyond them – the Arimaspians, and the Hyperboreans themselves. Between these lay a country rich in gold, with 'griffins' guarding it. Somewhere in that remote region was a cave where the wind Boreas lived. The Hyperboreans, naturally, were on the far side of it, 'beyond Boreas'.

Aristeas' route can be followed, more or less, far into

Siberia. A difficulty might seem to arise over Boreas, because we persist in thinking of Boreas as strictly the *north* wind. However, as already observed, this exactitude is a later sophistication. To a Greek of the seventh century B.C. Boreas meant, essentially, the strong cold wind which in Greece does blow from the north – but in Russian Asia, blows from the east. Hence, to a traveller who had arrived in that area, Boreas' cave might well (in terms of modern compass-bearings) have lain eastward rather than northward, and the Hyperboreans beyond would have been logically located in that direction. While the motif of a wind dwelling in a cave was un-Greek, it can be paralleled in the lore of the steppe country towards the Altai mountains, where the winds are tremendous. This hint at first-hand or good second-hand information converges with several others, such as Aristeas' report of gold, and the legend he tells in connection with it. The clues plausibly guide us to the upper Irtysh river, and the approaches of the Altai, as the limit of his specific knowledge. If the Hyperboreans (the earthly ones at any rate) are just beyond, they are in territory where shamanism flourishes to this day. The support for Guthrie is impressive. Aristeas' story, moreover, is very nearly the oldest of all allusions to them, and the one likeliest to have authentic tradition behind it.[9]

CHAPTER SEVEN

Inhabited Skies

1

Whether or not these northward-looking motifs were inspired by anything actually *in* the north, they show us where to look for the origin of the seven-mystique. The linkage of seven with the earth's sacred centres was by way of analogy with their great prototype. At the earthly centres, Meru in its various guises was evoked or imitated. Mesopotamian temples were named to show that they represented the world-mountain; Zion was twinned with a Zion 'in the far north'; the god of Delphi was also the god of the Hyperboreans, in their supra-terrestrial paradise. With that mystical connection the heptad came southward. The earthly centres do not account for it. Perhaps the mountain does not account for it either, in itself. But the mountain's character as sky-centre suggests an answer. The septenary began in the heavens. It was first descried and revered in some sort of relation to the celestial pole, the upper centre, not the lower. Its home was in the circling sky as centred on that, pivoted on the summit of Meru (or whatever the axle place was called).

Psychologically there is much to be said for the sky, and especially the night sky, as a source for patterns at the centre of the world below. It is mandalic, a multiple rotation around its own centre the pole. In the second and third millennia B.C. its polar constellation was Draco, the Dragon, a heavenly analogue to the coiling serpent of primitive maze dances. Around the pole, a 'self' symbol in Jung's language, the starry circlings were traced by visible motion, immense, majestic, eternal. To look for the original Seven here is a plausible action.

There is no need to credit the nascent Sumerians, or anyone else, with an improbably sophisticated process of thought. Stellar myths do not presuppose an advanced culture. They are familiar among, for example, the Australian aborigines. The full-scale planetary astrology invented in Babylon was junior to the seven-mystique, but star-gazing and star-worship, and a consequent notion of 'as above, so below', flourished long before. Mesopotamian priests, under their clear heavens, regarded constellations as the abodes of gods. Below on earth, natural features, cities, and even temples corresponded to celestial diagrams. This mode of thinking began among the Sumerians and was carried further by their Babylonian heirs. The presiding star-group of the great rivers, Tigris and Euphrates, was Pisces. The city of Sippar was matched to Cancer, Ezida to Capricorn, Eridu to Vela, Babylon to Aries and Cetus taken together.[1]

Given a cosmos already known to be complex, it would be rash to jump to conclusions about the aspect likeliest to have imprinted 'seven' on star-gazers below, in such a way that they connected the number with the sky-centre. They might have discerned it in a single circling constellation. Or in the ring of the Zodiac. Or in a cycle of time rather than space, an ever-recurring period marking some celestial change.

The only prototype-seven even tentatively proposed by Jung was in fact a heavenly one. As we saw, he detected it in the planets – 'the seven planetary gods of the ancients'. Several authors, notably Franz Cumont, offer the same idea. The statements already made – that it will not work, because the astrologers' set of 'planets' was not defined till long after the appearance of the magical seven – needs now to be given more exactitude. The process of doing so can help to open lines in other directions.

Mesopotamia's embryonic astrology had no place for the planets at all. As a result, the system was static and somewhat barren. Earthly events could not be correlated with star-patterns that never changed. Astrology proper required two things: first, the identification of those few bodies that move on paths of their own, and alter the celestial scene; second, the working out of an accurate

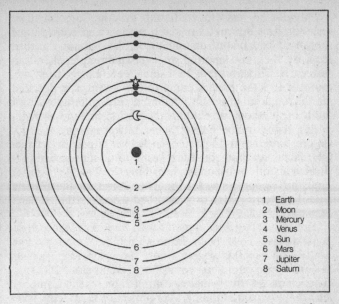

1	Earth
2	Moon
3	Mercury
4	Venus
5	Sun
6	Mars
7	Jupiter
8	Saturn

The planetary system according to ancient astronomy, with the earth in the centre

calendar by which their movements could be plotted. Sumerians divided the year into twelve lunar months with periodic adjustments, giving a slipshod result. Little by little, however, it was observed that during the year the sun passed through a tract of sky that never varied. Hence the Zodiac, with twelve 'signs' marking the sun's position each month.

The so-called planets of developed astrology were (to repeat) the sun itself, plus the moon, plus the five genuine planets then known apart from Earth itself – Mercury, Venus, Mars, Jupiter, Saturn. 'Planet' means 'wanderer', and not only the sun but all the others move about in the Zodiac, which is a belt of sky extending about 8° on either side of the ecliptic. Its twelve divisions or signs were named from the constellations – the Ram, Bull and so forth – which were conspicuous in each. (That is, when the belt was charted. They have shifted since.)

Babylonian astrology, based on the ever-changing relationships between the seven planets and twelve signs, began to find favour among the Greeks about the third century B.C., and exerted an overwhelming spell during the early Christian era. Its claims were exaggerated to a point where the planets came to be viewed, and dreaded, as the agencies governing mankind. Entire religions were built on methods of eluding their clutches, and escaping into a higher realm above them. Astrology's prestige was so crushing that it affected even Jewish minds, in defiance of official teaching on the Lord's total supremacy. The Jewish historian Josephus, describing the Temple, asserted that the Menorah's seven branches stood for the planets, and the twelve loaves of shewbread stood for the zodiacal signs.[2]

But all such development was late. For the seven-mystique to have been inspired by the seven planets, something like this system would have had to exist, with a similar grip on human convictions, well before 2000 B.C. That claim is actually made or implied by Joseph Campbell in his study of mythology, *The Masks of God*. This takes its author as close to advocacy of Ancient Wisdom as any recent anthropologist gets. Campbell argues that all civilizations, even the pre-Columbian in America, go back to Sumeria. The wheel and writing and decimal counting all began among the Sumerians towards 3200 B.C. The powerhouse of their civilization was the 'sacred city': that is, the centre, conceived more or less as we have seen. Other themes such as the world-mountain are duly recognized, but are all said to have been derived from the sacred city, as it existed in Mesopotamia. Its temple tower was the model for Meru, not the other way round, and it was also the model for Olympus, and Dante's Mount of Purgatory, and Aztec pyramids.

According to Campbell the sacred city mediated between the macrocosm, i.e. the universe, and the microcosm, i.e. man. It was a 'mesocosm', living by a system of myth and ritual which related human beings to the phenomena round them – to earth and heaven, day and night, birth and death, the seasons. The inspiration, says Campbell, came from the sky. Priests discovered order in the celestial movements and transferred it to earth, correlating one with the other. They invented astrology. In particular, they observed how the seven planets roved through the Zodiac erratically yet intelligibly, and from this drew all sorts of inferences.[3]

Some of this is plausible, but the issue of priorities and relationships, of what-influenced-what, is hopelessly confused; and much of the confusion is due to a mistake in the septenary part. Campbell's Pan-Sumerianism depends largely on Sumeria having an advanced cosmic ideology inspired by the planets. But although astrology of a sort may go back as far as he says, the pseudo-scientific scheme with the planets does not, because the requisite knowledge was slow to come. In particular, exactitude over the calendar could not be achieved till it was regulated by the sun instead of the moon. From about 1000 to 600 B.C., Babylonian priests were perfecting a solar year. They were also tracking the 'wanderers' in the Zodiac. However, astrology as we know it was not even in provisional working order till the sixth century B.C., and it only attained final precision through contact with Greek astronomers. There is no proof that the planets were invested with sovereign status any earlier, or even that they were regarded as seven in number before (to be specific) 722 B.C.[4]

Why did this happen as it did? The reason is fairly plain. The priests realized that by lumping together all the Zodiac-wanderers, however different the sun and moon were from the rest, they could make up seven. *And seven was already established as magical.* Because it was, the group of planets became so. As astrology gained ground, many further sevens followed on from the set of planets. But the set itself followed on from previous sevens, and from the ultimate prototype further back which we have yet to identify.

It might be objected that this is making the set of planets sound arbitrary, as if the priests forced the number to come out right when no forcing was needed. If we define 'planets' as 'those celestial objects regularly seen by the naked eye which move on paths of their own', surely the tally of seven is a fact of astronomy? Of astronomy, yes.

But when astronomy is harnessed to magical and religious ends, such logic ceases to be decisive. We have already taken note of the different planet counts in Iran, India, China. Some schools of astrology included (and still do) the head and tail of the constellation Draco. Hindu astronomers knew the five true planets by the fourth century B.C.; Hindu astrologers adopted the whole quintet as *grahas* or celestial powers, and added the sun and moon like their Babylonian colleagues. But they did not stop there. They further added two 'nodes' or foci of influence, Rahu and Ketu. For whatever reason, they wanted not seven *grahas* but nine (by this time the old seven-mystique of the *Rig Veda* had died out in Hinduism) and rigged their heavens accordingly. The Babylonians would have been perfectly equal to rigging theirs, but they wanted seven. We do catch hints in Mesopotamia of seven cosmic powers antedating the planets. The ziggurat at Borsippa was known as the Temple of the Seven Rulers of Heaven and Earth as early as the twelfth century B.C. The seven fate-decreeing gods of Sumeria are older than that. Whatever heptad we are pursuing in the sky, it must account for these.[5]

2

The planets, however, are helpful in another way. They direct attention to one of the most outstanding heptads of all, and one of the most long-lived – the seven-day week, so awkwardly yet insistently fitted into the twelve-month years. It is connected with the heavens now through our names for its days; maybe it can claim such a connection far enough back to be of value. The names of the days are based on an astrological plan which assigned a day to each planet. A day was given to the sun, the next to the moon, the next to Mars, the next to Mercury, the next to Jupiter, the next to Venus, the next to Saturn, and so round to the sun again. English retains Sun-day, Moon-day and Saturn-day, and allots Nordic deities to the rest, in hazy equivalence to the classical ones.

Gods were first assigned to the planets in Babylon, the

fountainhead of astrology itself. When the Babylonians had sorted the 'wanderers' out, they named them after seven divinities. For the sun they already had a deity, Shamash, and for the moon another, Sin. The planet which we call Mercury they associated with Nebo; Venus, with Ishtar; Mars, with Nergal; Jupiter, with Marduk; and Saturn, with Ninib. Under their influence, beginning in Alexandria during the second century B.C., Greeks did likewise, naming the planets after roughly corresponding gods of their own: Helios, Selene, Hermes, Aphrodite, Ares, Zeus, Cronus. Then they allocated a planet with its presiding god to govern each day, in an endlessly repeated cycle of seven. Romans imitated Greeks, using the names of their own gods. By the second century A.D. the planet week from which our own Sunday, Monday and so on are derived was popular through most of the Roman Empire.[6]

But it was popular only as an astrological formula, in an age when astrology was potent. It had no role in the calendar till the triumph of Christianity caused it to be assimilated to another seven-day week, which had nothing to do with the planetary scheme and was far older – the week of the Jews, six days plus sabbath. The Church transferred the sabbath from the seventh day to the first, Sun-day, in memory of Christ's resurrection, and imposed the resulting week on the calendar of the converted Empire. It has been going on ever since. Europe's phase of dominance, and its adoption by Islam, together carried it everywhere.

The question worth asking is where the Jewish week came from. It is a question that holds out hope of discoveries, because of the way the week was regarded. The biblical God makes the world in six days and rests on the seventh, giving it a special blessing. Israel planted this particular heptad at the very heart of his cosmic work, and the thinking behind it was certainly religious rather than practical. At the same time it was so completely innocent of astrology that the days, apart from the sabbath, did not even have names.

A survey of the world's calendars shows that the Jewish week has nothing absolute about it, or even convenient. While most nations have broken up the year into months, only some have employed a shorter day-series within the month, and those have not all made it the same length. The usual reason for it is economic. People need market days – days for buying and selling rather than producing – at regular intervals, and the interval of a month is apt to be too long. The period chosen depends largely on the nature of the economy, and the distances traders have to travel. Some West African tribes have a 'week' of only four days. Ancient Central Americans preferred five, and so did Scandinavians. Ancient Assyria had six. Republican Rome had a nine-day cycle counted as eight-plus-one – eight days of normal activity, then a distinct market day. Egypt, and Peru under the Incas, made it ten. The Chinese had a double cycle of ten and twelve, coinciding every sixtieth day. Regular holidays like the sabbath were no part of these schemes. Work ceased, when it did, on public occasions such as festivals which were fixed in other ways.

Trade was not everywhere the sole reason for the week. Egyptians regarded their ten-day cycle as one-third of a month, a time unit related to another time unit. Conversely, trade has not always produced a week at all. The Hindus had no such time division. Nor did the Greeks till they came under foreign influence. As for the biblical week itself which, through Christianity, we inherit, it implies other ideas again and the imposition of a religious pattern on what was elsewhere a purely practical matter. Its special day was not set apart for marketing or for any other business, but for abstention from business. The sabbath was for rest and worship.

And – a crucial point – not only was the Israelites' week seven days long, it seems to have been the only one in any calendar that ever was. No one else had a seven-day week independently. The period occurs in legend and ritual, but it nowhere ran on in a continuous cycle, independently of the month. It is the one 'week' which is never found to be economically natural. It enters Israel with a charge of septenary mystery, and, in due course, ousts all its practical rivals. Indeed, it may have begun its career by ousting a more practical 'week' in Israel itself. The patriarchal Hebrews doubtless had a marketing cycle like other peoples, and one clue suggests that it was – as we might

Helena Petrovna Blavatsky, the foundress of Theosophy

Medieval map showing Jerusalem at the centre of the
disc-shaped earth (known as the Ebstorf map, 13th
century)

Apollo with his seven-stringed lyre. (On a Greek bowl,
5th century B.C.)

Artemis as Mistress of Animals, on a gold plaque from
Rhodes, 7th century B.C.

Artemis with a bow and young deer, from Corinth,
c. 500 B.C.

A bear dance of North American shamans, as painted by
Catlin, and a bronze plaque honouring the bear, from
the Perm' region in Russia (*c.* 5th century A.D.)

Nicholas Roerich, artist and anthropologist, investigator
of the legend of Shambhala

The Siberian marshland directly under the Tunguska explosion, showing trees stripped of their foliage

Glastonbury Tor, Somerset. According to a theory developed by Geoffrey Russell the horizontal ridges are the remains of a septenary spiral maze

almost expect – the same as in the dominant civilization of nearby Egypt. In Genesis 24: 55, an early-written passage, Rebecca's relatives want to detain her for 'at least ten days'. But when Israel's week as we know it comes into view, its six-plus-one pattern already reveals a unique outlook. Here is the text:

> Remember the sabbath day, to keep it holy. Six days you shall labour, and do all your work; but the seventh day is a sabbath to the Lord your God; in it you shall not do any work . . . for in six days the Lord made heaven and earth, the sea, and all that is in them, and rested the seventh day; therefore the Lord blessed the sabbath day and hallowed it. (Exodus 20: 8–11)

That edict in the Ten Commandments was treated more and more reverently with the passage of time. By the Roman era many Jews were unwilling, when at war, to fight on the sabbath, because it counted as work. They were therefore beaten. Rabbis of pacific temper used to cite this dilemma to refute the dream of a conquering Messiah. If he was a faithful Jew he would have to halt military action every sabbath day, and his Gentile enemies would win.[7]

Certainly the Commandment has a vast solemnity, with its firm ruling for all the people, and its appeal to a divine model. It rather appears, in fact, that the week and the divine model were established together, when the holy awe of seven took hold of Israel. Creation itself was revised so as to give the week a cosmic significance and sanction. Genesis 2: 4, which is drawn from the oldest stratum of source-material, speaks of 'the day' when the Lord God made the earth and the heavens. Genesis chapter 1, and the first three verses of chapter 2, was composed much later, spelling out the process in seven days. That is, a primitive Hebrew notion of the world's having been made in one day was overridden in favour of the holy number, even though the change meant a discrepancy in scripture. This was still causing disquiet thousands of years afterwards. St Thomas Aquinas showed immense ingenuity in grappling with it.[8]

111

Where then did the holy number come from, related thus to time and the procession of the heavens, with such weight that God himself had to be pictured scheduling his work by it? The specific reason why Israel, and Israel alone, should have made this calendric application is perhaps (humanly speaking) beyond fathoming. However, it is a Jewish commentator, anatomizing the Week of Creation, who supplies the only ancient discussion of the seven-mystique in general; and embedded in this – 'embedded' is the right word – we have, at last, the answer.

The commentator is Philo of Alexandria. Born about 10 B.C. in a cultured family of Egyptian Jews, he learned Greek philosophy, and tried to expound Judaism as a system perfecting the wisdom of the pagans. To do this he had to treat many parts of the Old Testament as symbol and allegory, often exploiting the alleged inner meaning of matters that failed to explain themselves. These included numbers, and he found numerology, in the style of Pythagoras, extremely helpful.

Philo's adroitness at making almost anything mean almost anything ensured that he need not stumble over the first chapters of Genesis. Ascribing them, as everybody then did, to Moses in person, he dissects them in two essays entitled *On the Creation of the World* and *On the Allegories of the Sacred Laws*. The 'days', he assures us, are not periods of time at all. Moses allots six to the making of the visible universe, not because it actually took that time, but because of the symbolic qualities of six. As for the seventh 'day' when God rested, it is meant to guide our minds, through the nature of the number itself, to God's higher invisible creation – a realm of spirits and ideas which is the inwardness of the world we see, and the source of its design.

It all sounds very far-fetched. Yet biblical scholarship is not quite as adverse to Philo as we might expect. The author of Genesis 1–2: 3 does weave seven into his story cryptically as well as openly. An esoteric purpose is present which goes deeper than providing a pattern for the calendar. The author describes God's work by ringing the changes on seven literary elements: (1) an introductory 'God said'; (2) the creative command 'Let there be so-

112

and-so'; (3) the fulfilment 'And so it was'; (4) a description of the act of creation; (5) God's blessing or naming what he makes; (6) his approval, 'God saw that it was good'; and (7) the conclusion, 'evening and morning'. These elements do not all occur every time, but their permutations and interlockings have a symmetry which is not due to chance. Underlying the overt septenary plan the narrative has another, subtler one which an ordinary reader does not suspect. When Philo not only stresses the secret symbolic virtue in the number but specially relates this to the seven-day week in general and the Week of God in particular, he seems to be justified.[9]

His discussion leads, however, not directly to any enlightenment but through an amazing medley of pseudo-science and fantasy, some of which we have already had glimpses of. 'I know not', he says, 'if anyone would be able to celebrate the nature of the number seven in adequate terms, since it is superior to every form of expression.' Beginning with straight numerology, he remarks that seven is three plus four, but not with any implication that its magic is due to being made up from them. He goes on to observe that in the series of basic numbers, one to ten, seven alone is neither a product of others nor a producer of others: it is a prime itself, and if you multiply it by anything else you overshoot ten and are outside the series. Within that first fundamental group it neither generates nor is generated. 'On which account other philosophers liken this number to Victory, who had no mother, and to the virgin goddess, whom the fable asserts to have sprung from the head of Jupiter; and the Pythagoreans compare it to the Ruler of all things.' The 'virgin goddess' is Athene, the Roman Minerva, goddess of wisdom.

Philo reels off some of the more obvious sets of seven – the strings of Apollo's lyre, the Greek vowels, the Pleiades. He tries to trace heptads in the structure of man. He quotes Hippocrates as dividing life into seven ages (the original of Shakespeare's in *As You Like It*, perhaps); he makes out – not very cogently – that the soul has seven faculties and the body seven main parts, together with seven internal organs, seven secretions, and so on. He turns from anatomy to astronomy to define seven circles

113

in the heavens – the arctic, the antarctic, the summer and winter tropics, the equinoctial line, the Zodiac, and the Milky Way. With a great deal more in the same manner.

There is no suggestion, however, that any of these groupings are more than symptoms. They manifest a truth which it takes wisdom to penetrate. Seven, Philo declares, 'is honoured by those of the highest reputation among both Greeks and barbarians who devote themselves to mathematical science. It was also greatly honoured by Moses.' We are back with the Creation story and whatever mystery it embodies. Notice, Philo does not claim that seven has honour because of Moses. On the contrary, the Creation story is Moses' way of steering us towards certain truths, and it assumes the unique quality of seven in advance. The number could not have the symbolic value in the story which Moses intends, could not direct the wise reader of it to spiritual heights, without a prior holiness.

What then is special about seven? Where and how is it written into the cosmos with an objective clarity that makes its majesty plain? To rephrase this question in our present terms, what is the celestial prototype-seven? In his first essay, Philo never singles one out; he merely goes on and on with his list. In the second, he indicates three possible answers.

> Nature delights in seven. For there are seven planets, going in continual opposition to the daily course of the heaven which always proceeds in the same direction. And likewise the constellation of the Bear is made up of seven stars, which constellation is the cause of communication and unity among men, and not merely of traffic [i.e. it is used in navigation]. Again, the periodical changes of the moon take place according to the number seven, that star having the greatest sympathy with the things on earth.[10]

The planets, the Great Bear, the phases of the moon. For Philo these are the supreme heptads, visible in the order of nature, written by God's hand in the sky.

Despite the importance of the planets in Philo's time, and despite their connection with the week, we have seen that they cannot be the source of the seven-mystique. The moon's four phases also relate to the week. Here Philo foreshadows another theory about seven. Richard Cavendish has aired it thus:

> The significance of 7 comes from its connection with the moon. It is a widespread primitive belief that the cycle of life on earth – the birth, growth and decay of plants, animals and men – is connected with the waxing and waning of the moon as it goes through its endless cycle of births and deaths in the sky . . .
>
> The moon's cycle is made of four phases, each lasting about seven days. The Sumerians based their calendar on this cycle.[11]

Is this the explanation, not only of the week but of the seven-mystique as a whole? It is hard to see how the wide-ranging motions of the moon could have been associated with a sky-pivot above a northern mountain. Still, that hypothesis must not be allowed to block inquiry, and the lunar theory does look more hopeful. For one thing, it seems to take us back far enough. In remoter Middle Eastern antiquity the moon was honoured above the sun. To people who had to endure that climate it was a cool, kindly orb, lighting the traveller by night instead of scorching him by day. It was easier to watch, and its changes marked the passage of time. The earliest calendars were lunar. The discovery that the moon had no light of its own reduced its importance but failed to destroy its glamour.[12]

Over a large part of the ancient world, not only the tides but all the rhythms of life were thought to be governed by its rising, setting, waxing and waning. In a book ascribed to Ptolemy, whose astronomical system held the field till Copernicus, we are told that the moon,

. . . as the heavenly body nearest the earth, bestows her effluence most abundantly upon mundane things, for most of them, animate or inanimate, are sympathetic to her and change in company with her; the rivers increase and diminish their streams with her light, the seas turn their own tides with her rising and setting, and plants and animals in whole or in some part wax and wane with her.

To this day the moon remains a focus of weather lore and beliefs about omens. A ring around it portends storms. Full moon on Sunday is unlucky, and at Christmas it indicates a poor harvest next year. The moon determines the best times for planting and sowing. It also affects the brain, whence 'lunacy'.[13]

All of this carries us back behind planetary astrology, into a realm of thought which is more primitive and therefore more promising. One witness to a lunar spell surviving into the Roman era is Apuleius. Like Ptolemy he lived during the second century A.D., and he was initiated into the Mysteries of the goddess Isis, whose many forms included the moon. Some of his experiences are narrated (and much improved upon) in his serio-comic romance *The Golden Ass*. The hero tells of waking up suddenly by the sea-shore in dazzling moonlight:

It is at this secret hour that the moon-goddess, sole sovereign of mankind, is possessed by her greatest power and majesty. She is the shining deity by whose influence not only all beasts, wild and tame, but all inanimate things as well, are invigorated; whose ebbs and flows control the rhythm of all bodies whatsoever, whether in the air, on earth, or below the sea. Of this I was well aware, and therefore resolved to address the visible image of the goddess.

Jumping up and shaking off my drowsiness, I went down to the sea to purify myself by bathing in it. Seven times I dipped my head under the waves – seven, according to the divine philosopher Pythagoras, is a number that suits all religious occasions.[14]

Whether or not Pythagoras really taught it, the use of this

number on this particular religious occasion, by an author steeped in myth, seems encouraging.

The point about the lunar phases, in relation to the week and to seven in general, is – as Richard Cavendish says – that they are roughly seven days long: new to half, half to full, full to half again, half to new. Furthermore the complete twenty-eight-day cycle corresponds to the monthly cycle in women, and thus to processes at the root of life. (In the Jungian vision quoted on page 73 above, the four rows of stones, totalling twenty-eight, may have been prompted by the month.) Furthermore again, seven and twenty-eight have an arithmetical link, of the sort that delights numerologists. Philo himself remarks that if you add together the numbers up to seven $(1+2+3+4+5+6+7)$, their sum is 28. He also remarks that 28 is a perfect number, equal to the sum of its divisors apart from itself: $1+2+4+7+14=28$. Perfect numbers are rare and therefore significant. The only one below 28 is 6, and there are no more till 496, and none after that till 8,128. Such fancies were unknown before Pythagoras, and could not have inspired an earlier notion of septenary moon-linked magic, but they could have helped to confirm it.

Let us see whether the moon would explain specifically the great heptad we have been considering, the seven-day week of Israel. This can hardly be directly lunar. Scripture has its traces of pre-Israelite myth, but it has very little about the moon – except as an orb with a function in the calendar whenever it is full or new. Biblically speaking the moon has no numen, and it is not brought into relation with the week. We might suppose, however, that the week was formed by the moon in Mesopotamia, and then adopted by Israel with its pagan lunar basis suppressed.

Historically, this might have happened. The patriarch Abraham is said to have come from Ur, a Mesopotamian city. It was a centre of moon-worship and its chief building was a lunar temple. Abraham's saga is founded on a real Semitic migration round the Fertile Crescent. This began a little after 2000 B.C. and carried myths and traditions to Palestine, where some were converted into biblical stories such as that of the Flood. Abraham's clan could have taken a lunar week with them when they migrated. They could not have taken the scheme of seven planets, since it had not then been invented; and arguably, that is the reason why Israel had the seven-day week but never assigned planets to the days.

All this, however, depends on the assumption that there actually was a seven-day week – or at least a time-division foreshadowing one – in Mesopotamia. In Babylon, certainly, there was a period when the first, seventh, fourteenth, twenty-first and twenty-eighth days of the lunar month were accounted ominous. On those days the King never offered sacrifice, or pronounced judgement, or ate roasted meat, or changed his clothes. But previously it was not so. In Ur, and in the reign of Hammurabi, the taboo days were the first, seventh, fifteenth and twenty-eighth. The regular septenary spacing came later, long after Abraham had left. It cannot have supplied a model for the Israelite week.[15]

On scrutiny, in any case, the 'phases-of-the-moon' theory about seven looks highly dubious for a simple reason: that it is not normal or natural to regard the moon as having four phases, or to make its phases equal in length. Primitive people scarcely ever do. The Australian Kakadu recognize only two phases, waxing and waning; the Andamanese and others have three, waxing, full, waning; the Karaya in central Brazil split these up into five. The Greeks originally reckoned two phases, waxing and waning, and later added 'full' like the Andaman islanders, making three. The familiar four phases seem to have been invented by the Babylonians, and – here is the theory's death-blow – to have been defined so as to break the lunar cycle into seven-day periods, *because seven was magical already*. This is the implication of the Babylonian Creation Epic, which is far older than Genesis. It is the case of the planets over again. The Babylonians settled on a plan of four phases, to fit the scheme of taboo days in the month. But the scheme originated, and was then moulded into its second, regularly septenary form, through the pressure of a prior septenary magic, which the moon itself fails to account for. Seven came first; the lunar cycle was redefined in four parts so as to be septenary. As for the Israelite week, it has no convincing relation to any of this.

118

Nor did lunar magic (despite its power) inspire a seven-day week anywhere else. The Israelite week, it must be insisted, began as a lonely anomaly in the world's calendars. It expressed a magic in the number, which eventually triumphed over practicality, but the magic was not lunar.[16]

It need not be doubted that moon-magic reinforced the septenary, once the phases were fixed at that length and the septenary was linked with the moon. In much the same way the planets reinforced it also, once their number was fixed at seven. The moon's spell is a fact, but it cannot be the ultimate fact. The truth lies further back still, and we must renew the search for a prototype. This ought, surely, to be something plainer and more direct, a clear-cut image in the sky, taken in as a whole without prolonged stargazing or computation. Also there ought to be evidence for a linkage with the celestial pole, and, via the pole, with at least one of the sacred centres affiliated to it. Given a primary impulse from such a source, there would be no trouble in accepting that the rest followed: that the moon and then the planets were brought into numerical correspondence; that the numen of the centre caused sacred sevens to proliferate, branching out from Nippur, Babylon, Zion, Delphi, with a psychic charge accumulating at compound interest. The results are still with us in astrology and religion, in the calendar and the musical scale, in fairy-tales and films. But what was the starting-point?

CHAPTER EIGHT

The Primary Image

1

Philo anticipates two modern theories about the heptad – planets and lunar phases – though neither can be the whole answer. It will be recalled that he mentions another cosmic pattern of seven: the Great Bear, Ursa Major. And this at last is almost certainly the prototype we are looking for, the celestial source of the mystique – whether or not we will find any Ancient Wisdom symbolized in it.

The Bear has much to be said for it even at first sight. To begin with, it is not inferred or constructed but simply there, a fixed shape, presented to the eye as a whole. One of its stars is of the third magnitude only, but in Middle Eastern and Mediterranean skies it is a well-defined group of seven, and even in less lucid climates the pattern is distinct on a clear night. As many as eighteen dimmer stars have been counted with it, but the main group totally outclasses them. Hyginus, a Roman astronomical writer, explains very frankly that they were added to it merely to make the figure more like a bear.[1]

This is the only northern constellation which is easily found and recognized at all seasons, and at all times of night. It is also the only one picked out by ordinary people who have no knowledge of myths or astronomy, and given popular names. As we have noted, they called it after familiar objects – the Plough, the Waggon, the Dipper – or made it a vehicle for sky-riding folklore heroes. The latter aspect is oddly persistent. The Rider is Charlemagne or King Arthur (so that the constellation becomes Charles's or Arthur's Wain); or he may be David, Elijah, Thor, Odin, even Christ. In the counting song 'Green grow the

120

rushes, O', 'seven' is 'the seven stars in the sky' – the pre-eminent seven, as if no others existed. The Bear is so described in *King Lear* without further explanation.

Scattered and unconnected nations, most of them little given to star-mapping, have singled out this group and told stories of it. For Egyptians it was the astral shape of the god Seth, or perhaps only his thigh. For Mexicans it was the foot of the god Tezcatlipoca, bitten off by an alligator, this being the reason why he walks with a limp. It was the chief constellation (in fact virtually the only one) of the early Lapps, and the only one to be universally acknowledged by Eskimos and North American Indians. To the Lapps it was the bow of a celestial hunter. To Sioux it was a bier or coffin, and so likewise to Arabs. A Siberian Kirghiz legend calls the seven stars the seven watchmen, who are guarding the 'horses', the two brighter stars of Ursa Minor, from a wolf; when the wolf kills them, the world will end. Other legends from the same general area make out that the seven are wolves themselves, who pursue the horses and, just before doomsday, will succeed in catching them.[2]

In most of the northern hemisphere Ursa Major never dips below the horizon. Its constant presence night after night is not only an argument for its being the prototype, but a much more striking argument than appears on the surface. Those nations which had the seven-mystique at an early period all lived far enough north to see the Bear continually. Southward, in latitudes where it sets, the mystique fades out. Seven is conspicuous in early Hindu material originating in what is now Pakistan. It is not conspicuous in the mature Hinduism which took shape further south, in the Indian peninsula. Australian aborigines, who look to the south pole and see different constellations, have a detailed star-lore but no special attitude to seven.

As Philo says, Ursa Major has a plain practical value to mankind because of its use in direction-finding and navigation. The word 'arctic' is from the Greek for 'north' and means, literally, the Bear's place. More important still, the portion of sky which it dominates is more than a mere vague area. It is centripetal. The constellation sweeps round it. Ursa Major's two pointer-stars guide the eye inward to the celestial centre; some northern folklore speaks of the constellation as tied to Polaris. It was even more consciously seen as central when no single star defined the pole. Homer speaks of it as 'always wheeling round in the same place'. Its circlings marked the hub of heaven, the axle, the pivot above the world-mountain.[3]

Giorgio de Santillana and Hertha von Dechend suggest outright that observation of Ursa Major led on to planetary astrology, through a notion of correspondences. 'The Seven Stars of Ursa are normative in all cosmological alignments on the starry sphere. These dominant stars of the Far North are peculiarly but systematically linked with those which are considered the operative powers of the cosmos, that is, the planets as they moved in different placements and configurations along the Zodiac.' Elsewhere: 'Each planet is represented by a star of the Wain.' Such an explicit linkage is perhaps a shade conjectural, but there is no doubt that in several myths Ursa Major was held to be the motive-power of the heavens. The Latin for 'north', *septentrio*, refers to this constellation just as 'arctic' does. It is a contraction of *septentriones* and means the Seven Oxen, probably implying a team turning a mill.[4]

Nor was this a primitive fancy forgotten afterwards. With the passage of time it was restated in more sophisticated forms. It surfaces in the early Christian era when Asian cults were asserting themselves among Greeks and Romans. Thus a Greek mystical tract surprisingly depicts a Great God 'in a white robe and trousers, with a crown of gold on his head, holding in his right hand the golden shoulder of a heifer, that is the Bear that sets in motion and keeps the heaven turning in due seasons'. This exotic deity is attended by seven virgins, and by seven youths who are Pole-Lords and supervise the rotation. He is a form of Mithras, whose cult travelled westwards from Iran to become a major factor in Roman religion.

The Bear's supremacy leaves its imprint on a more famous body of writing, the Corpus Hermeticum. The so-called Hermetic texts were supposed to enshrine the wisdom of the primeval Egyptian sage Hermes Trismegistus, Thrice-Greatest Hermes, identified with the god

Hermes as teacher of the 'Hermetic' system, with a symbolic seven-branched lamp

Thoth. These were the books that did so much to inspire 'Ancient Wisdom' theories in the Renaissance. Actually they are not Ancient Egyptian at all; they were composed in Greek during the first two or three Christian centuries, under a medley of influences. They draw, however, on older traditions, including some which come from Asia.

Hermetic doctrine is strongly septenary. Its God has features in common with the Lord of the seven-day week, at least as he figures in the writings of such metaphysical Jews as Philo. 'Hermes', however, leads up to him by way of a question which is not in the Bible (though Job 38: 32 partly foreshadows it): 'The Bear up there that turneth round itself, and carries round the whole cosmos with it – Who is the owner of this instrument?' 'Hermes' has got hold of the same notion as the Mithraic mystic – that Ursa Major is the power-source which drives the system. Elsewhere he speaks of the Bear 'composed of seven stars' as being in the centre of the Zodiac. This is inaccurate, but vital to an astrological point he wants to make, which is all the more noteworthy if the bibilical translator Moffatt was right in identifying the Hebrew names in Job 38: 32 as meaning the Zodiac and the Bear. Of Ursa Major, 'Hermes' says: 'Its energy is as it were an axle's, setting nowhere and nowhere rising, but stopping [ever] in the self-same space, and turning round the same, giving its proper motion to the Life-producing Circle [the Zodiac], and handing over this whole universe from night to day, from day to night.' In Revelation 1: 16 the apocalyptic Christ, ruler of the universe, has seven stars in his right hand.[5]

'Hermes' may have helped to start Madame Blavatsky thinking on septenary lines. It is disconcerting to read what she herself says about the prototype-seven. 'The first form of the mystical SEVEN was seen to be figured in heaven by the Seven large stars of the *great Bear*.' The idea is not her own. She is citing Gerald Massey, author of a book called *The Natural Genesis*, published in 1883. Massey affirms that 'the constellation of the Seven Great Stars (Ursa Major) was probably the primordial figure of Seven'. By the standards of approved scholarship, Massey is almost as mad as HPB herself. Yet here at least the lunatic advocates of Ancient Wisdom are right, and the responsible scholars, with their talk of planets and lunar phases, are wrong.

Incidentally it was in his occultish phase, and only then, that Jung himself almost hit on the answer, though not quite. His alchemic study *Mysterium Coniunctionis* contains the following: 'The "chariot" in the sky, Charles' Wain (Ursa Major or Big Dipper) . . . marks the celestial Pole, which was of great significance in the history of symbols. It is a model of the structure of the self.' What Jung fails to do, as we might predict in the light of other passages, is to note the number of stars. As elsewhere, he shies away from that number when its psychic importance threatens to be forced on him.[6]

A crucial test remains. Can we connect Ursa Major, through the heavenly centre, with the known mythology of the ancient earthly centres? We can, and at early levels of myth-making.

Meru, the Hindus' world-mountain, was centre of the heavens and of earth as well, uniting both main functions. Among the beings frequenting it were the Seven Rishis, semi-divine sages, the sources of all sublunary wisdom. These – as Madame Blavatsky knew, and pointed out – were identified in plain terms, and as early as the *Rig Veda*, with the stars of Ursa Major. Its principal Hindu name was Saptarshi, 'the Seven Rishis'. Their homes were in the sky, and from there they made periodic descents on Meru. In other words Hindus associated this constellation, not only with their world-centre, but with the whole conception of Ancient Wisdom as they understood it.[7]

Next, Mesopotamia. The earliest major earth-centre distinguished from the heavenly one was apparently seven-gated Nippur. In the old astral system matching constellations with places on earth (page 104 above), Nippur actually was matched with the Bear, Mar-gid-da. Burrows enlarges on this point:

> The Great Bear is the most notable constellation near the celestial pole, the centre and axis of the heavens; thus it is analogous to Nippur, the old summit and centre and perhaps navel of Sumer. It is noteworthy that a ritual gives the Great Bear the title *markas samē*, bond of Heaven, for we have seen that *markasu*, Bond, is the term applied to central *cities* in the hierocentric pattern.

While the same attitude to the Bear persisted in Babylon, its link with the original centre at Nippur seems to have been strong enough to prevent an astrological transfer to the new city.[8]

The Israelites had no use for such heathen fancies. What they inherited they censored, if not always successfully. Zion, therefore, has nothing so specific to offer. Nevertheless the earliest completed book of the Bible, Amos, refers to the God who dwells in the Temple as 'he who made the Seven Stars and Orion' (5: 8). In some English Bibles the first phrase is translated 'the Pleiades', but 'seven stars' is the literal meaning and the Bear is more likely. It was the Greeks who insisted that there *were* seven Pleiades. We have no reason to assume that Israelites in Amos' time, the eighth century B.C., did likewise.

When we turn to the Greeks themselves, the road to Delphi is roundabout as it was before. But it can be traced, and the exercise is fruitful.

2

To track the Bear in Hellas we cannot apply Asian ideas bodily. Greek is the language of the Hermetic and Mithraic writers, but they come too late to be relevant. They are not close to ancient Greece even in spirit. Their language is simply a by-product of Alexander's conquests, which spread Hellenistic culture to the Nile and the Indus. The quest must be pursued further back, in classical and preclassical myth, where the constellation itself and the Delphic shrine are both accessible to inquiry.

One Greek myth of the starry Bears, Ursa Major and Ursa Minor, gives them a Cretan origin. The tale is told by Aratus, who is the poet quoted by St Paul in Acts 17: 28. He lived about 270 B.C. and composed an *Astronomy* in verse. Aratus calls Ursa Major 'Helice' and Ursa Minor 'Cynosura'. Once, he says, they were both she-bears living in Crete. When Zeus was born they took care of him in a hiding-place near Mount Ida, so that he should not fall prey to his murderous father Cronus. After he grew up and ousted Cronus from the throne of the universe, he promoted his ursine guardians to the heavens. This may be a fragment of authentic tradition, or it may not. A

126

Minoan cult of a she-bear as a divine nurse is thought to have flourished in a cave on the Akrotiri peninsula near Canea.[9]

Aratus' chief point of interest is the name Helice, meaning 'that which turns'. It would apply not only to the constellation but to the circling Cretan dances and maze-spirals which seem to go with the mystique of the centre. However, that is not very helpful; after all, the god of the Cretan Labyrinth was not a bear. Nor does Aratus face the obvious question: why was this particular constellation made out to be a bear? To take a star-group which, if pictured as a quadruped, must have a long tail, and then identify it with almost the only one that has hardly any tail – this, on the face of it, is a perverse way to behave. It is repeated with Ursa Minor, where the length of the tail becomes completely absurd.

For more promising clues we must get behind Aratus, and plunge into the mainstream of Greek literary legend. The constellation makes an early appearance. At that period it has few named companions. The Greeks were slow to develop a detailed star-lore. Homer, however, refers in the *Iliad* (XVIII: 486ff.) to '. . . all the Constellations with which the heavens are crowned, the Pleiads, the Hyads, the great Orion, and the Bear, nicknamed the Wain, the only constellation which never bathes in Ocean Stream, but always wheels round in the same place and looks across at Orion the Hunter with a wary eye.' In the *Odyssey* (V: 275) he repeats most of this, adding that when Odysseus sailed for home from Calypso's island, she advised him to watch the Bear and 'keep it on his left hand as he made across the sea'.

This constellation, then, was thought of as perpetually there, eternal, unchanging; as a guide, relevant to human needs; and as Helice, 'that which turned', rotating around the fixed polar centre. A chorus from Sophocles' *Trachiniae* gives it pride of place in the heavenly circlings. Aratus himself follows up his Cretan story with a more factual passage revealing that in his time, the third century B.C., Greek seamen still steered by Ursa Major as Odysseus did, even though Ursa Minor was known to be a better

127

north-pointer, and was used by the more nautical Phoenicians.

So far, we have nothing to connect the Bear with the Delphic earth-navel or with its god Apollo. The sole evidence is circumstantial and tenuous. As god of the Hyperborean paradise in the northern sky, Apollo *may* have had something to do with a cosmic axle 'beyond the north wind', a function which would have made Helice a special constellation for him. He *may*, in his undisclosed ancestry, have been like the Mithraic god who held it in his hand as the cosmic power-source. But is there anything solid to connect the seven stars with Apollo and, through him, with the sacred map below?

We can edge towards it by insisting on that obvious question, how this group came to be called a bear when it was not like one – when, moreover, it was also seen plausibly as a plough or waggon. The more usual Greek myth about it is quite different from that of Aratus. Hesiod put it in written form in the eighth century B.C. His version is lost, but the gist is reproduced in Hyginus' *Fables* and *Poetic Astronomy*. The goddess Artemis (known to Romans as Diana) had a girl companion, Callisto, who became pregnant by Zeus. Artemis preferred her attendants to be virgins, and angrily turned Callisto into a bear. In that form she bore Zeus a son, Arcas. To save them from hunters Zeus raised them to the sky, Callisto as Ursa Major, and her son (despite the gender difficulty, the Bear being a 'she') as Ursa Minor.[10]

As Hyginus is aware, the story is open to dispute. Some writers assert that it was Zeus' jealous wife Hera (Juno) who turned Callisto into a bear, the intention being that Artemis should shoot her in error. Some claim that although it was Zeus who worked the change, he did it for a different purpose – to throw Hera off the scent. Another query overhangs the transformation of Arcas. Between his birth and his ursine apotheosis, he seems to have had time to become the ancestor of the Arcadians, a perfectly human tribe in southern Greece. Perhaps, however, they merely named their habitat after him.

Whichever version we choose, we are far back among prehistoric animal cults. In that context the worry over the bears' tails resolves itself. Early religious images were often non-representive, 'aniconic'. A stone could stand for a god. In the age when these constellations became bears, there was no need for them to be pictorial, and the issue did not arise. They were symbols of beings identified with them for other reasons. It was only later, when pictorial fitness came to matter, that fainter stars were added to Ursa Major to make it more bear-like.

The immediate problems are two. First, why those constellations? Second, who or what were the ursine beings who were associated with them? . . . With special reference, of course, to the greater Bear.

To take the second question first, it is natural to think of totemic ancestors, and to suppose that the Arcadians were *arktos*-people or People of the Bear. But even if they were, the myth was simply one variation on a widespread and ancient theme, and the central figure was not Arcas but Artemis herself. She entered Hellas from Asia Minor. There she was one of the many forms of the Great Goddess who appears in various guises over a vast expanse of the ancient world. Her chief shrine was at Ephesus, where she was venerated as Mother and was still popular in St Paul's time ('Great is Diana of the Ephesians', as the anti-Christian protesters shouted). Motherhood may sound a strange thing to connect with a notorious virgin. Artemis' virginity, however, meant at first only a refusal to submit to any male as permanent lord; her virgin-motherhood can be paralleled in other manifestations of the Goddess, such as the Canaanite Anath and the Egyptian Neith. Even in her later and chaster guises, when reduced to a member of the Olympian Twelve, she was a protectress of women in childbirth.

Among many divine roles the goddess was Mistress of Wild Animals, and Homer gives Artemis that title. She was especially close to bears. She ruled over them, and received homage under an ursine image. Her unlucky nymph Callisto was not in origin a separate person but an aspect of Artemis herself, the-Goddess-as-Bear. The Arcadians had a shrine of her, Artemis-Callisto. In the Attic festival of Artemis Brauronia, a girl of five and a girl of ten, wearing dark yellow bear-skin robes, danced in ceremonies that were still performed in classical times. Astrally they corresponded to the Little Bear and the Great Bear, and Callisto's name did not figure at all. The roots of the cult were pre-Hellenic. Most probably the Artemis who arrived from Asia Minor was a composite. There had been fusion between Anatolian elements and a bear-goddess who can be traced back along the north littoral towards Russia. The stellar connection may have been a part of that combination. Astral myth, in general, was not native to Greece or the lands near it.[11]

Does Artemis bring her seven stars within the field of Delphi or of its god Apollo? She does. She was known to Greeks as Apollo's twin sister. In several places they were worshipped together. Olympian myth, giving them (as was its custom) a revised birth-story, alleged that they were the offspring of the Titaness Leto, and born in the island of Delos. This was where Apollo's Hyperborean offerings were delivered each year, wrapped in straw. Delos may have been the first locale of their combined cult in Greece. But they had both been worshipped in Asia Minor before that, and, it appears, jointly. According to Homer they shared a temple in Troy, on the Asian side of the Dardanelles, in the twelfth century B.C. Like other pre-Olympian deities both were adopted into the family of Zeus, and their real background was obscured.

When they emerge into view, at all events, Artemis has the required affiliations. She does not actually share her brother's oracle, but vase paintings depict them together at Delphi. A very clear specimen shows Apollo with a staff on one side of the navel-stone, Artemis with a torch on the other. At least one ancillary Delphic ritual was performed in her name as well as his. She was there, at the centre. She even had septenary traits quite apart from the Bear, and in conjunction with her brother. It may be too fanciful to remark that Apollo's name in classical Greek, 'Apollon', has seven letters and so has 'Artemis', whereas only one other Olympian, Demeter, has a name of that length. It is *not* too fanciful to recall the legend of Thebes, with its seven gates named after the seven daughters of King Amphion. By his wife Niobe he also had seven sons. When Niobe boasted of having a bigger family than Leto's,

130

as indeed she had, Leto's divine twins appeared with bows and arrows and slaughtered the entire brood: Apollo shot the sons, Artemis the daughters. So one of the oldest heptads in Greek heroic tradition, the Seven Gates of Thebes, is connected with a story of seven victims of Artemis, in alliance with the god of Delphi.[12]

In that setting her septenary aspect might seem to be a mere by-product of Apollo's. But her undoubted monopoly of the seven-star Bear suggests that Apollo, just possibly, derived his own from hers, or that they were twinned partly because a septenary quality was common to both. Artemis, moreover, had other celestial interests. Almost the only constellation besides Ursa Major which the early Greeks defined and named was Orion. Before his translation to the heavens, Orion was a giant. Artemis killed him when he intended a massacre of wild life. The brightest stars of Orion also total seven – the four at the corners, and the belt. Further astral ramifications draw us away from Artemis in person, but support the view that her Great Bear was the prime septenary. The star-groups named in the *Iliad*, besides the Bear itself and Orion, are the Pleiades and Hyades. Both these clusters were also reckoned by the Greeks to be seven despite ocular obstacles – the Pleiades always, the Hyades sometimes – and the Pleiades at least were mythically linked with Orion. They were the seven daughters of Pleione. Orion pursued them for seven years, till Zeus enabled them to escape to the sky, where the giant huntsman, slain by Artemis and translated aloft, still chases them. There is a distinct sense of a kind of Artemisian network in the sky, with sevens recurring. Incidentally a kindred tale from a Jewish source makes the Bear itself the pursuer of the Pleiades.[13]

Where were Artemis and Apollo first paired? Nobody knows. Certainly they reached Hellas from the same quarter, across Asia Minor. Almost certainly a close relationship already existed. If the story of Apollo's Hyperborean sojourns does recall an origin among northern shamans, it is noteworthy that Artemis too has a Hyperborean presence. The golden-horned hind captured by Hercules in his third labour belonged to her; it was one of five, which had escaped when she harnessed the other four to her chariot; and it has been pointed out that this 'hind' is probably a reindeer, because, within the range of Greek knowledge, female deer of other types do not have horns, and also because reindeer are the only kind that can be harnessed for drawing vehicles. Thus the tale seems to contain northern information, from reindeer country. Hercules, furthermore, had to track the hind into the land of the Hyperboreans. The pursuit took him a whole year, and when, after what must have been an enormous journey, he overtook the animal, he met Artemis herself in that land. There was also a story told at Delos of two Hyperborean maidens, called Arge or Hekaérge, and Opis. They came at the time when the Apollo–Artemis cult was founded there, and died on the island. Their supposed tomb was in, or behind, Artemis' temple, and semi-divine honours were paid to them. Both can be interpreted on other grounds as aspects of Artemis herself, like Callisto. In other words she had a Hyperborean character as did Apollo.[14]

All this might suggest that whatever considerations united her with Apollo in Asia Minor and Greece, the union had a prior logic because she came from the same region and travelled down the same path; or to be more precise, that we should look in the same northerly direction for one of the forms of female deity that went into the making of the complete Artemis. This was doubtless the bear-goddess element. On separate grounds, it can be proved that her seven-star constellation became ursine at a great distance from Greece, whatever her own involvement in the original process. The Hindus called it the Seven Rishis, and that was what it principally meant for them, but as the *Rig Veda* attests, they also called it the Seven Bears. That name is never explained in any recorded Hindu myth. Since bears were uncommon in the country where the *Rig Veda* was composed, the name would not come naturally to mind. The choice of the same animal as in Greece, if with a different arrangement, points to a common inspiration far back in the pre-Vedic past, affecting the astronomy of the migrant Indo-Europeans, somewhere in what is now the Soviet Union.[15]

Very dimly, then, we have a possible picture of some ursine myth about the seven-star constellation taking shape in 'Hyperborean' country, Russia or Siberia; of this myth vestigially reaching India, and also being conveyed south-west in the cult of Artemis-Callisto, the bear-goddess, partnered with Hyperborean Apollo; of their both having septenary traits because of it, and because of their joining hands around the celestial pole; and of their uniting the heavenly and earthly centres by occupying Delphi. Ursa Major was there because Artemis was — Artemis, of whom Ursa Major was an image – in addition to any personal link with the northern world-axle supplied by Apollo. The later literary myth-making that projected a separate Callisto obscured the origins, but there were always Greeks who knew better.

If the speculation is to be given any more substance, it is perhaps by way of that other question, still unanswered. Why was this supreme constellation, this one in particular, associated with bears? Ursa Minor could have been simply an offshoot of Ursa Major. Myths of bears and bear-goddesses could perfectly well have been projected into the heavens; there is no call to make a special mystery of it. But why into that most potent of stellar patterns? What (if anything) happened in the Hyperborean remoteness where arguably the myths took shape?

CHAPTER NINE

Myth, Reality or Both?

1

Before tackling the questions which were left hanging in the last chapter, let us take stock. From Greece to the Indus Valley, we find people holding Ursa Major in reverence almost as far back as we can document them. In various ways (and the variousness itself is a weighty point), they introduce the Bear into beliefs that connect the centres Above and Below. Because it has seven stars, their action builds seven into the myths of the centre, giving the first impulse to its peculiar magic which is prior to the magic of other numbers.

We have enough here to reconstruct a common myth that *might* underlie all primary versions of the seven-mystique, Indian, Sumerian, Semitic and Grecian, from which the rest follow. The immediate purpose of doing so is not to contend that it must actually have existed, as a conscious whole, but to show that it can be put together; that the myths we do know, diverse as they are, can all be construed as fragments of a single original.

In the far north (it might have run) *there is a high and paradisal place, peopled by an assembly of beings of superhuman longevity and wisdom. They have associates and contacts at lower levels. Access to it is difficult. This is the place where earth rises to join the celestial centre, the pole of heaven. Here is the axis of the sky, and above is the power that keeps it turning. The visible and sovereign sign of that power is the great constellation of seven stars, which possess a divine life, and circle in the centre without setting.*

Our disc-shaped earth has a sacred centre which is in

union with this centre where the heavens are pivoted. As above, so below. The visible stellar 'bond', that is, the great circling constellation, is septenary. The numen of the earthly centre is the same as that of the heavenly centre. Seven, therefore, is its number, which is superior to other numbers.

Consider the data as they can now be summed up. To begin at the east, early Hindus believed in a 'high and paradisal place' on the world-mountain which they called Meru. The sky pivoted on Meru's peak. The mountain was frequented by many exalted beings. Among these were the Seven Rishis, who were identified with the stars of Ursa Major, in endless majestic motion around the pole. Their spiritual glory infused all wisdom into the world below. Meru had seven sides or tiers, and was the centre of the whole universe, earth as well as heaven. For Hindus it remained so. They had no earthly centre distinct from it, so the second part of the myth, for them, would have referred simply to Meru itself. They never did anchor the seven-mystique to a visible temple or city in their own country. When they pressed on into the Indian peninsula, with Ursa Major sinking horizonwards, they almost forgot it.

Their cousins in Iran said the mountain was inhabited by seven gods. They too never had an earthly centre with cosmic dignity. But they passed on the mountain to Islamic legend, from which Dante reconstituted it in a new setting, united along the earth's diameter with the Christian centre Jerusalem.

Sumeria supplies both a tradition of a 'mountain of heaven and earth' which was a home of gods, and a separate earthly centre at Nippur. In the early astral scheme Nippur was explicitly linked with Ursa Major, as the constellation of the divine sky-centre. It had a temple called 'the bond of heaven and earth' and 'House of the Mountain'. It also had seven gates in its walls, and, in myth, a seven-gated netherworld underneath.

Babylonians called Ursa Major the bond of heaven. They left nothing in writing about the world-mountain itself, but to judge from Isaiah 14: 13 they preserved something of the Sumerian notion of it, and perhaps located it more correctly. At their own earthly centre, the Etemenanki ziggurat seems to have been a deliberate magical model of the world-mountain. It had a seven-tiered ascent, and a shrine on top where the city's priest-king encountered gods.

Greek ideas were more complex. By classical times, however, the northern paradise was clearly defined as the home of semi-deified Hyperboreans, dwellers-at-the-back-of-the-north-wind. It was no longer apparent whether this place was on top of any mountain, but it was certainly high up, and reached by an aerial journey, being inaccessible by ship or on foot. There, at the back of the north wind, was the cosmic axle; and the seven-star constellation was Helice, That Which Turns. Associated with that region were the divine twins Apollo and Artemis. Apollo was the Hyperboreans' god and rode to visit them in his flying chariot. Helice was the constellation of Artemis-as-Callisto, the Bear.

Both these beings arrived in Greece with septenary attributes. Apollo took charge of Delphi, the Greeks' earthly centre, and made its oracle the mouthpiece for all Hellas. By living part of the year at Delphi, part of it with his Hyperboreans, he linked the upper and lower centres in person. His companion Artemis was at Delphi also, if less prominent. Since Ursa Major was her celestial image as Artemis-Callisto, Ursa Major was implicit; the literary myth of a separate nymph Callisto never effaced the essential theme.

As for Jerusalem, though seven was more exalted here than anywhere else, the hardening of Judaism and the rewriting of scripture almost obscured the antecedents. Official Israel tried to do the opposite of what India did, not merely insisting on its earthly centre but making this out to be the only one, the holy hill of Zion with Yahweh in residence. On the one hand, however, biblical editing never quite censored out the northern mountain and Zion's mystical identity with it, as in Psalm 48 and the 'Safon' references; while on the other, the God of the prophets defied confinement. His divine Wisdom could build her seven-pillared house in Jerusalem, but he himself was apt to be elsewhere. Ezekiel, in Babylonia, locates the

136

earthly paradise on a mysterious 'holy mountain of God', and when Yahweh's chariot appears to him it whirls out of the north, from an abode which is not Zion. The prophet's imagery is baffling, and rabbis in later ages claimed that it concealed a great secret, an occult wisdom. Only the wisest and holiest could expound the 'Work of the Chariot'. Robert Graves has maintained that the God of the Chariot actually is Apollo, riding out of his northland in a Hebrew disguise. I will not reproduce his argument; I simply underline the fact that such a view can be seriously argued at all.[1]

Thus the principal data, spread across the homelands of the seven-mystique, can all be fitted into the myth as constructed. So can the Mithraic and Hermetic imagery of a later mysticism. It is at least *as if* such a myth existed. To use the world 'myth' is not to imply anything, either way, about a factual basis. The myth (if it did exist) may have been pure imagination, grounded perhaps on Freudian symbolism or on a Jungian mandala. But then again it may not. The problem brings us face to face again with the Ancient Wisdom issue. Is there reason to think that the northern Something was literally there, that the related themes found in India, Mesopotamia, Palestine, Greece, were diffused long before from a real centre, that a cosmic system was actually taught by the Rishis (so to speak) on a real Meru, and carried south and west along several routes? The inquiry has not yet led to an Ancient Wisdom, but it has led to what no one ever identified before – an arguable locale, to which the search can be narrowed down.

Further, the results suggest that behind all the absurdities of Ancient Wisdom's advocates, an elusive esoteric tradition may somewhere be lurking. Madame Blavatsky's septenary insistence does turn out to be more than fantasy. She and Gerald Massey do turn out to have been right in picking Ursa Major as the original heptad, whereas scholars of repute have missed it, and blundered into the anachronism of planetary astrology. These are facts which it would be less than fair to ignore.

For those who care to scent secret traditions, the *Divine Comedy* is also worth attention. Dante's reassembling of the world-mountain from its disintegrated fragments, and his realization that it has to be central in spite of obvious difficulties, are striking enough. But even in detail, he has apparent traces of a remote and exotic past. When his imagined pilgrimage brings him to the highest circling path of the Mount of Purgatory, a company of spirits, undergoing purgation for the sin of lust, praise two examples of chastity. One is the Blessed Virgin. The other is Diana (Artemis). They do not, as we would expect, praise the 'queen and huntress chaste and fair' for her own virtue. They recall only that she expelled a lustful nymph from her presence. This is the nymph, formerly an aspect of the goddess herself, who was turned into Ursa Major. Moreover they refer to her not by the mythic name Callisto, but by the astronomical name Helice. In some way which Dante's text fails to divulge, the heights of the Mount evoke not only Artemis but the constellation. Afterwards, in the Earthly Paradise on top, he sees an allegoric pageant in which seven candlesticks are displayed. These stand for the seven gifts of the Holy Spirit headed by wisdom. He calls them 'the First Heaven's Septentrion' guiding the pageant, and makes Ursa Major, our known Septentrion, an analogue to them. This image is close to being a Christian version of the descent of the Seven Rishis on Meru.[2]

If we consider the bear-goddess theme which the seven stars have incorporated into Greek legend, two dreams recorded by a patient of Jung's are seen to be stranger than Jung acknowledged. In his own view they illustrate 'the antique Mother-image', 'expressing itself in Cybele-Artemis' (Cybele being another form of the ubiquitous Supreme Goddess).

i. 'I am wandering over a great mountain; the way is lonely, wild, and difficult. A woman comes down from the sky to accompany and help me. She is all bright with light hair and shining eyes. Now and then she vanishes. After going on for some time alone I notice that I have left my stick somewhere, and must turn back to fetch it. To do this I have to pass a terrible monster, an enormous bear. When I came this way the first time I had to pass it, but then the sky-woman protected me. Just as I am passing the beast and he is about to come at me, she stands beside me again, and at her look the bear lies down quietly and lets us pass. Then the sky-woman vanishes.'

(Here, Jung comments, we have 'a maternally protective goddess related to bears, a kind of Diana or the Gallo-Roman Dea Artio'.)

ii. 'We go through a door into a tower-like room, where we climb a long flight of steps. On one of the topmost steps I read an inscription: "*Vis ut sis*." The steps end in a temple situated on the crest of a wooded mountain, and there is no other approach. It is the shrine of *Ursanna*, the bear-goddess and Mother of God in one. The temple is of red stone. Bloody sacrifices are offered there. Animals are standing about the altar. In order to enter the temple precincts one has to be transformed into an animal – a beast of the forest. The temple has the form of a cross with equal arms and a circular space in the middle, which is not roofed, so that one can look straight up at the sky and the constellation of the Bear. On the altar in the middle of the open space there stands the moon-bowl, from which smoke or vapour continually rises. There is also a huge image of the goddess, but it cannot be seen clearly. The worshippers, who have been changed into animals and to whom I belong, have to touch the goddess's foot with their own foot, whereupon, the image gives them a sign or an oracular utterance like "*Vis ut sis*".'[3]

No classical legend would account for these dreams. In both, there is a mountain. In the second, the mountain has a temple on top and Ursa Major is seen at the zenith (hence, the mountain is in a fairly high latitude). The magical and barbaric atmosphere is scarcely in key with the cool, virginal Artemis of convention. Both dreams, the second especially, read as if they were prompted by some ancestral memory – or some obscure tradition – of the bear-goddess's cult as it might have flourished in Central Asia or Siberia, before it arrived in Greece and was re-edited.

But setting aside such literary and clinical puzzles, we are justified in reverting to Guthrie's theory of Apollo. If this god was brought to Asia Minor and thence to Greece from a Siberian birthplace, a real Land of the Hyperboreans, then he implies a northern Something which actually was there: a centre of an influential species of shamanism, with Hyperborean Apollo as one of its gods, perhaps the chief. This is Guthrie's view of the matter. He shows that Apollo-worship was anomalous among the Greek cults, not only in inspiring weird shaman-like conduct among its devotees, but in being a missionary religion. Travelling apostles carried Apollo to mainland Greece in the first place, and despite all acclimatization, he was remembered as an intruder. As the Greeks spread into Sicily and beyond, Apollo's ministers tried to extend his cult to the new colonies. These campaigns, of course, happened long after any original transmission through Asia. But at least the idea of wandering prophets is not incongruous to Apollo, as it would be if applied to most of the other Olympians.[4]

We have seen that if Apollo did make this journey from Siberia, the bear-goddess Artemis (in some sense) was probably paired with him at an early stage. Since, as we have also seen, her constellation acquired its ursine character a long way east and north of Greece, the picture of a double migration from that quarter is all the more plausible. What we have yet to appreciate at its full value is the significance of the 'bear' motif itself, quite apart from any particular deities.

2

To survey the role of bears in religion, ancient and not so ancient, is to catch glimpses of a very strong magic. Artemis is only a special case, important, but not isolated. Their status is high, their dignity is deeply rooted. The bear, in fact, is the oldest of verifiable divine beings.

Neanderthal men in Switzerland and south Germany, a hundred thousand years ago, made sacred niches and altars in their caves where they arranged the skulls of bears they had killed. This treatment, it is inferred, returned the animal's spirit to its home without injury or thoughts of vengeance. In Austrian çaves, bear thigh-bones were carefully oriented.

There are several reasons for the spell which the bear exerts. Popularly supposed to be born a shapeless lump and licked into shape, he symbolizes primordial chaos transformed into an ordered world. His winter sleep makes him symbolic also of the seasonal cycle, death-and-rebirth, like the Young Gods (Attis, Adonis and the rest) made famous by *The Golden Bough*. One spring ritual of American Indians is a 'grizzly bear dance' imitative of his waking up. A more mundane source of awe is his eerie combination of bone-crushing strength with a half-human look, especially when he stands on his hind legs. He takes the postures of human beings and eats the same foods. According to some psychologists the she-bear is a powerful maternal symbol. Conversely, Apache Indians politely call the male bear 'the Old Man'. A feeling that these creatures are at once immensely formidable and not-quite-animal has inspired various legends of bear-men and bear-women who mate with humans and produce marvellous offspring. Beowulf may once have been a bear-son. So may Odysseus, who is of the House of Arceisios, the Bearish House. Several of his adventures are matched in bear-son legends.

The bear – more often, of course, the male bear – has lingered on as a god into modern times. Ursine cults are spread over a vast region stretching from Scandinavia across northern Asia and far into America. The Finnish epic *Kalevala* refers reverently to bears. The Ainu of Japan have elaborate bear-rituals. Eskimo shamans in Labrador are visited by the Great Spirit in polar bear disguise. Until recently, several tribes of North American Indians would never kill a bear at all, or lay a hand on a dead one. Others echoed Neanderthal custom (Lapp custom also) by killing bears for food but apologizing and laying out the remains with respect, so as to assure them an intact future in the spirit realm. Many of the tribes – Sioux, Chippewa,

Pueblo, Iroquois – had benign bear-gods who were healers. Their medicine-men could assume the god's identity; and in this they resembled the shamans of north Russia and Siberia, who may dress up in a bear's skin and be considered to turn into it.[5]

Artemis' form as a bear was no mere barbaric incidental. Nor was the ursine quality of the great constellation. Whatever was expressed here, it was ancient and deep-seated. The vital point is that these elements in the mythical cluster take us back through time and space to the same region where Guthrie places the beginning of Apollo himself. In just that Siberian homeland, in just that religious context, the bear is traditionally a mighty being who can instruct shamans and take possession of them. So Hyperborean Apollo and Hyperborean Artemis, the god of shamans and the goddess in the form of a bear, would have belonged together. The credible outline of an early cult, in the north under the seven wheeling stars, begins to solidify.

We may now have an answer to that more difficult question – why this constellation, this one in particular, acquired the ursine character. Early Hindus called it both the Seven Bears and the Seven Rishis. It is almost like a riddle: Who is the 'wise man' or 'seer' who can also be a bear? Evidently a shaman. The double Vedic name points in the same direction as Apollo and Artemis, and, in doing so, offers a solution. There is no obvious reason for the constellation to be regarded either as seven bears (in Hindu myth) or as one bear (in Greek). But the heavens' master-constellation would have been quite naturally regarded as a group of superhuman beings – sages, wizards, pole-lords – and the Hindus preserved that view of it. In shaman country the seven became 'bears' as well because the most powerful shamans did become bears. The migrant cult that branched off, taking Apollo and Artemis to Greece, transformed the group into a single Bear identified with the bear-goddess. But the tradition that survived in the *Rig Veda* kept the dual meaning.

Suppose then that having glimpsed this possible solution in Siberia, a very long time ago, we ask what can be said about shamans now, and inferred about their past. Does their cult look like an Ancient Wisdom? As it stands, hardly. Yet it is interesting in the first place that they assert something of the kind themselves. They say that in former ages all men had access to the gods, whereas now only shamans have it. In effect, shamanism presents itself as the remnant of an Ancient Wisdom which once flourished in the same part of the world.[6] Anthropologists have patiently pieced together this alleged remnant. The question to ask is whether it has any relation to the seven-mystique, centre-mystique and so forth; whether the Ancient Wisdom which shamans claim to preserve, vestigially, could be the same as the 'Hyperborean' set of ideas embodied in the myths of the south. If so, we may be in sight of the common source, the ancestral northern Something; and in sight (who knows?) of a real Wisdom which did once flourish.

It is worth while to grasp what a shaman is. Though correctly described as medicine-man and visionary, he is neither a mere purveyor of superstition nor a mere holy lunatic. His initiation and training are rigorous, and when he comes through he really does seem to be more intelligent and stronger than his fellow-tribesmen, a healer, spiritual guide and general helper to the community. The vocation and the techniques are not confined to males. There are shamanesses as well as shamans. Both have psychic gifts that set them apart. They are certainly mediums of a sort. They are at least able to convince others, and themselves, that they can leave the body and voyage astrally through space, or even travel physically without normal locomotion. A shaman may look barbaric in his ritual gear, representing an animal or bird; he may not suggest a sage exactly; yet he is credible as heir to a heritage of value, however decadent it is now, and however poorly he understands it.[7]

Undoubtedly a great deal has been lost. But the modern shamanism that still exists to be studied yields an astonishing harvest. It discloses the same motifs as in the ancient civilizations. In Hellenic, Mesopotamian and Hindu lands these have to be picked out, as we have seen, from a confusing mass of material. In Siberia they are not merely present but crucial and highlighted.

The main feature of the shamans' universe is – here too! – the cosmic centre, a bond or axis connecting earth, heaven and hell. It is often pictured as a tree or a pole holding up the sky. In a trance state, a shaman can travel disembodied from one region to another, climbing the tree into the heavens or following its downward extension. By doing so he can meet and consult the gods. There is always a numerical factor. He climbs through a fixed number of celestial stages, or descends through a fixed number of infernal ones. His key number may be expressed in his costume – for example, in a set of bells which he attaches to it. The key number varies from shaman to shaman and from tribe to tribe. But in one of the most important fields of shamanistic activity, the Altaic area stretching from Lake Baikal west and south-west, seven is dominant. In a typical Altaic descent to the nether world, the shaman goes down through seven levels to encounter Erlik Khan, lord of the dead, who has seven sons and seven daughters. (It is much the same infernal scene as in Inanna's ordeal.) A shamanistic variant of the cosmic tree is a world-mountain like Meru, with seven storeys and the 'navel of the sky' above. One Altaic myth tells how the god who made the world sat on this mountain, which was then in the sky. After creation he lowered it so that it rested on the earth. It was made of gold. The name 'Altai' itself refers primarily to a mountain range and actually means 'golden'. In the *Mahabharata* (VI. vi. 10), Meru is said to be made of gold.[8]

Pure coincidence can be ruled out. In some versions the shamans' world-mountain even has a name like the 'Sumeru' variant of Meru – Sumyr, Sumbyr, Subur. The leading authority on shamanism, Mircea Eliade, accepts that there was influence but prefers (as several others do) to trace it in the reverse direction. The shamans borrowed the world-mountain from India and the seven-mystique from Mesopotamia. However, as to the first theory, it is at least odd that the Indians should have originated the world-mountain and then located it far north in the shamans' country, whereas the shamans do not see it as exotic at all. As to the second theory, it is weakened by the recurring delusion that all sevens are derived from the

Babylonian planets. We have amply seen that the septenary is far older, and that although some of its earliest forms are Mesopotamian, its beginnings cannot be pinned down in that area with any confidence. Eliade casts further doubt on his case by an apparent approval of Guthrie's view that the Apollo cult was an export from shaman territory. It seems dubious to imagine movement in both directions – *from* Siberia to Greece, but *to* Siberia from Mesopotamia – while with India the movement would have had to be in both directions along the same path, since, even if the 'mountain' motif travelled from south to north, the 'bear' motif, as applied to the seven stars, undoubtedly travelled from north to south.[9]

It is worth noting that Aristeas, narrating his quest for the Hyperboreans (see pages 101–2), seems to have adapted a piece of folklore which spread out from North-Central Asia in very much the way conjectured. He describes 'griffins' as watching over deposits of gold. This is probably a variant of a tale of monstrous ants doing the same thing, which is almost certainly Mongolian, and is found in Greece, Persia, India and China. Here we have a specific case-history of a motif being diffused from North-Central Asia. Furthermore, Aristeas' version of it appears in a context of Hyperborean lore and Apollo-worship.[10]

Since no one would deny connections of some sort, it is fair to remark that the Ancient Wisdom hypothesis is, after all, the simplest. It is genuinely easier to start off the entire complex – world-centre, mountain, septenary – from a single Altaic source; not crudely from tribal medicine-men, but from a culture whose degenerate heirs the medicine-men are. The myth constructed or reconstructed on pages 134–5 is then a reminiscence of an Altaic sacred centre that actually flourished – a reminiscence that is fragmented over a vast area, but can still be put together again.

Shamans' assertions about a past golden age are of minimal value. Yet certain clues suggest that shamanism did evolve (or rather decline) from an earlier state, when it was more unified and more like a coherent system. That state may have resembled the antique phase of Middle

Eastern and Aegean religion, shading off into prehistory, when divinity was female rather than male – Robert Graves's 'White Goddess' era – and the status of women was higher, perhaps through a monopoly of the arts of magic. One reason for thinking so is that whereas there are many local terms for a male shaman, there is only one term for a female shaman. The Altaians, Mongols, Buryat, Yakut and other tribes call a woman-shaman a *utagan*, with variants such as *udagan*, *ubakhan*, *utygan*. For a man-shaman they all have different words. Shamanism, it appears, was formerly a women's cult, which was united when the people themselves were. It only passed into male hands and required a new word for its male practitioners after the tribes were separated and drifted out of touch with each other. Furthermore the old word for a woman-shaman awakens echoes. It is like Etugen, a Mongol name for the Earth Goddess. The Siberian Earth Goddess, in her turn, has affinities with the Bear constellations. In one Tartar dialect *utygan*, the word for a woman-shaman, also means 'bear'.[11]

Whatever the implications about a Siberian Artemis, it is well known that male shamans in modern times have often shown an odd tendency toward sex-change, as if the femaleness of a lost golden age were the historic source of their powers. The shaman who follows this path does his hair like a woman, dresses like one, takes up feminine crafts such as sewing, and adopts a feminine style of speech. The change is not, as a rule, homosexual. It reflects an idea lingering on from a distant past that inspiration is female. Another hint of the same kind is a belief that shamans are closely akin to smiths. As two Siberian proverbs put it, 'The blacksmith and the shaman are of one nest', and 'The smith is the elder brother of the shaman'. The explanation – or part of it – may be that male shamans originated as smiths who made metal amulets for the female ones, and then usurped magical functions themselves. A shaman who becomes a woman is trying to reconstitute in his own person the pristine state of affairs before the change.[12]

We have, then, at least a possibility that the themes noted in ancient civilizations are due to diffusion from a

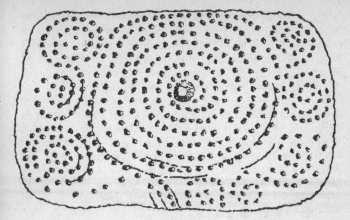

A septenary spiral on a mammoth ivory from Mal'ta in Siberia

Siberian culture, with a cohesion and character of its own, since lost. One or two archaeological findings are consistent with such a view. At Mal'ta, fifty-five miles north-west of Irkutsk, in country where the remnants of Altaic shamanism are still active, carvings have come to light which far antedate anything in the civilized Middle East. They include an oblong panel of mammoth ivory with designs on it. The dominant design is a spiral of dots which goes round seven times, and winds in to (or out from) a central hole. This is the oldest known heptad in the world, and it already relates the magical number to a centre.

As will be recalled, the sevenfold spiral appears in the Middle East and Europe, both in the simple form and in a more complex one that goes in and out and in again. A version of the second form, which is less likely to have occurred independently, is also found among the Hopi Indians of the American south-west, who call it the Mother Earth symbol. Hopi copying from the Middle East or Europe is almost incredible. Diffusion of a sevenfold spiral from Siberia, in both directions, can at least be conceived, since Siberian tribes did cross to America. This is obviously a guess, the more so as the objects found at

147

Mal'ta give a simple spiral only. However, the impression of a loosely Altaic source of diffusion is encouraged in other ways. The Mal'ta objects include 'goddess' figurines in a well-marked style, and the motif can be traced spreading west, producing imitative but inferior figurines; the Altai-Baikal region supplies the model.[13]

Such facts as exist, and such inferences as are not mere dogmas about what 'must have' happened, are in favour of some sort of dissemination from an Altaic homeland. This would have included the Altai mountains – which extend from Siberia into north-western Mongolia – and the country towards Lake Baikal. We might fix on it tentatively as the Land of the Hyperboreans: their earthly land, at any rate. Greek ignorance, and the westward drift of peoples, later caused the Hyperborean legend to find footholds in other northerly areas, and to absorb details from other quarters. But even in Greece one of the earliest sources, Aristeas, does point towards the Altai country. There could have been a real sacred mountain: Belukha, the highest Altaic peak, might qualify. For anyone actually living there, the pole of the sky would still not have been overhead and the peak would hardly have been acceptable as a literal pivot. But accounts of shamanistic ascents of the world-axis, mythified by people thousands of miles away, could have converted Belukha into a Meru in contact with the heavens.

The Altaic Wisdom may be imagined spreading out into lower latitudes, taking various forms, mostly scrappy, but always with some of the reconstructed essence present – ideas about the cosmic centre, the circling heavens ruled by the Bear, the heptadic linkage of above-and-below, the mountain, the paradisal assembly, and so forth. Whether this Wisdom could have been anything more profound than a bundle of mythological imagery is a question still to be raised. But not yet. Other ground has to be explored first.

Note
Mention was made on page 124 of Gerald Massey, author of *The Natural Genesis*, who pointed out Ursa Major as the primal heptad, thereby being right where better

scholars have been wrong. Massey is a puzzling case. His ideas are so grotesque that it would have been improper to cite him as an authority for any part of the foregoing argument. But now that the argument has been developed without him, it is fair to concede that he foreshadows parts of it very shrewdly: so shrewdly as to make one wonder further about secret traditions and sources of information, such as occultists have always alleged.

The Natural Genesis is the second part of his immense work *A Book of the Beginnings*, published in 1881 and 1883. Its general thesis is an 'Ancient Wisdom' theory very different from the one proposed here. All myths, symbols and religious motifs originated in Africa. The Egyptians made them into a system and spread them to other countries. To prove it, Massey resorts to such devices as deriving English place-names from an Egyptian sacred vocabulary. Some of his etymologies are fiendishly clever. He can even handle two names for the same place. He is aware, for instance, that the Somerset hill-fort of Cadbury is also known by the more romantic name Camelot. Both names, he declares, imply a burial-site where the dead were preserved in Egyptian style. 'Camelot' is from the Egyptian *kham*, a shrine, and *ret*, to retain form – in other words a preservation-shrine; while 'Cadbury' is from the Egyptian *khat*, a corpse, plus 'bury' which is a corruption of 'barrow'. This is the kind of pseudo-erudite rubble in which Massey's insights are embedded. Yet the insights are genuine, or at any rate interesting, and well worth hunting for. In view of his African obsession it is all the more remarkable that the best things in his book suggest northern rather than southern motifs.

He has a good deal to say about sets of seven, and grasps that some of the best known are artificial and imply an earlier septenary magic forced on the facts. There is nothing absolute, he observes, about the seven planets; these, and the Pleiades, were only counted as such by those who had a prior reason for wanting a heptad. As for Ursa Major itself, the real prototype, that was numinous partly because it was the visible symbol of a Great Goddess. Artemis was born in the celestial circle which it traced. Speaking of the female scriptural figure of Wisdom,

149

she of the seven pillars, he says: 'Her foundations were laid in the seven stars which made the first circle in heaven.'

From the divinized Seven Stars he goes on to the Seven Rishis, Seven Spirits before the Throne of God, and other groupings which have become familiar, deriving them all from the Great Bear. He also connects this constellation both with the world-mountain and, more surprisingly, with the spiral labyrinth.

According to Massey the first mountain of mythology is 'the Mount of the Seven Stars . . . which represented the celestial north as the birthplace of the initial motion and the beginning of time'. It was a seven-stepped Meru where the Great Goddess was enthroned. Everything was believed to revolve round it. Other sacred mountains were, so to speak, copies of it, and some artificial hills such as the mound of Silbury were models of it. As for the labyrinth, he picks out the right one, the double-spiral. 'The Troy city that was overthrown is still figured in the children's games in Cornwall and Wales, and consists of seven circles round a centre cut in the grassy sod. These represent . . . the seven encirclers of the Great Bear.'

Madame Blavatsky, who quotes Massey several times in *The Secret Doctrine*, seems to have regarded him as learned but uninspired, 'an initiate in the mysteries of the British Museum', and a rationalist – certainly not a vessel of occult truth like herself. On the other hand I have heard him claimed by a modern Neo-Druid as a member of the revived Order. His curious possession of a few most acute ideas, not only embedded in nonsense but at odds with it, could be taken as hinting at access to a valid secret tradition, quite on occultist lines. Few of those who assert such a tradition give any impression of having actually been in contact with it themselves. Massey, without making any such claim, occasionally does.[14]

CHAPTER TEN

The Hidden Kingdom

1

Having found plausibility in Apollo-of-the-shamans, and a certain wider relevance also, we might wonder whether the legends of Russia have anything to add. They have. Curiously enough, however, it is not strictly Russian. It is a key unlocking a fresh storehouse of data, among peoples we have not yet considered. Russian clues point to the same Altaic region in quite a different way. By doing so they strengthen the case for focusing attention on it.

During the seventeenth century, Russians began to tell stories of a wonderful place called Belovodye. The name means 'White Waters'. Belovodye was a sort of eastern paradise, a lost valley. To the oppressed sect of Old Believers it was a yearned-for refuge from persecution, beyond the reach of the Tsar and his bishops, where a favoured few might discover haven. In that respect, it resembled the 'Land Promised to the Saints' which the Irish legend of St Brendan located across the western sea; and it was equally hard to find.

Two centuries and more after it began to be spoken of, old men in Russia were still whispering directions for the long journey. In 1923 a party actually searched, and vanished. The route was then alleged to be 'over the Kokushi mountains, through Bogogorshi, and over Ergor', to a 'snowy lake' where Belovodye nestled among the peaks. This itinerary, so far as it can be deciphered, fixes it in or near Tibet. But by that time, like other semiphantasmal places, Belovodye had been shifted on from its early site into a more august inaccessibility. There is good reason to believe that when first reported it was closer to Russia, and somewhere in the Altai mountains.[1]

It is a shock to find the Hyperborean paradise being spoken of again in such a different context. The legend's lateness might be held to destroy its value. In this Russian form, perhaps. But the legend is not native to Russia. It travelled westward with the Kalmucks, a migrant Mongol people, and it is actually Buddhist or more precisely Lamaist. 'Belovodye', almost certainly, is a Russian name for a place of transcendent mystery which is known to Mongolians and Tibetans as Shambhala.

Shambhala is not very familiar to Western students of mythology. Once introduced, however, it illuminates the whole scene from a fresh angle. Shambhala, or White Waters, or whatever we choose to call it, apparently *is* the Land of the Hyperboreans coming down through a separate tradition, Asian instead of European. Its independent appearance in two contexts makes the case for an underlying reality very powerful indeed. When we explore its legend in Lamaistic Buddhism, we find some of the same themes that confronted us earlier with an air of Altaic provenance. Furthermore the Asian legend is living as the Greek and others are not. It speaks of a creativity which belonged to Shambhala many ages ago *and still does*. However cryptic, however fanciful this notion, it attests the vitality associated with the place.

But what place? To what extent is it real, to what extent mythical? Its full name is Chang Shambhala, North Shambhala, a title planting it in the north from a Mongolian or Tibetan point of view, despite attempts to transfer it elsewhere. (Shambhala is the original, or part-original, of James Hilton's Shangri La. *Lost Horizon* seems to reflect a theory locating it in the Himalayas, but this is a modern fancy with no basis in authentic legend.) 'Shambhala' means 'quietude', with a connotation of bliss. 'Chang Shambhala', the northern place of quietude, conveys much the same idea as 'Hyperborean', at-the-back-of-the-north-wind. Though the place figures in Tibetan literature, the consensus locates it outside Tibet, in a north vague enough to fit the Altaic site. It makes its début in writing in Buddhist works. However, it may well belong to an older Central Asian tradition, preserved through a religion known as Bön which preceded Buddhism in Tibet.

One of the earliest things said about Shambhala – and here it begins to look really interesting – is that it was the homeland and source of a system of esoteric wisdom. The system is still taught by a surviving Lamaistic school. It is called Kalachakra, the Wheel of Time. Kalachakra has – or had – its headquarters at the Tibetan monastery of Tashi-lhun-po in Shigatse, where the Tashi or Panchen Lama, next in authority after the Dalai Lama, used to preside. It is one of several systems broadly described as Tantric. Since these are Indian, and Kalachakra as it is now known was first taught in Tibet by an Indian guru, it would be natural to assume that Kalachakra was Indian like the rest; so the insistence on a prior source in Shambhala is most significant, and points to a strong northern tradition.[2]

The truth seems to be that while Kalachakra used Indian teachings, it combined them with a 'Shambhalic' ingredient . . . whatever meaning we attach to the phrase. Lama tradition assigns the Shambhalic part to a date earlier than the Buddha himself, that is, before the sixth century B.C. Kalachakra texts unfortunately do not help with the geography. One of them mentions the river Oxus (today the Amu Darya), but this probably refers to a supposed route of transmission rather than a real origin. We can, however, make a fair guess at the nature of the Shambhalic ingredient, the doctrine which issued from Shambhala well before the Christian era. The distinctive, non-Indian features of Kalachakra can be disentangled; they stand out clearly and, in view of what has gone before, impressively.

Shambhala's apparent teaching echoes what we have projected into the Land of the Hyperboreans. The name Kalachakra, Wheel of Time, is the key. The system looks to a Supreme Being who personifies the circling heavens. In art he stands at the centre of the universe, with a mandala of stars and planets around him. A prominent feature of Kalachakric practice – a feature admittedly foreign to mainstream Buddhism – is a stress on astronomy and astrology. We even come across septenary touches. Kalachakra texts divide astrology into seven branches.

Kala, 'Time', appears in poetry driving a seven-wheeled chariot with seven reins, which may, to judge from the 'Charles's Wain' kind of folklore, be Ursa Major itself.[3]

Such parallels are at least arresting. However, a greater fact about Shambhala is that it is more than an antiquarian wraith. Though never a very conspicuous legend, it has been a marvellously stubborn and vital one, held to possess meaning for the present and the future as well as the past. In Lamaist belief, Shambhala is still there (wherever precisely 'there' is), and so are its sages, or their successors. It still has a role to play in the world. The mark it made long ago was presumably so intense, so special, that it could never be thought of afterwards as dead and finished. The living, modern, even contemporary Shambhala, fictitious or not, is a case-history of the notion of Ancient Wisdom and its home. It shows that Blavatsky-style thinking is not simply irresponsible fantasy. It also shows how much better HPB might have done than she actually did.

Much of this lore of Shambhala is hard to date. Jesuit missionaries were hearing tales of it as early as the seventeenth century. Father Casella, who died at Shigatse in 1650, was invited to visit it. When the Jesuits' reports reached Europe the name found its way on to a map printed in Antwerp. What we have today is a composite account assembled by Western inquirers from the Jesuits onward, which brings together lamaistic ideas as they have been expounded during the past half-millennium. Some are certainly very much older.

The writings of various lamas make Shambhala's status as a hidden paradise clear. As such, it was carried over Siberia in the traditions of the migrating Kalmucks, to become the Belovodye of Old Believers in Russia. Access is said to be by a route which profane travellers cannot find, like Pindar's 'wondrous way' to the Hyperboreans. A Tibetan abbot describes the route after a fashion in a book, *The Red Path to Shambhala*, locating the entrance in Mongol country. However, no one can simply go there, even with the aid of the abbot's itinerary. A would-be pilgrim has first to be called. If he tries without being called, he perishes. Given enough holiness or mental powers, the route can be short-circuited. One Tashi Lama was transported there in an ecstasy.

Shambhala, in the words of a Western writer, is 'the Holy Place, where the earthly world links with the highest states of consciousness'. This linkage exists because Shambhala is double. It is earthly and heavenly – another Hyperborean echo. The rays of the heavenly one can be seen in the far north (Aurora Borealis?); it is, perhaps, a mental rather than a physical place. The earthly one is sometimes spoken of as an island, or as a 'legendary height' in the north, comparable to Meru. Other indications suggest a more complex image – a mountain-cluster enfolding secret valleys, barred from easy approach by a lake or dried-up lake bed, and entered only through a cave or narrow defile. Hidden away in Shambhala is a tower or citadel, the headquarters of its king. Buddha himself went there for initiation, and, in turn, expounded Kalachakra in the king's presence. The monarch wrote it down and a copy of his book was preserved. He was an incarnation of Manjushri, the God of Divine Wisdom. Atisha, the guru who came from India to teach or revive Kalachakra in Tibet, was a later incarnation of the same god. With unconscious aptitude, the scholar Evans-Wentz speaks of Manjushri as an eastern form of Apollo. Yet again the Hyperborean link.[4]

Like the shamans' world-tree, and the Middle Eastern 'bond' temples, Shambhala is pictured extending downwards as well as upwards. It has a subterranean realm under it, branching out over a wide area. This may once have been a separate legend, but in the Lamaism of Mongolia it blends with Shambhala, and the same sovereign is ruler of both. It is called Agharti or Agarttha, the 'inaccessible'. After countless centuries the entire sacred kingdom, above ground and below, is still potently alive. Its inhabitants are immensely advanced in science and virtue. Its rulers reign for a hundred years each.

The advent of Communism has confined these ideas to small groups, but they still exist; and their popularity and potency on the eve of suppression is attested by several Western travellers during the early decades of the twentieth century. The legends, in fact, had then taken a

Messianic turn. That aspect may have been present all along, but it had become sensational.

Especially in Mongolia, the unseen ruler was said to be the true King of the World, in direct touch with God. He and his council wielded telepathic influence over persons in power outside. Shambhala and Agharti might be hard to enter, but a chosen few did enter, and go out again as the King's secret agents. Royal messengers emerged at intervals to confer with these agents, scattered among the nations.

Occasionally, it was asserted, the King of the World came out in person. He would visit some holy place, arriving and leaving mysteriously. He had done so at a temple in Narabanchi, Outer Mongolia, in 1890. Thirty years later the Hutuktu or monk in charge gave this account to a Russian visitor, Ferdinand Ossendowski:

'Do you see this throne? One night in winter several horsemen rode into the monastery . . . Then one of the strangers mounted the throne, where he took off his *bashlyk* or cap-like head covering. All of the Lamas fell to their knees as they recognized the man who had been long ago described in the sacred bulls of Dalai Lama, Tashi Lama and Bogdo Khan. He was the man to whom the whole world belongs and who has penetrated into all the mysteries of Nature. He pronounced a short Tibetan prayer, blessed all his hearers and afterwards made predictions for the coming half century. This was thirty years ago and in the interim all his prophecies are being fulfilled. During his prayers before that small shrine in the next room this door opened of its own accord, the candles and lights before the altar lighted themselves and the sacred braziers without coals gave forth great streams of incense that filled the room. And then, without warning, the King of the World and his companions disappeared from among us. Behind him remained no trace save the folds in the silken throne coverings which smoothed themselves out and left the throne as though no one had sat upon it.'

The King's 'predictions for the coming half century' –

actually a good deal more than a half century, though the later part is dealt with in a few words – foretold much war and upheavel, after which the peoples of Agharti would come up to the surface, ushering in a new era. Ossendowski and other Westerners discovered a widespread and confident expectation that this would happen. A Shambhalic King of the World would presently step forth as Messiah, leading a Buddhist crusade, and subduing the forces of evil throughout the earth . . . especially European imperialism. This coming King's name was usually given as Rigden Jye-po, and perhaps he was already reigning.[5]

Some associated this advent with that of Maitreya, the next Buddha. It was maintained, not only that Maitreya would be born in the north among Mongols, but that Gautama Buddha himself had been a Mongol and a northerner. The whole Buddhist scheme of things was thus made Shambhalic, and Shambhala, or its affiliated realm Agharti, was named as the source of world power and the destined fountain-head of salvation. Mongolians were apt to think of the hope in political terms. Others gave it a more spiritual sense. Evans-Wentz summed this up: 'The prophecy that the King of Shambhala, who is sometimes called the Chief of the Secret Tibetan Brotherhood of Initiates of the Occult Sciences, shall govern mankind, implies the coming of a Golden Age and the enthronement of Divine Wisdom on earth.'[6]

2

Here of course we are right in the territory of the Blavatsky Masters. The King and his companions sound like HPB's secret chiefs, who have preserved the Ancient Wisdom and guide human destiny. She may have heard some garbled form of this very legend. But before we consider that, and before we draw all the threads together and ask what the Ancient Wisdom (if any) actually was, we should appreciate the strength of the belief well within living memory, and its ability to impress outsiders who came in contact with it. For about a decade it figured in an upsurge of Asian nationalism which Europeans not only recognized and investigated, but judged to be worth trying to harness. As a result, many relevant facts came to light, favouring Shambhala's assimilation to the Hyperborean 'high place' indicated in Greek and Middle Eastern mythology.

One of the first Westerners to become fully aware of the belief was the alarming Ungern von Sternberg, a Russian baron and army officer descended from the Teutonic Knights. During the First World War he scented approaching revolution and travelled East, with a dream of organizing the confused region of Central Asia into a Greater Mongolian state, as a bulwark against Bolshevism. After the war he pressed on with counter-revolutionary intrigues. He was a Buddhist himself, though remote from the compassion which Buddhism teaches, and he was also a fanatical White, not merely as a matter of politics but in a spirit of crusading against satanic evil. One of his phrases was 'the depravity of revolution'. Somehow or other he persuaded many Mongols that he was a reincarnation of Jenghiz Khan, destined to renew their career of conquest. He also proclaimed himself the ally and forerunner of the hidden King of the World. Von Sternberg was killed in 1921 on an anti-Bolshevik foray into eastern Siberia, but he had prophesied that a new leader would carry on the campaign. His propaganda took effect, giving a fresh impulse and a more specific and pressing form to Mongol aspirations. There was talk of the creation of a vast Asiatic Empire, with the 'purification' of depraved Russia as part of the programme.

Ossendowski, the same who recorded the tale told at Narabanchi (see page 156), revealed all this to the West in a bestseller entitled *Beasts, Men and Gods*. A Russian doctor of White sympathies, he escaped from Siberia and met Baron von Sternberg at Urga in Mongolia, where he collected stories about the King of the World. He fancied that he had witnessed the dawn of a new age, which would include the overthrow of Lenin and all his works by Sternberg-inspired conquerors from Asia. His book, published in 1922, closes with a kind of vision:

Afterwards, as I travelled farther through Eastern Mongolia and to Peking, I often thought:

'And what if . . . ? What if whole peoples of different colours, faiths and tribes should begin their migration toward the West?'

And now, as I write these final lines, my eyes involuntarily turn to this limitless Heart of Asia over which the trails of my wanderings twine. Through whirling snow and driving clouds of sand of the Gobi they travel back to the face of the Narabanchi Hutuktu as, with quiet voice and a slender hand pointing to the horizon, he opened to me the doors of his innermost thoughts:

'Near Karakorum and on the shores of Ubsa Nor I see the huge, multi-coloured camps, their herds of horses and cattle and the blue *yurtas* of the leaders. Above them I see the old banners of Jenghiz Khan, of the Kings of Tibet, Siam, Afghanistan and of Indian Princes; the sacred signs of all the Lamaite Pontiffs; the coats of arms of the Khans of the Olets; and the simple signs of the north Mongolian tribes . . .

'There are innumerable crowds of old men, women and children and beyond in the north and west, as far as the eye can reach, the sky is red as a flame, there is the roar and crackling of fire and the ferocious sound of battle. Who is leading these warriors who there beneath the reddened sky are shedding their own and others' blood? Who is leading these crowds of unarmed old men and women? I see severe order, deep religious understanding of purposes, patience and tenacity . . . a new great migration of peoples, the last march of the Mongols . . .'

Karma may have opened a new page of history!
And what if the King of the World be with them?
But this greatest Mystery of Mysteries keeps its own deep silence.[7]

For Ossendowski the King's own realm is always the subterranean power-centre Agharti. He seems to take no interest in its upper and more significant portion Shambhala. At the time of his wanderings the chief authority on Shambhala and its doctrine was still the Tashi or Panchen Lama. In his monastery at Shigatse, he claimed, a predecessor of his had received a message from the King of the World written on golden tablets. No one could read the characters, but their meaning 'penetrated the Lama's brain'. The Tashi Lama of Ossendowski's time was said to have been King of Shambhala himself in a previous life, and he was expected by many to reincarnate as the Messianic one. In 1923 political pressures built up against him. He was pro-Chinese, whereas the more powerful Dalai Lama was pro-British. The Tashi Lama was forced to leave his monastery as a refugee. Escaping from Tibet, he travelled through Inner Mongolia and north-western China founding Kalachakra colleges. These were alleged to be in direct touch with the Shambhalic Masters.

Coming when von Sternberg's propaganda was still current, his actions fuelled an apocalyptic excitement, with a literature and oral lore of its own. The Mongols now spoke openly of a great liberating war, the 'War of Chang Shambhala', in the words of a soldiers' song. Power in Asia, they declared, has passed from India to China to Russia, and would soon pass to Shambhala. The warriors of Shambhala were being prepared, the people of Agharti were saddling their horses. War, however, was only a preliminary. After it the 'Teachers' would appear and enlighten the earth. There was no other salvation: the way was 'only through Shambhala'.[8]

Meanwhile the King of the World bided his time in his northern fastness, above and below ground. In the words of a cryptic popular Mongolian saying, 'As a diamond glows the light on the tower of the Lord of Shambhala'. His apparition at Narabanchi in 1890 was eagerly recalled. The reigning King might himself come forth as the Messianic leader, or it might be his successor. The Messiah was variously named. The name specifically linked with the Shambhalic hope was Rigden Jye-po. But figures already famous in other settings were sometimes introduced into this one. Many purveyors of Shambhalic lore continued to speak of Maitreya, who was (and is) prophesied as the founder of a spiritual golden age. The view usually taken was that the coming Ruler would not himself be Maitreya, but would conquer the forces of evil and clear

160

the ground for Maitreya's reign. A third name, with deeper roots, was Gesar Khan.

Gesar had been a hero in his own right for many centuries. His saga existed in a number of versions from Tibet through Mongolia to the Altai mountains and the area around Lake Baikal. Its canonical literary form is a long epic composed in eastern Tibet, which is said to have been his native land. This, however, is inflated with philosophic interpolations, and a simpler Mongol text is closer to the original story. Gesar flourished, if he was a real person, about the eighth century A.D. In the epic he is a wonder-working champion of righteousness and true religion, vanishing at the end with an implication of rebirth and return.

During von Sternberg's activities Gesar's 'return' became a living belief. He was made out to have been a Mongol, and identified with the coming Ruler. He would reappear from a place of concealment in the north, and the place, normally, was Shambhala. His career would take the form of a crusade for justice, enlisting peoples outside Mongolia in the revival of Asia and the crushing of the white races. Alexandra David-Neel, the translator of the Gesar epic, met a Tibetan woman in Peking who took her to a lamasery where they had a statue of Gesar, and said she prayed to him for a son who would serve him in his imminent war. Mme David-Neel was informed several times that Gesar had already been reborn and would manifest himself within fifteen years. When she was writing the epic down at a bard's dictation, he told her he had visited Gesar's court. She gave him a paper flower which he promised to offer to 'the King'. Some days later he came back with a present from Gesar – a fresh blue flower, a real one; it was the middle of winter with snow deep on the ground, and the flower was of a species that blooms in July.[9]

All these ideas form the background of an obscure chapter of politics which has become part of neo-occultist secret history. Louis Pauwels and Jacques Bergier, in *The Morning of the Magicians* (originally published in 1960), claim that the Central Asian mythos became a major though unpublicized factor in Nazism. They have been followed by other writers, such as Trevor Ravenscroft, author of *The Spear of Destiny* (1972).[10]

As the key character, Pauwels and Bergier pick out General Karl Haushofer. Thus far they are on credible ground. Haushofer, a military pundit born in 1869, invented the 'science' of Geo-Politics, which based a programme for German world power on the configuration of the continents. Among much else he said that Central Asia was the heartland from which the Indo-Germanic master race had emerged; Germany must recover and dominate it to achieve control of the rest. He taught at the University of Munich, where Rudolf Hess was his assistant. Hess introduced the professor to Hitler, and parts of his theory went into *Mein Kampf*.

But according to the alleged secret history, Haushofer's public teachings were only a pseudo-rational disguise for beliefs held on other grounds. He had been in the East and was specially interested in Japan. 'While in Japan,' Pauwels and Bergier assert, 'Haushofer is said to have been initiated into one of the most important secret Buddhist societies and to have sworn, if he failed in his "mission", to commit suicide in accordance with the time-honoured ceremonial.' As a general in the 1914 war, the story continues, he showed a kind of second-sight, accurately predicting the weather, the times of enemy attacks, and other events. In his later relationship with Hitler he held the status of a magician rather than an adviser. 'Behind the Geo-Politician there was another personality – a disciple of Schopenhauer who had taken up Buddhism, an admirer of Ignatius de Loyola who wanted to govern men, a mystic in search of hidden realities, a man of great culture and intense psychic sensitivity. It seems that it was Haushofer who actually chose the swastika as an emblem.'

In this version, the true motive behind Haushofer's insistence on Central Asia was not strategic or economic but magical. The mystic sources of future world power were concealed in Shambhala and Agharti (or, in the spelling employed, Schamballah and Agarthi). But Haushofer had his own views on these places. They were in Tibet. Both were underground, and sharply distinct, because the ancient Masters who founded them had split

162

into two parties. Agharti was a place of retirement and meditation peopled by sages. Shambhala was 'a city of violence and power whose forces command the elements and the masses of humanity, and hasten the arrival of the human race at the "turning-point of time" '. Germany's aspiring world-leaders should make contact with Shambhala, conclude a pact, and tap its resources. Though Agharti was less interesting, they might also be able to draw upon the occult wisdom preserved there.

The story further declares that from 1926 onwards the Nazi Party sponsored a series of expeditions to Tibet, and that these brought back Tibetans who were supposed to have some connection with the secret communities. One of them, a monk known in Berlin as 'the man with green gloves', was a clairvoyant. His success in forecasting the results of elections caused Hitler to place great reliance on him. Tibetans fought for Germany, and the Russians found a thousand of them dead in Berlin, wearing German uniforms but without the usual insignia of rank. Haushofer committed suicide in Japanese fashion. His son, who had been arrested for plotting against Hitler, left a manuscript poem accusing the General of releasing the Evil One from prison.

Trevor Ravenscroft, in *The Spear of Destiny*, gives a slightly different account. Adepts of the inner circle of Nazism were equally interested in both centres. Agharti was regarded as a 'Luciferic' headquarters concerned with astral projection and thought-control, Shambhala was an 'Ahrimanic' one exerting power over material nature. Both, it was believed, could provide the means for sowing confusion among inferior races. Nazi emissaries made contact with their governing Orders, but only the Luciferic party proved willing to support Nazism. The Tibetans who came to Germany belonged to this group and were known as the Society of Green Men. They were joined by seven members of the Green Dragon Society of Japan – presumably the group Haushofer belonged to. Instructed by him, the Tibetans were employed by Himmler to teach occultism to the Nazi élite. Agharti and Shambhala were mentioned in testimony at the Nuremberg War Crimes

Trials, but nobody understood what the witnesses were talking about.

As far as Haushofer is concerned, it seems doubtful whether there is any way of getting beyond rumour. However, Ungern von Sternberg's notions may well have become known to the Nazi leadership through Ossendowski's book, and suggested hints for disrupting the Soviet Union from the rear. Ossendowski alludes to the swastika as a Mongolian emblem. Though German extremists had already adopted it before his book was published,[11] the allusions could have, suggested a Central Asian rapport to minds obsessed with race-mysticism. Did the process really go any further? In view of the assortment of fantasies that found their way into Nazism, nothing can be excluded. Ideas about subterranean peoples, drawn from other sources, certainly influenced fringe thinking in Germany. Soon after D-Day in 1944, two Tibetans were reported among the prisoners of war. Their presence, however, was explained by their having been employed in Russia as labourers and captured by the Germans. There remains one major fact which is at least consistent with a belief that Agharti carried weight in Nazi policy-making.

As already stated, when the King of the World appeared at Narabanchi in 1890, he uttered a prophecy of events for the next half-century and, more briefly, for the decades following. Ossendowski gives the text.[12] It begins with a vague series of horrors which more or less fits the First World War. The King goes on to speak of the war's aftermath, and the action he will take through his own secret influence. 'Then I shall send a people, now unknown, which shall tear out the weeds of madness and vice with a strong hand and will lead those who still remain faithful to the spirit of man in the fight against Evil. They will found a new life on the earth purified by the death of nations. In the fiftieth year only three great kingdoms will appear.' The first two sentences could have been applied, by Hitler and his associates, to the rise and assumed mission of the Nazi movement. Purifying the earth 'by the death of nations' could mean the extermination of Jews and other lesser breeds; the term 'genocide' was coined to describe this aspect of Nazi policy. The 'fiftieth year' from the prophecy was 1940. In that year Germany, Italy and Japan, 'three great kingdoms', formed the Tripartite Alliance which was intended to dominate the earth. The attacks on Russia and the United States followed, both of them acts of apparent lunacy which might yet have been supposed to make sense if the Alliance had the King's blessing. According to the rest of the prophecy, the three great kingdoms were to flourish for seventy-one years. There would then be eighteen years of renewed war and destruction, after which – that is, in 2029 – the peoples of Agharti would 'come up from their subterranean caves to the surface of the earth'.

So much for the possible fantasies of the Hitler élite. From our present point of view, the main point about this short-lived ferment in Central Asia is that it attracted the notice of other, more responsible Westerners, so that many Mongolian and Tibetan traditions were placed on record. The Tibetan aspect was studied by Alexandra David-Neel, translator of the epic of Gesar. More wide-ranging were the researches of Nicholas Roerich.

Roerich was a Russian of immense talent and versatility, a painter, archaeologist and anthropologist. His name endures on thousands of record sleeves, because he was Stravinsky's collaborator in *The Rite of Spring*. Stravinsky had conceived the idea of a ballet based on paganism in ancient Russia, but lacked the necessary knowledge; he consulted Roerich, and in July 1911 they worked together to reconstruct the series of rituals which the music evokes. Roerich also designed scenery for Diaghilev's productions, and worked with Stanislavsky. After the Revolution, the Bolsheviks offered him a high post at the Ministry of Culture, but he left Russia for the United States. He did not stay long. Rumours had reached him of the stirrings in Central Asia. He took them seriously, but gave them a less violent interpretation than Ossendowski's, hoping, himself, for a new age of enlightenment, with stress on Buddhist wisdom rather than Buddhist militancy. (He was a Theosophist for a while.) From 1923 to 1928 he led an expedition through Central Asia, accompanied by his son George, an anthropologist of a more academic stamp.

165

Being a Russian White, if a pacific one, he was able to collect much information from the Mongols.

His travel diary, published in 1930 under the title *Altai-Himalaya*, supplies valuable insights into most of the beliefs already reviewed. But it also discloses motifs already identified by an approach from Greece and the Middle East, appearing again when the same region is scanned from Tibet and Mongolia. First, as to geography. In the entry for 13 May 1926, Roerich notes:

> Our friend T. L. . . . spoke of the significance of the future of Maitreya. 'We knew it a long time ago,' says the lama, 'but we did not know how it would come about. And now the time has come. But not to every Mongol and Kalmuck can we tell it but only to those who can comprehend.' The lama speaks about different proofs and no one would have suspected such knowledge in this modest man. *He speaks about the spiritual meaning of Altai* [italics mine].

Later Roerich refers again, with some wonderment, to the 'general reverence for Altai' and to 'the coming of the Blessed Ones to Altai' and 'the true significance of Altai'. In another entry he records that the constellation Orion is associated with Gesar (or as he spells it, Gessar), and that the mountain Belukha, the principal peak of the Altai range, has a name meaning 'Orion-dwelling-of-gods' – which, he says, correlates it with the world-mountain of other mythologies. This may or may not be right. The striking fact is that he should think of the world-mountain at all.

Elsewhere he writes: 'The cults which surround some constellations such as the Bear and Orion amaze you by their widespread popularity. The wisdom of the Shamans designates them for worship.'

Here (noted on 10 May 1926) is a Mongol legend of Gesar, who, it should be reiterated, was linked with Shambhala and destined to come again from there:

> To Gessar-Bogdo-Khan were sent seven heads, cut off from seven black blacksmiths. And he boiled the seven heads in seven copper kettles. He fashioned

166

out of them chalices, and inlaid these chalices with silver. And so out of seven heads came seven chalices; and Gessar-Khan filled these with a strong wine. Thereupon he ascended to the wise Manzalgormo and bestowed upon her the chalices. But she took the seven chalices fashioned from the seven heads of the blacksmiths and scattered them into the heavens and the seven chalices formed the constellation Dolan-Obogod (the Great Bear).

Roerich comments: 'How remarkably the symbols are fused into these unclear and apparently meaningless words which bind Gessar-Khan with the seven-starred constellation of the north.' We could now add more. Manzalgormo, who creates the constellation, might be the Bear-Goddess again. The repetition of seven is almost as relentless as it is in the Bible's Jericho narrative. Also, the seven stars are formed out of seven smiths; and the seven sages, in the Hindu account of them, may originally have been shamans; and in Siberian lore, but not further south, shamans and smiths are closely related (see page 146 above). Both this Mongol story and the Rishi myth of the Hindus could be rooted in a single Altaic concept of the seven stars as seven undifferentiated Wise Ones – smith-shamans.[13]

Alexandra David-Neel, in her introduction to the main Gesar epic, concludes that the oldest traditions about him (like the oldest traditions about Shambhala) may derive from the pre-Buddhist Bön religion, and this, she says, was more or less shamanistic. The epic, though given a Buddhist form, is 'impregnated with shamanism'. So by this route also we are led again to shamans, just as we were led to them by Apollo, and seemingly in much the same area.[14]

CHAPTER ELEVEN

What Was the Ancient Wisdom?

1

Here then is a living, vigorous tradition extending to a time well within living memory. What is more, it is fairly specific. It belongs to Central and North-Central Asia. It survives in quite a number of contexts, but especially in two which are related, Kalachakra and the legend-plus-prophecy of Gesar. Both of these point to a Shambhala which is viewed as a home of Ancient Wisdom. Shambhala is best located in the same broadly Altaic country indicated by clues from Middle Eastern and Greek sources, such as the myths of Apollo. Matching motifs appear, such as the Great Bear. So in both cases does the probable shamanistic background. Shambhala in fact will do very well as the original Land of the Hyperboreans, or its capital. If we want a literal mountain as Meru, Belukha is a good candidate.

At this point an occultist or astronaut-seeker might regard the problem as solved, the case as proved, the Ancient Wisdom as run to earth. It would be safer to say that we have got the problem under control rather than solved it. If an Ancient Wisdom did make its way into the various cultures, this Altaic zone is the most promising place to look for its cradle-land. If we wish to picture Masters or alien visitors, teaching prehistoric humanity and leaving legends behind, this is the most promising place to locate their earthly headquarters. The original and greater shamans, or shamanesses, were their trainees.

But have we been guilty of sustained question-begging? We started with Madame Blavatsky's septenary clue, found it helpful, and assumed that whatever it might lead to would count as Ancient Wisdom. This is plainly open to question. What it has seemed to lead to is a bundle of mythical–magical motifs – the world-centre, the seven stars of Ursa Major, the rotating heavens, and so on. Traces of these appear, as we have amply seen, in a variety of settings, and it looks as if all of them may go back to a single 'Shambhalic', or 'Hyperborean', body of doctrine. But would this have amounted to any sort of Wisdom? Could the intellectual development of the nations it reached have been in any sense due to it? Was anything of real value wrapped up in the bundle?

Suppose we return to Greece for a moment, after the oriental excursion. Greece is the one place where the tradition is well enough documented in ancient times to pursue further. A thousand years or so before Christ, Apollo arrived at Delphi with his Hyperborean lore, and made himself one of the Olympian company. That was the end of a long story of migration, but it was also the beginning of other stories. Apollo's cult presently spread, becoming more like a missionary church than any other form of Hellenic religion. Furthermore a second stream of shamanistic influence flowed into it in the seventh century B.C., as Greeks explored the Black Sea coasts, and came into contact with Scythians and kindred wandering peoples of Asia.

Some of Apollo's best-known votaries were credited with powers suggesting an impulse from those quarters. When Aristeas went on his Asian quest, Apollo is said to have inspired him, and having got to where he at least heard of the Hyperboreans, he returned (it is asserted) capable of strange shamanistic feats. The tradition has no great value as biography, but it is interesting that such notions should ever have been attached to him. He and a kindred initiate, Hermotimos, are described as bilocating, vanishing in one place and appearing in another, and so forth. In this Apolline context we hear also of astral travelling, a wandering of the discarnate spirit which is out of keeping with traditional Greek beliefs, but is familiar in shamanism. Similar offbeat characters are Epimenides and Zalmoxis. Epimenides, a Cretan, is supposed to have lived for 290 years and to have been divinely inspired in his sleep; St Paul quotes him as a Gentile 'prophet' in Titus 1: 12 ('Cretans are always liars, evil beasts, lazy gluttons'). Zalmoxis preached to a Thracian tribe about a happy Otherworld, and then, by vanishing for three years and reappearing, convinced them that he was the god of the Otherworld himself and could conduct them to it.[1]

According to one account Zalmoxis was a disciple of Pythagoras. Pythagoras is the great figure in whom these cryptic hints become illuminating. We met him as the inventor of numerology in the sixth century B.C., but that description is far short of doing him justice. He was one of the first major geniuses of Western history, the chief founder of Greek philosophy, a mathematician of the highest order. He was also a devotee of Apollo, asserted in legend to be the god's son. Like Aristeas and the others he performed shamanistic feats such as healing and bilocation. The point, of course, is not the reality or otherwise of the performance, but the fact that feats of this type were ascribed to him. He founded a mystical community which admitted women – shamanistic rather than Hellenic behaviour – and he is credited in legend, most curiously, with taming a bear, another touch reminiscent of northerly regions.

In Pythagoras, while we have a huge forward stride in Greek culture, we also have this backward contact with Apollo and the shamans. Indeed we have details which are more specific. Pythagoras is said to have been instructed himself by a Hyperborean guru called Abaris, who carried – and in a later story, rode through the air upon – a golden arrow. Arrows as magical vehicles, or as emblems of magical flight, are part of Siberian lore to this day. If Abaris existed he was a shaman himself, and since 'Altai' means 'golden', his golden arrow could really have been an Altaic arrow. If he did not exist, he still stands for Hyperborean wisdom, trickling down to Greece via the Apolline succession. There are also strong indications that Pythagoras was influenced by Aristeas' book describing his pilgrimage.[2]

Pythagoras surely received and applied the Altaic Wisdom, or part of it, if anyone did. What special teaching did he offer that advanced the Western mind? In a word it was numerology; but, once again, to say so is to give a poor opinion of an extraordinary man. He taught that 'all

170

things are numbers', meaning that by the use of numerical methods – measurement and calculation – we can build up an intelligible, harmonious system of the universe. One of his discoveries was that a musical string twice as long as another gives a note exactly an octave below it: hence a relationship between number and sound. Not so literally correct, but very fruitful, was his belief that different kinds of matter were made from different three-dimensional patterns of atoms which, again, could be defined numerically (so many sides, so many atoms to the side). With this sense of exactitude in nature, attained by no Greek before, he was able to arrive at the first clear notions of proof, in geometry for instance.

What this amounts to is that Pythagoras was the first Greek to form the conception of a Cosmos – a conception of order, inter-relation, measure, replacing the primitive anarchy of gods and spirits. If, now, we glance once more at Babylon, where – as has been supposed – the same Altaic scheme made an imprint, we do not find a Pythagoras. Yet we do find the same conception struggling through. Babylonians express it in the astrology that takes shape about Pythagoras' time – the system of seven planets and twelve zodiacal signs, articulating a universe centred on Babylon. Here too a Cosmos, if a dubiously conceived one, is emerging instead of chaos. Here too there is stress on numbers.

So could it be that in the Altaic mythology of centre and septenary and the rest, a more profound general idea was implicit? Is it absurd to see these forward strides of the mind as Hyperborean-inspired, whether through continuing actual contact or through the rediscovery of the implications? After all, even a modern shaman has similar ideas, however little use he makes of them. He too has a Cosmos of sorts. His key numbers anatomize the heavens and hells. His central world-tree unifies the realms above and below, bringing everything within the scope of his superior knowledge.[3]

This is not a fantasy concocted to justify the word 'Wisdom' in the Altaic connection. The idea of a Cosmos is one on which all later science and rational thought depend; and the fact that it had to start somewhere, somehow, has been recognized by authors with no occult axes to grind. Joseph Campbell has even proposed to trace its origin, as here, to the mystique of the world-centre. So have the collaborators Giorgio de Santillana and Hertha von Dechend. They actually face the possibility that it could have come down from shamans in North-Central Asia. That notion, of course, is too radical for them. They dismiss what they call the blunder of 'taking the conception of several skies and underworlds' – the shamans' cosmic conception – 'as natural, ergo primitive'. The source *must* have been in civilized Mesopotamia.

> The shaman climbing the 'stairs' or notches of his post or tree, pretending that his soul ascends at the same time to the highest sky, does the very same thing as the Mesopotamian priest did when mounting to the top of his seven-storied pyramid ... Says Uno Holmberg: 'This pattern of seven levels can hardly be imagined as the invention of Turko-Tatar populations. To the investigator, the origin of the Gods ruling those various levels is no mystery, for they point clearly to the planetary gods of Babylon, which already in their far-away point of origin, ruled over seven superposed starry circles.' ...
>
> Whether Shamanism is an old or a relatively young offshoot of ancient civilization is irrelevant. It is not primitive at all, but it belongs, as all our civilizations do, to the vast company of ungrateful heirs of some almost unbelievable Near Eastern ancestor who first dared to understand the world as created according to number, measure and weight.[4]

For the statement in the last sentence there is no evidence whatsoever. It rests wholly on the assumption that the civilized Mesopotamians *must* have thought of a Cosmos first, after which a garbled version of their ideas drifted northward to the savages of Siberia. We have seen some of the difficulties in regarding shamanism like this, as an offshoot of 'higher' things, and they are no less manifest here. Santillana and von Dechend admit the parallels. Why should the explanation not be simply the other way round? Pythagoras smooths the path. There does not seem to be anything indebting him to an 'almost unbelievable Near Eastern ancestor'. But the Abaris tradition and other clues do indebt him to shamanism. Moreover, the septenary line of argument has apparently made the Altaic Something ancestral to Babylon as well as Greece. Why not frankly credit the Cosmos conception to Altaic sages? They would have been earlier and greater shamans; perhaps female ones.

Until recently, such a theory would have shipwrecked on the assumption (the general form of the Santillana–Dechend assumption) that a society with creative thoughts must also be advanced in arts and technology; and that creative thoughts never occur in societies which are not advanced in other ways. Since, as far as we know, the Altaic region was never advanced in that sense, its inhabitants could not have had creative thoughts. That assumption, however, is no longer secure. As we have seen, Thom, Renfrew and perhaps Hawkins also, working on the megaliths of the British Isles, have shown that ancient societies could know and devise remarkable things while leaving archaeological traces suggesting near-savagery. Altaic thinkers could have had profound insights while lacking a context of what we call civilization; though, of course, there may be more to discover.

It is feasible to picture the Altaic people as the first to conceive of a true Cosmos, an intelligible universe. In view of the consequences, this would have been Wisdom indeed, even if they achieved nothing else. They could have reasoned it out through an 'as above, so below' analogy, linking the heavens and the earth and the presumed underworld. They had their holy place – the central mountain, the original Meru, pattern for all other centres – and there perhaps inspired or initiated persons could gather in a temple and spiritually ascend, descend, bring the realms together, and expound the correlation. They expressed the above-and-below cosmic pattern in number, seeing the great septenary of the Bear as powering the heavenly rotation; and they set up earthly septenaries to match it, such as spiral labyrinths and a college of seven principal teachers, remembered in India as the Rishis.

Such ideas and practices, if they existed, were mythically stated, but their meaning transcended myth. Apollo's

Hyperborean missionaries carried some of them south-westward. Wandering Indo-European tribes picked up fragments. Sumeria related the Bear to its own centre at Nippur. Babylon's ziggurat imitated the sevenfold mountain. Presently the thought at the heart burst out again into new systems, such as Pythagoreanism and astrology. On its home ground the Ancient Wisdom declined into shamanism as it now is, yet never lost its grasp of the essentials, however superstitiously understood. The shamans still have their world-uniting centre and their numerical keys.

In Mongolia and Tibet, meanwhile, Altaic teaching that went into Kalachakra bore the stamp of its primary inspiration, just as Babylonian astrology did: Kalachakra too dwelt on a divine centre and skies that spelt out messages in their eternal circling. Lamas preserved their traditions of the source as Shambhala, a secret place of enlightenment in the northern mountains.

2

On this showing, we have made occultist theory look tenable up to a point. Only up to a point. We may have located an Ancient Wisdom which gave an impulse to early movements of the mind. However, if it existed, it would seem to have become a purely historical topic with no lasting relevance. Once Pythagoras had planted the idea of a Cosmos in Western society, and shown that numbers could be crucial in understanding it, the Altaic impulse was surely exhausted. We may care to imagine it lingering on at unconscious levels, and surfacing again in such mathematical world-organizers as Newton, who did see himself as a rediscoverer rather than a discoverer. But it has no place in anything that has happened since.

If that is the whole story we have still found no hint of an Ancient Wisdom in the full-blown occultist style, a Wisdom which was, in essence, greater than anything possessed now, and is far from being entirely recovered. To test the remainder of the occultist theory we would need to raise several further questions, and at present, it must be acknowledged outright, we cannot do much more than raise them. They might be worded as follows. Whatever the original agency was – call it the Shambhalic community – have we now said all that can be said about it, at least until archaeology reveals more? Beyond the myths and ideas already inferred, did it launch anything else, was its Wisdom more extensive? And is it still active, not purely a thing of the past at all? Could it produce any fresh phenomena in the future, as the prophecies of modern lamas imply?

These last two questions, however bizarre they sound, have to be asked if we are to take even a step towards assessing the second part of the occultists' belief; and for the moment, only a step is possible. Inquiry may open up a vista, but exploration is for another day. Stated in their own terms, this second part of the belief asserts that the Masters of Wisdom (or Rishis or UFO sky-people) are still concerned with humanity, and liable to intervene again with further enlightenment. Stated in less flamboyant terms, it asserts that the original agency *is* still active. Whatever it was that happened long ago has in some sense continued, at least as a potentiality, and may recur in a new form.

Obviously this is in keeping with the lamas' ideas about the King of the World, and the Messiah destined to appear from Shambhala. With most occultists, however, such tangible support is almost ignored. They rely on alleged telepathic revelations, or secret lore which cannot be checked. The only useful approach to them is by way of comparison. We have arrived at Shambhala, with its downward extension Agharti, as a source of Ancient Wisdom which can be equated with other sources, and seriously contended for as a real place however mythified. We have related it to known motifs, such as the world-centre and the septenary. Now what have esoteric authors said about it themselves? And if their statements agree with what we have discovered, thereby inspiring some slight measure of trust, do they add anything further to which the same trust might extend?

Do they, in fact, show any signs of genuinely possessing knowledge which has escaped everybody else – knowledge which might imply a secret tradition of Shambhala and its teachings, a secret Shambhalic activity that is still going on? We have seen that Madame Blavatsky and Gerald Massey deserve at least a touch of respect on similar grounds. They and they alone, for whatever reason, stress the importance of seven and Ursa Major. Have they or their kind said anything of value about Shambhala or Agharti?

The truth is, they have said a certain amount but not much. Madame Blavatsky herself was too deeply committed to India and Tibet. In *The Secret Doctrine* she glances once or twice at 'Śambhala', variously spelt, but her remarks are made in passing only, and are less than illuminating. She quotes an alleged ancient book as saying that 'elect' survivors from the lost continent of Lemuria took shelter on a sacred island which, she explains, 'is now the "fabled" Shamballah, in the Gobi Desert'. The desert, it must be presumed, was then mainly under water. Further on we are told that the heart of Mother Earth 'beats under the foot of the sacred Shambalah'. Two notes hint at an association with Meru, but it is all too muddled and obscure to pursue. In her earlier book *Isis Unveiled* she discusses shamans, and the shamanistic background of Tibetan religion. She takes a poor view of Siberian medicine-men, yet thinks they are decadent heirs of something higher, with vestigial mental and psychic powers which they no longer understand. Here she seems on the brink of a real insight, but she fails to connect shamanism with Shambhala, and the clue peters out. One does not feel that she knows anything. As for Massey, he is silent.[5]

Shambhala bulks larger in the writings of Alice Bailey. Born in 1880, she came rather late to the Theosophical Society, and edited its magazine; but having the temerity to contact the same Master as Madame Blavatsky, and to receive teachings from him, she was expelled. Several semi-theosophical groups owe their origin to her. The Bailey doctrines are best known through books written in the 1930s by a disciple and popularizer, Vera Stanley Alder.

The Bailey–Alder 'Shamballa' is elusive. It is 'the vital centre in the planetary consciousness'. It is the earthly home of the great spiritual Hierarchy, and was founded by superior beings who came over from Venus eighteen million years ago. The first part of this sentence, if not the second, might be taken to imply that it has material reality and a geography that can be pinned down. Somewhat dauntingly we are informed that it is built of 'etheric physical matter'. Perseverance, however. yields a few data. The trouble is that they are contradictory. Shamballa is in the Himalayas. Shamballa is beyond the Himalayas. Shamballa is on what was once an island in the Gobi Lake (since desiccated) and was linked by a bridge with a city of Atlantean colonists on the south shore of the lake. Today it is still there, a sacred city of seven gates ruled by the 'Lord of the World', and hidden in the Gobi Desert. Since the Masters meet there, one would suppose that it must be above ground and visible. One gathers, however, that any search for it would be doomed to failure.

As for Shamballa's current programme, it appears that a sort of AGM is held called the Wesak Festival. The Hierarchy discuss their activities, and the Buddha resumes contact with earth. Christ – not exactly the Christ of the Gospels, however – is involved in all this. In keeping with the Masters' plans, he will return before the end of the twentieth century, being the same person as the Maitreya foreseen by Buddhists.[6]

It is hard to see anything in this but the play of theosophical fancy round a few bits of lamaistic legend, probably learnt at third or fourth hand. The curious Gobi location is from Blavatsky. So much for the occultists' Shambhala under that name. With its subterranean portion Agharti, their version is a shade more impressive. Again the spelling varies. The place is first mentioned, as 'Agartha', by a Frenchman named Saint-Yves d'Alveydre, whose book *Mission de l'Inde* was published posthumously in 1910. Saint-Yves was an advocate of various racist and political doctrines. He borrowed some ideas from the pioneer Socialist Fourier, and transmitted some to Rudolf Steiner. Peculiar to himself, however, was the 'underground city of Agartha', described as a centre of mystic initiation. He claimed two sources of knowledge: telepathic messages from the Dalai Lama, and conversations with a 'high official of the Hindu Church'. The high official was perhaps not very high. He was an expatriate Indian who kept a pet shop in Le Havre.

Nevertheless the name and legend did somehow get through.[7] When taken up by a more notable writer in these fields, René Guénon, they have undergone a striking development. Guénon has read Ossendowski, and draws on him for the title of his book, *Le Roi du Monde*. But he leaves Ossendowski far behind. His 'Agartha' is a Holy Land which is the prototype of all other holy lands. It is a place of immortality. If it is anywhere, it is in Central Asia, and although spoken of as a cave, it is not to be wholly identified with this. Now we begin to tread on familiar ground. Guénon introduces Meru and other versions of the world-mountain, saying that the cave is inside it. He also argues at length that this mountain-and-cave complex was regarded early as the world's centre or navel, and that all other centres, such as Delphi, are representations of it. He even connects it with the Great Bear.[8]

How does he arrive at all this? He never fully explains. He shows no sign of awareness of the arguments that have taken shape in this book, arguments associating the earthly centres, the world-mountain, the Bear, Shambhala–Agharti. The Aghartic lore in Ossendowski never speaks of centrality or of a mountain on top. Guénon simply seems to 'know' it all, on very slight grounds. A critical reader would be inclined to view him as pontificating in a void, like so many others. Only . . . he is not. His work, like Massey's, could be construed as evidence that a secret tradition may exist after all. Unhappily it takes us no further. It sheds no light on the nature of Aghartic, or Shambhalic, Wisdom.

3

If the occult trail as such leads to a dead end, however tantalizing, the same is not quite true of its offshoot deriving from science-fiction concepts. Enthusiasts for flying saucers, and for astronauts from other worlds, may be just as confused in their reasoning. But the UFO saga yields two genuinely interesting case-histories, both of which can be related to the Siberian area as defined, suggesting further thoughts as to what has happened there or is happening now. One of them involves a distinguished figure we have already met, a person actually concerned with the Shambhalic problem.

A word of preface may be in order. The flying saucer epidemic is commonly said to have begun on 24 June 1947, when a businessman named Kenneth Arnold, piloting his private aircraft near Mount Rainier in the State of Washington, saw 'a chain of saucer-like objects ... flat like a pie-pan and reflecting the sun like a mirror', flying among the peaks. His report inaugurated the first wave of sightings. Since then, while the phenomenon has waxed and waned, it has never entirely ceased.

Sceptics have argued that UFO-sighting is all in the mind, and was touched off by Arnold, with a snowball effect following. Some reports, it is pointed out, are evident hoaxes. Others arise from misinterpretation of natural objects, such as clouds of unusual shape. Other alleged saucers are real, but are discovered to be man-made objects such as weather balloons and satellites. All these cases are due to mass suggestion in part, and when they have been refuted and set aside we are left with a residue of sightings which are products of mass suggestion alone. Once the notion of flying saucers was publicized, people duly saw them. It has also been remarked, snobbishly but with some truth, that they are seldom seen by the well-educated and hardly ever by trained observers.

UFO zealots have tried to rebut this line of argument by denying that Arnold was the first. Similar objects, they insist, have been seen for thousands of years, so the modern media cannot have done it all. But to make this out they have to list every strange thing ever rumoured to have been seen in the heavens, and count them all as flying saucers. Many are no more than unexplained lights observed in the sky at night. Many others are visionary or mythical portents from ancient writings – winged dragons, Ezekiel's chariot, and so forth – arbitrarily given the UFO classification. On the whole, such attempts to reach back before 1947 are unconvincing.

Two cases, however, remain formidable. The first is the Tunguska event, as it is now described for want of a better term. At 7.17 a.m. on 30 June 1908, in central Siberia, an

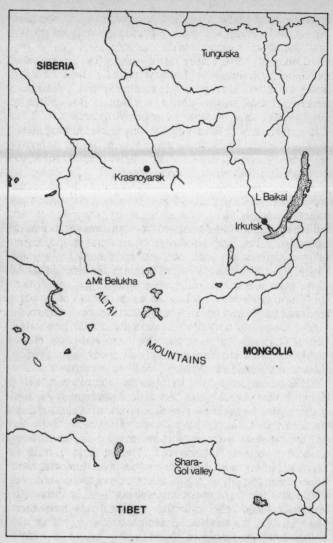

Map of Siberia, Mongolia and Tibet

immense bright object hurtled across the sky. It was seen over a wide area; witnesses included passengers on the Trans-Siberian railway. With an explosion heard five hundred miles off, it – apparently – struck the ground near the upper reaches of the Stony Tunguska river. Fire and cloud rose into the air in a vast column. Herds of reindeer were wiped out, and so were two villages, though luckily the disaster happened in a thinly peopled region.

Unfortunately no investigation was made till long afterwards. In 1921 Professor Leonid Kulik began gathering eye-witness accounts, and in 1927, after much trouble, he succeeded in leading a party to the spot. The scientists expected to find a colossal meteorite. That was the obvious explanation, and Kulik maintained it to his death, but his colleagues felt obliged to abandon it. At the place where the object would have had to fall, there was no crater or other sign of anything having hit, and no meteor fragments were found. For at least twenty miles on all sides the forests were flattened. The fallen trees showed marks of burning, and their tops pointed outwards from the centre. The impression was not of an impact but of a huge explosion in the air, generating terrific heat. Further study during the 1950s and 1960s revealed radioactivity in the soil and the fallen tree-trunks, and abnormalities in the new growth. These and kindred after-effects suggested that the explosion was atomic.

UFO advocates have claimed that the object was a flying saucer. Others, including Russian scientists of high standing, have argued in all seriousness that it was an alien space-ship that tried to land, had an accident and blew up. Perhaps its crew were seeking a landing site used long before by previous expeditions? The surprising truth is that although the Tunguska is outside our proposed Shambhalic territory, it is not too far outside, and the object was moving approximately northwards from that direction. A few minutes earlier, it might well have been over the Altai mountains. Attempted renewal of an old earthly contact would at least stand up as a viable speculation, and bring us back to much the same place.[9]

The second case has received less attention from UFO enthusiasts than it deserves. It is the strongest single argument for the reality – in some sense – of flying saucers. It reintroduces Nicholas Roerich, and is a point of intersection between the UFO tradition and the older occult one.

Roerich's travel diary *Altai-Himalaya*, quoted in the previous chapter, covers his Central Asian expedition during 1923–8. He had joined the Theosophical Society some time before. His status in it was ambiguous. On the one hand, his works show little trace of the wilder theosophical fantasies. On the other, he was regarded by some as belonging to the very highest élite. In an introduction to *Altai-Himalaya* Claude Bragdon insinuates that he was in touch with the Masters.

> Without attempting to elucidate, explain or justify it, therefore, I shall simply say that there is a tenable point of view from which one may regard Roerich as an envoy of those powers which preside over the life and evolution of humanity in the same sense that gardeners preside over a garden: that he journeys into desolate and forbidden lands for the fulfilment of a mission the purpose of which will increasingly reveal itself.

This view of Roerich was taken up by Andrew Tomas in *We are not the First*, one of the recent crop of speculative works on prehistory, UFOs, and so forth. It can scarcely be claimed that the purpose of Roerich's mission ever did reveal itself. Weird rumours circulated about a black stone, a fragment of a great meteor which had fallen in Shambhala. He was alleged to be restoring the stone to its parent body. Certainly he believed himself to be engaged on a task of deep and mysterious importance, in which a stone, whether material or symbolic, played a part. Equally certainly the full truth never emerged.[10]

In *Altai-Himalaya*, however, Roerich does manage to spring a major surprise, and for his readers it remains very surprising indeed. During the summer of 1927 his party was encamped in the Shara-gol valley between Mongolia and Tibet, a little over 39° N, a little over 95° E, near the Humboldt mountain chain. Here he set up a shrine. His own word for it is *suburgan*. His son George, recording the same event, uses the familiar Buddhist term *stupa* and describes it as a 'stately white structure', clearly given much hard work and regarded as important. As to its purpose, George says simply that his father built it to commemorate the site of the camp. Roerich's own account shows that he had a more esoteric motive, and felt himself to be acting under orders. He dedicated the shrine to Shambhala and thereby marked a crucial step in his own career, though the diary leaves its nature obscure. 'On July twentieth directions of the utmost importance reached us. They are difficult to execute but they may lead to certain results. No one in the caravan as yet suspects our immediate programme.'

On 24 July the 'Suburgan of Shambhala', as he called it, was complete in its main structure. Friendly Mongols had helped to build it, and about this time messages were sent to various lamas and other notables, inviting them to the consecration. Now comes another cryptic entry: 'The end of July: "I am going joyously into the battle." *Lapis exilis* – the wandering stone. Yesterday the Buriats foretold something impending. Precisely, "I am sending the best currents for the happy decision of the works." ' Early in August the shrine was finished. The Elder Lama of Tsaidam came to consecrate it, and other guests also assembled.

Then comes this entry:

On August fifth – something remarkable! We were in our camp in the Kukunor district not far from the Humboldt Chain. In the morning about half-past nine some of our caravaneers noticed a remarkably big black eagle flying over us. Seven of us began to watch this unusual bird. At this same moment another of our caravaneers remarked, 'There is something far above the bird.' And he shouted in his astonishment. We all saw, in a direction from north to south, something big and shiny reflecting the sun, like a huge oval moving at great speed. Crossing our camp the thing changed in its direction from south to southwest. And we saw how it disappeared in the intense blue sky. We even had time to take our field glasses and saw quite distinctly an oval form with shiny surface, one side of which was brilliant from the sun.

Obviously this is a classic flying saucer report. George Roerich is silent about the incident, but in another book, *Himalayas, Abode of Light*, his father gives a second version:

A sunny, unclouded morning – the blue sky is brilliant. Over our camp flies a huge, dark vulture. Our Mongols and we watch it. Suddenly one of the Buriat lamas points into the blue sky. 'What is that? A white balloon? An aeroplane?' – We notice something shiny, flying very high from the north-east to the south. We bring three powerful field glasses from the tents and watch the huge spheroid body shining against the sun, clearly visible against the blue sky and moving very fast. Afterwards we see that it sharply changes its direction from south to south-west and disappears behind the snow-peaked Humboldt Chain.[11]

This second paragraph shows that the sky was cloudless; that they could fetch binoculars from their tents – in other words that the object's speed, though great, allowed them time to do so; and that the change of direction was (as the first version implies but does not say) 'sharp'.

In view of the term 'spheroid' in the second account, there is a slight query over the object's shape. However, if it had been like a Rugby football, suggesting, to a Western eye, a balloon or airship, it is unlikely that Roerich's immediate diary entry would have made it sound so alien. What was seen from below was, apparently, an oval form with a certain convexity – enough to explain the impression of sunlight catching one part, with the rest in shadow. UFOs of both shapes, discs and spheroids, have been reported since. Far more significant in the UFO connection is the object's behaviour – flight with no visible means of propulsion or support; rapid motion in a straight line and then an abrupt turn. Such movement is typical of flying saucers, and the abrupt turn is peculiar to them. It has been cited, with good reason, to prove that they cannot be manned vehicles, or indeed physical things at all. No swiftly flying machine could make a sharp turn in the air, and if it did the crew would be killed, through being flung forward by inertia and smashed against the interior.

UFO sightings as such have no evident place in the present discussion. Roerich's, however, does matter, not only because of its Shambhalic context, but because it is exceptional. It cannot be lumped together with all the rest and explained away with all the rest. Not only is it relevant in itself, it compels a reappraisal of standard UFO theories, and hints that later sightings may be relevant too, if hardly in the way many enthusiasts would wish to believe. It is strange in fact that UFO enthusiasts have made so little of the Roerich report, because it defeats the 'anti' case completely. None of the would-be rational explanations will work.[12]

To begin with, Roerich was anything but an untrained or uneducated observer. He was a man of impressive learning. He was also a gifted painter with hundreds of canvases to his credit, many of them careful studies of scenery, buildings and living models. Suppose we discount his companions, who left no record of what he says they saw; his own story remains decisive. The sky had no clouds in it to be misconstrued. At that date and in that country, there could be no question of weather balloons or satellites. The lama who mentioned balloons and aeroplanes had probably never seen either. Other explanations collapse on the time factor. The event took place, and was published, nearly twenty years before Kenneth Arnold's sighting. Granted that Roerich was in a state of mystical expectancy, and on the alert for some sign or wonder: still, how did he come to imagine this one? How could he have been mass-suggested into it, when the sighting occurred in total isolation long before flying saucers were thought of? If he was hallucinating, or inventing, how did he manage to hallucinate or invent a flying saucer two decades ahead of time? If the lamas hypnotized him, how did they hit on such an image themselves? Furthermore – a disturbing converse – Roerich's books were almost certainly unknown to Arnold and other saucer-seers, from 1947 on; so how did they come to see very much what Roerich saw, independently, unless there was something to be seen after all?

Roerich's explorations lead us to a surprising result. Here is the first clear-cut flying saucer report of any real interest, and unlike most, it really is compelling. Here perhaps, if we could find how to use it, is the key to the notorious UFO mania of recent years. And it is linked with Shambhala and the Ancient Wisdom territory. The aerial oval came from the north, which was the direction of the Altai mountains (just as the Tunguska object came from the south, which was also the direction of the Altai mountains). It came on the solemn occasion of Roerich's putting up his Shambhalic shrine, and sensing a crisis in his life. Whatever it was, it was not an intrusive space-ship that just happened to fly over, indifferent to events below. Its advent was connected with what Roerich was doing and thinking about. A psychological factor was present, as any sceptic would urge. The problem is to see what it was and how it functioned.

In the book containing his second account, Roerich mentions that the lamas who shared the apparition called it 'the sign of Shambhala'. He also mentions a discussion with a lama who was not present, but who spoke of the 'sign' with a knowing mien. Roerich told him of the vulture and the 'something shiny and beautiful' flying south over the camp. The lama asked if they smelt a perfume of temple-incense. Roerich thought he could recall some such whiff in the air. The lama replied:

'Ah – you are guarded by Shambhala. The huge black vulture is your enemy, who is eager to destroy your work, but the protecting force from Shambhala follows you in this Radiant form of Matter. This force is always near to you but you cannot always perceive it. Sometimes only, it is manifested for strengthening and directing you. Did you notice the direction in which this sphere moved? You must follow the same direction. You mentioned to me the sacred call – *Kalagiya!* When some one hears this

186

imperative call, he must know that the way to Shambhala is open to him. He must remember when he was called, because from that time evermore, he is closely assisted by the Blessed Rigden Jye-po. Only you must know and realize the manner in which people are helped because often people repel the help which is sent.'[13]

Since the help was from Shambhala, and the object approached from the Altaic area, the lama's discourse seems to establish Shambhala's whereabouts, at least in his own opinion. The sequel, unhappily, is an anticlimax. After receiving his obscure orders and seeing his 'sign', Roerich broke camp and moved south and south-westward across Tibet. But no fruition or revelation ensued – none, at any rate, that he put on record in his books. *Altai-Himalaya* tails off in cloudy apocalypse. Roerich went to live in the Himalayas, and engaged in international work for culture and peace. But he had no very specific aim or message. He died in 1947.

4

Two cryptic incidents, however puzzling, must not be allowed to get out of hand and inspire a theory. Yet it remains true that the Tunguska event and Roerich's aerial sighting are among the few bits of UFO-type 'evidence' which really are forceful; and it also remains true that, because of the objects' flight path, they both direct attention towards the same region, which is the region converged upon by the Ancient Wisdom arguments. The notion that parts of the earth are somehow mysterious, and the scene of strange happenings, is familiar. It is as old as voyage-romances such as the *Odyssey* and probably far older. A popular modern instance has been the Bermuda Triangle, a patch of the Atlantic where aircraft and ships are alleged to vanish. The Triangle theory itself may be as erroneous as sceptics maintain, resting on a few accidents at sea plus a mass of hearsay. But the Altaic country has now become genuinely interesting, not only because of what may have happened there long ago, but because of what may still be happening there. Is it actually 'live'? If so, we are within hailing distance of that other occultist doctrine: that the Masters (or priestesses or whatever they were) still survive, or at any rate that their influence does, so that we might hope to recapture more of the Wisdom in its original fullness.

So – again – can we say anything more about it?

CHAPTER TWELVE

Possibilities

1

We have defined what might have been the great 'Cosmos' insight arising in Altaic Shambhala. Occultists, and fellow-travellers with the occult, would claim that the Altaic sages arrived at this (and presumably at much else) because they functioned on a level which humanity at large has fallen away from. They would further claim that although the falling-away has occurred, this level has never passed wholly beyond human attainment. It has gone on being reached by a few of the sages' spiritual heirs, both inside and outside their own territory. Hence, for example, the belief that the hidden King of the World talks with God directly. Hence also the supernormal powers ascribed to the lamas.

Madame Blavatsky weakened her own position by claiming that through her privileged contact with the Masters, she herself possessed supernormal powers. Her feats were petty and semi-comic, like allegedly restoring a broken cup at a picnic. Worse, several of them were exposed as clumsy conjuring tricks. Yet behind her posturing and faking there was, as usual, a serious idea. She insisted that those who came nearest to being public inheritors of Ancient Wisdom – lamas of course, and even the despised shamans in some degree – had the abilities which she claimed herself, and often much greater ones. Material wonder-working, astral flight, telepathy, and many other things beyond the scope of everyday mortals, were part of the Wisdom.[1]

With the advance of theosophical studies, HPB promised, such powers would be recovered more and more fully. This notion led her to put her trust in charlatans who pretended to have invented mind-driven machines and kindred devices. But it was far from being confined to her, or to dupes of hers. By the inter-war period it was affecting the thinking of learned orientalists such as Evans-Wentz, who predicted that Tibetan techniques of mind-control would soon short-circuit Western science. Heat Yoga would supersede central heating, Illusory Body Yoga would reveal secrets about the nature of matter which escaped physicists, and Teleportation Yoga would solve the parking problem.[2]

Suppose we meet the occultists on their own ground, and ask more precisely what these superhuman powers are, and what is distinctive about them. The first question is not so much whether Central Asian wonder-working actually happens, as what sorts of wonder-working are reputed to happen. The second question is whether Central Asia professes any species of wonder-working which is unique, unparalleled elsewhere, and might therefore be a clue to whatever it was that Shambhala produced and handed down. To a certain extent the exercise imitates the work of those classical scholars who have traced Siberian shamanism in the cult of Apollo. We have seen that by following this line of argument through to Pythagoras, we can guess at what an older and higher shamanism, an Altaic Wisdom, might have taught. Do the alleged powers of the lamas shed any comparable light from another angle?

A fairly sweeping elimination can be carried out quickly. Quite a number of lamaistic feats, real or otherwise, are not distinctive enough to suggest a special Shambhalic ancestry. Hypnotism and teleportation and levitation and invisibility are all asserted, but can be matched in other contexts, by yogis, medicine-men, wizards and mediums, even in the West. Other feats such as astral travelling are simply shamanistic, and take us no further than the exploits of Greeks under the same influence.

These matters were studied on the spot in the early decades of the twentieth century, when Lamaism still flourished, by Alexandra David-Neel, the French Buddhist who examined and translated the tale of Gesar. She dismissed miracles, but accepted that strange things happened, attributing them to mental or physical techniques which had been preserved in Tibet and Tibetan-influenced areas but were little known outside. Two phenomena interested her specially. Since both are peculiar to the lamas' world, both might seem to put us on promising tracks. Actually only one of them does. By way of preface, however, it is worth looking at the other, in order to show why it does not, and so draw a contrast.

Certain Tibetans, Madame David-Neel learned, could walk at an astounding speed. The term for such an athlete is *lung-gom-pa* or wind-man, and she saw one herself.

I noticed, far away in front of us, a moving black spot which my field-glasses showed to be a man . . . As I continued to observe him through the glasses, I noticed that the man proceeded at an unusual gait and, especially, with an extraordinary swiftness. Though, with the naked eye, my men could hardly see anything but a black speck moving over the grassy ground, they too were not long in remarking the quickness of its advance. I handed them the glasses and one of them, having observed the traveller for a while, muttered: '*Lama lung-gom-pa chig da.*' (It looks like a lama *lung-gom-pa*.) . . .

The man continued to advance towards us and his curious speed became more and more evident. What was to be done if he really was a *lung-gom-pa*? I wanted to observe him at close quarters, I also wished to have a talk with him, to put him some questions, to photograph him . . . But at the very first words I said about it, the man who had recognized him as a lama *lung-gom-pa* exclaimed: 'Your Reverence will not stop the lama, nor speak to him. This would certainly kill him. These lamas when travelling must not break their meditation . . .'

By that time he had nearly reached us; I could clearly see his perfectly calm impassive face and wide-open eyes with their gaze fixed on some invisible far-distant object situated somewhere high up in space. The man did not run. He seemed to lift himself from the ground, proceeding by leaps. It looked as if he had been endowed with the elasticity of a ball and rebounded each time his feet touched the ground. His steps had the regularity of a pendulum.

The secret is said to be a yogic technique which lightens the body. Indeed, a *lung-gom-pa* who wishes to remain grounded must weight himself down with chains. Evans-Wentz mentions a case in 1931 of a *lung-gom-pa* covering twelve miles in twenty minutes, though he did not witness it himself. Fosco Maraini, visiting Tibet nearly twenty years later, heard of the same accomplishment. A Tibetan assured him that a competent wind-man could walk all round Tibet in a week. On Evans-Wentz's figures he would have to walk at least ten hours a day, but, of course, perhaps he could. Maraini never saw it done either.[3]

Such hyper-walking is not easy to trace in other nations, even as a legend. Saints, heroes, magicians may fly or levitate, they seldom simply walk very fast. The fairy-tale theme of seven-league boots is the closest obvious parallel, but it does not imply that the wearer need possess special powers himself; the magic is in the boots. The technique of the *lung-gom-pa* does seem to be distinctive. The trouble is, however, that it has no visible link with the Shambhala tradition. It has no clear dependence on any philosophy or doctrine which might be part of the Ancient Wisdom. Nor is it associated with the right people, the ones who have Shambhalic connections. It is not ascribed to Gesar or to the teachers of Kalachakra. Further research might put the matter in a fresh light. At present, wind-manship does not appear to lead anywhere.

The other lamaistic technique which Madame David-Neel singled out is more interesting. Lamas claim that thought can create tangible things, thought-forms. This belief goes beyond all notions of apparitions, astral travelling or telepathy. Human beings, it is asserted, can project mental phantasms which are at least semi-physical. While extreme holiness is helpful, the feat can be performed without it if you try long and hard enough. A thought-form created in this way is called a *tulpa*. It can – sometimes – be seen by others, without any prior suggestion or hypnosis, just as if the object were there in the ordinary way. It can – sometimes – even have a temporary life of its own, so that it can break free from control and wander off.

A thought-form can be evoked inadvertently, with no awareness of what is happening. More usually, however, the adept does it with a purpose, by long-drawn and deliberate exercise. The potentialities are boundless. He can create a replica of himself, a doppelganger. He can create what appears to be another person. He can create an animal or a material object. The Dalai Lama told Madame David-Neel that with enough spiritual progress, it is possible to create 'hills, enclosures, houses, forests, roads, bridges'.

She tried it herself. She imagined a monk, 'short and fat, of an innocent and jolly type'. After months of lonely concentration and ritual the monk appeared, and went on appearing. He looked lifelike and consistent, not changing from one evocation to another. When she started on her travels again, the monk joined the party. He now manifested himself without her having to think of him. He also performed normal actions which she did not will him to do – walking beside her horse, halting, looking round. Occasionally he touched her, though very lightly. After a while he did start changing, but not as if her image of him were wavering, rather as if he were acquiring a character of his own. He grew thinner, and his face took on a malicious look. The phantasm was out of control, and he had reached a pitch of reality where a few other people were beginning to see him too. Madame David-Neel had had enough of her monk and decided to wipe him out. Easier decided than done. She had to concentrate again for six months before he gave up.[4]

Unlike the fast walking, which sophisticated lamas view as a stunt with no deep significance, *tulpa*-projection is held to be important and to express philosophic truth. Sometimes, when a master is training a novice (or was, before Communism), he tells the disciple to shut himself away in a hermitage and meditate till his *Yidam* or tutelary god appears. After a long time, if the course is successful, the *Yidam* does appear, and slowly takes on the same quasi-reality as the phantom monk. A disciple who has got so far may now simply go off in triumph, with his master's congratulations and the *Yidam* in attendance as his guardian angel. This, however, is not the end which the master hopes for. Sometimes the disciple goes further, into a sort of dark night of the soul, and confesses with anguish that although the *Yidam* is present, he no longer believes in it as an independent being. It is his own creation. 'That is exactly what it is necessary for you to realize', the master tells him. 'Gods, demons, the whole universe, are but a mirage which exists in the mind, "springs from it, and sinks into it".' In Evans-Wentz's words, 'Matter is a development of thought, "crystallized mental energy".' The world of normal experience is in fact a colossal thought-form sustained by the One Mind. Gods, demons and other unseen beings exist, but even they are not truly outside yourself because ultimately you *are* the One Mind.[5]

Such a belief might well have been part of the Shambhalic Wisdom. It might indeed have been the metaphysical aspect of the Cosmos conception inferred already; the two would fit together as a single great affirmation that *mind embraces all and can comprehend all*, which was differently followed up in different places that the doctrine reached. Stated abstractly the One Mind principle is not unlike the teaching of, say, Vedanta in India. But to state it abstractly is to miss the essence. The lamas not only expound a theory of mind and matter, they claim to know how to prove it in practice by the creation of thought-forms. The doctrine is alive, positive, even supposedly verifiable like the statements of science.

Moreover, it figures in the careers of people with Shambhalic associations. Gesar himself, he whose seven chalices formed Ursa Major in the heavens, and who is to come again from Shambhala, is portrayed in his epic as a master of the art of *tulpa*-projection. He uses it to defeat his enemies. Phantasms of himself appear bewilderingly where he is not. Phantasms of horses, tents, soldiers, cover the embattled landscape. Similar illusions occur in other Asian epics such as the Hindu *Mahabharata*, but they are visual tricks only. In the story moulded by Central Asian ideas the phantasms are, within their limits and life-span, real. The *tulpa* soldiers fight Gesar's enemies, and are solid enough to kill them with *tulpa* weapons. That is ancient legend, but another case is within living memory. In 1923, when the Tashi Lama fled from Shigatse, he is reputed to have left a mobile speaking phantasm of himself that deceived everyone till he was at a safe distance, and then vanished. He went his way founding Kalachakra colleges in touch with Shambhala.[6]

The thought-form idea not only reflects philosophic doctrine, it has a bearing on lamaistic theories of reincarnation. Here too Gesar is involved. If the concentration of thought and will is powerful enough – perhaps a joint effort by many people – a human *tulpa* can be more than a phantasm. It can come into being by normal birth, as a stable physical form with a personality. It is then called a *tulku* or 'phantom body'. A *tulku* child is not, or need not be, distinguishable from others by inspection alone. But he embodies a god or a demon or another person deceased, or an intention or hope: whatever it was that inspired the thoughts which formed him. Repetition of the process through a series of lives produces a chain of *tulku* persons who are fundamentally the same, though they may develop quite differently. This accounts for the mystic succession of Dalai Lamas. One of Madame David-Neel's informants told her that the Mongols would 'construct' the returning Messianic Gesar by their own thoughts, their own yearning for him. He would be reborn as 'the *tulku* of all of us whom the foreigners wish to make their slaves'.[7]

We certainly have something distinctive here. Other mythologies tell of phantasms with the same solidity as Tibetan ones. As a rule they are the temporary disguises of gods. Not always: in a late Greek legend, the Helen who went to Troy was an illusion, and the real Helen was in Egypt. But such things are unforeseeable quirks of heaven, altogether beyond mortal scope. No system outside lamaistic Buddhism recognizes the thought-form as a known phenomenon which the mind creates and can, with training, create at will. While reincarnation is a very widespread belief, nobody else has conceived the *tulku* version of it, even in other schools of Buddhism.

Arguably, then, the thought-form idea with its background philosophy was part of the Shambhalic Wisdom, and has survived for that reason in Shambhalic traditions – Gesar, Kalachakra. If the sages or priestesses of Shambhala expounded and applied the technique, and actually made it work, we must accept that they justified the occultists' claim. They functioned on a level which humanity at large has fallen away from.

2

All this would be very conjectural indeed, if it were not for Roerich's UFO. It will be recalled that the flying oval was described by his lama companions as 'the sign of Shambhala'. No one seems to have told him why the sign of Shambhala should have looked and behaved thus. However, it is surely beyond chance that this first and most impressive of flying saucers should have appeared just there, in the one earthly context where an explanation was ready to hand, and part of an accepted philosophy. The UFO may have surprised Roerich's lama friends, it did not baffle them. They made no special mystery of it. The one who spoke of it as 'the protecting force from Shambhala following you in this radiant form of matter' was alluding to the *tulpa* idea. Roerich quotes him as using the word 'manifested', and 'manifestation' is a world he uses himself to refer to *tulpas*.[8] Allegedly the UFO was a thought-form projected from Shambhala by its ruler Rigden Jye-po or some associate. It appeared (unlike any of its successors) precisely where it could carry its own interpretation and be understood. No conclusion follows as to whether Rigden Jye-po does or does not exist. The coincidence, and the interpretation, would remain arresting whoever projected the thing.

Curiously enough – and here is the last of our many glances at Jung – this is the explanation of flying saucers which Jung himself struggled to formulate in his essay on them, published in 1959. Though treating them as psychological in origin, he refused to accept that they were all 'nothing but' hallucinations. They were externalized somehow, only he lacked the vocabulary to say how. His theory, never succinctly stated by himself, is summed up by Colin Wilson: 'The flying objects *have* an objective existence, but as projections from the racial unconscious mind.' Apart from the word 'racial' this is close to the *tulpa* concept, which Jung seems not to have known.[9]

As remarked before, most flying saucer reports can be explained away easily. With a stubborn few dismissal is harder, and the *tulpa* theory, if we care to extend it beyond lama country, handles them rather well. It accounts for the saucers' odd behaviour, like physical objects, but not wholly or consistently like. It accounts for their evanescence. It accounts for the fact that only some people see them. It accounts for the conflicting and, on the whole, negative evidence as to whether they can be photographed, or picked up on radar. Thus far, the conventional theory of mass suggestion covers the facts equally well and a great deal more economically. But the *tulpa* theory also handles what is perhaps the strongest point made by advocates of UFOs as real objects – that they have often been sighted by people who never previously thought about them, had no opinion on them, were not looking for them, and had no occultish or 'fringe' interests. This does tell against suggestion as the whole truth. If the saucers are thought-forms, the difficulty dissolves. They have been projected by people who *are* thinking about them. Then, during their phantasmal life-span, they are seen by a few others, as a few saw Madame David-Neel's monk.

It would be rash to dwell on such a bizarre notion if it were not for the fact that Roerich's UFO is a genuine problem, and defeats rational explaining-away in any case. Nor can we stop at Roerich. Because of him, some of the flying saucers of later times also become genuine problems. Observers ignorant of Roerich have seen things in the sky that look and behave like his airborne sign of Shambhala. Hoax, delusion, suggestion can all be properly invoked. Still, that strange image had to impress itself on somebody in the first place, and probably on quite a number of somebodies. Flying saucers had to be seen in some way before they could be faked or imagined. Even if the prototype sightings were all optical illusions or hallucinations, it is very puzzling that they were so like Roerich's.

A fresh explanation is needed, which will cover both his and the later ones from 1947 onward; and Roerich's comes to us, not only with its own explanation, but with a clue (however weird) to its successors. This is foreshadowed by Alexandra David-Neel:

> Once the *tulpa* is endowed with enough vitality to be capable of playing the part of a real being, it tends to free itself from its maker's control . . . Tibetan magicians also relate cases in which the *tulpa* is sent to fulfil a mission, but does not come back and pursues its peregrinations as a half-conscious, dangerously mischievous puppet. The same thing, it is said, may happen when the maker of the *tulpa* dies before having dissolved it.[10]

We can pin UFOs down to a psychophysical phenomenon. It is not a hypothesis contrived for the purpose. It has been in print for decades, it has been known to lamas and perhaps their shaman precursors for untold centuries, and it may be open to impartial inquiry. If conceded as possible, it suggests a train of events. Whatever actual instance projected the object in 1927, repetitions began outside Central Asia twenty years later. Thought-forms of the same type started materializing and vanishing. The sign of Shambhala was seen everywhere. In view of the apocalyptic prophecies in the background, that may fit in with the belief of enthusiasts that UFO sightings herald a New Age.

3

But who has been doing the projecting? And while the first 'sign' was obviously for Roerich's benefit, what about the later ones which have been (up to now) so cryptic, aimless and dubious? If such questions are on the right track at all, they still cannot yet be answered. Doubtless many occultists and astronaut-seekers would cheerfully try. To think further along their lines, however, is not to

198

find answers but to bring this inquiry – for the moment – to a sudden and ironic conclusion.

On the completion of the main argument at the beginning of Chapter Eleven, I said: 'If an Ancient Wisdom did make its way into the various cultures, this Altaic zone is the most promising place to look for its cradle-land. If we wish to picture Masters or alien visitors, teaching prehistoric humanity and leaving legends behind, this is the most promising place to locate their earthly headquarters.' It may now be clear that modern occurrences have revealed more in this second sentence than an 'if'. There is a positive mystery, a double one, which is contemporary as well as ancient.

Nicholas Rocrich was believed by his friends to be in touch with the Masters. To judge from his writings he believed it himself. He connected them with Shambhala, which for him was not a dead legend but a living reality, a centre of their continuing influence. In that faith he built his shrine in the wilderness – and Shambhala responded: the shining oval 'sign' rushed through the heavens. It may be objected that we have only his word for this. His companions, however, cast no doubt on the incident, and even if he did invent it the invention is puzzling, because he described a flying saucer long before they had begun to be seen. It is simplest to suppose that his report is true and the sign appeared, flying towards him from the direction of the Altai mountains.

Because of this, Roerich is the only claimant to contact with the Masters who makes one feel that he may be trustworthy, and that they may actually exist. The so-called messages alleged by Madame Blavatsky and others can be explained away without trouble. Shambhala's signal to Roerich cannot. *Tulpa*-projection may account for it as the lama assumed. But even on the most credulous reading of this phenomenon, no ordinary Tibetan or Mongol adept could have created such a portent as skimmed over Roerich's camp. It belongs to the higher class of thought-form described by the Dalai Lama – 'hills, enclosures, houses, forests, roads, bridges' – which only a being advanced beyond normal human capacities can hope to produce. If the sign of Shambhala was a *tulpa*, it was assuredly launched by such a being.

As to the UFO sightings of later years, we may reserve judgement. That of 1927 stands by itself as an intelligible gesture implying conscious purpose, a will to communicate. Such a purpose and will must have been, from an everyday point of view, superhuman. If we reject thought-forms as fictitious the difficulty is greater, not less; in normal human terms, there is no explanation left at all. Roerich's experience does seem to be evidence that Masters exist. *And it points to the same location for them as the main 'Ancient Wisdom' argument:* an Altaic Shambhala, alive or reactivated after thousands of years.

Are we closing on a note of triumph for occultists? Not entirely. Their science-fiction confrères have a retort. According to them the real Masters are superior beings of a different kind – those aliens who visited Earth long ago, and may return. The proofs of such visits amassed by Erich von Däniken may nearly all be tenuous – but not quite all. We have one piece of serious evidence, respected by scientists, for an alien space-ship coming to this planet. It is, of course, the Tunguska explosion. It puts the visit in 1908, not in the remote past, although the astronauts may have been attempting a return to a known site. *And it too points to the same location as the main 'Ancient Wisdom' argument:* not precisely, but near enough to be interesting. The object came from approximately the direction of the Altai mountains.

So the proper statement of the case is no longer purely hypothetical. It is not merely what we may call Proposition A: 'If superior beings have ever lived on earth and instructed humans, this is the best place to look for them'. We must add Proposition B: 'There are just two pieces of evidence for such beings, and they both point to this place, independently of the data behind Proposition A'.

A surprising and thought-provoking result. Frankly, though, it would be easier with only one piece of evidence. We might manage to cope with Masters, or with astronauts. It is a large order to accommodate both. No doubt there are speculative ways of doing it, or of inventing a third class of super-being, whose activities can explain both the

200

UFO and the Siberian explosion. The immediate moral is more sober. This Altaic region is clearly a very strange place. It was once, apparently, a source of what can fairly be called Ancient Wisdom. It may have been, and may still be, something far more extraordinary. Ready-made theoretical fantasies, however, will not resolve the problem. They lead only to confusion. There is no substitute for patient research by rational methods, with imagination and intuition playing their part, but no more.

Another Centre?

A loose end remains which is too intriguing to ignore, yet which cannot be discussed on the same footing as (say) the legend of Shambhala, because the mere act of discussing it would make the evidence appear weightier than it is. The most that can be done is to note some obscurely associated facts, and hope that future research may disclose their meaning.

They concern Britain – the Celtic Britain of the last few centuries B.C. and the first few centuries A.D. The question is whether the Hyperborean Wisdom, or a portion of it, found a lodgement here independent of its main seed-beds in Greece and Asia. The chief motive for wondering – or rather, for inclining to wonder – is that the Greek historian Hecataeus of Abdera, writing in the fourth century B.C., moves the entire Hyperborean scene to an island which is not named, but can only be Britain.

> Opposite to the coast of Celtic Gaul there is an island in the ocean, not smaller than Sicily, lying to the north – which is inhabited by the Hyperboreans, who are so named because they dwell beyond the North Wind ... Tradition says that Leto [the mother of Apollo and Artemis] was born there, and for that reason, the inhabitants venerate Apollo more than any other god. They are, in a manner, his priests ...
>
> In this island, there is a magnificent precinct of Apollo, and a remarkable temple, of a round form, adorned with many consecrated gifts. There is also a city, sacred to the same god, most of the inhabitants of which are harpers ...
>
> The Hyperboreans use a peculiar dialect, and have a remarkable attachment to the Greeks, especially to

the Athenians and the Delians, deducing their friend-
ship from remote periods. It is related that some
Greeks formerly visited the Hyperboreans, with
whom they left consecrated gifts of great value, and
also that in ancient times Abaris, coming from the
Hyperboreans into Greece, renewed their family
intercourse with the Delians.

It is also said that in this island the moon appears
very near to the earth, that certain eminences of a
terrestrial form are plainly seen in it, that Apollo
visits the island once in a course of nineteen years, in
which period the stars complete their revolutions,
and that for this reason the Greeks distinguish the
cycle of nineteen years by the name of 'the great
year'. During the season of his appearance the god
plays upon the harp and dances every night . . .

The supreme authority in that city and the sacred
precinct is vested in those who are called Boreadae,
being the descendants of Boreas, and their govern-
ments have been uninterruptedly transmitted in this
line.[1]

What is Hecataeus talking about? Of course he may
simply have transferred the Hyperborean mythos to Britain on the strength of somebody's ignorant guess that this
was where the Hyperboreans lived; in which case his
'information' is not about Britain at all. Still it is interesting
that the transfer should have occurred, and also that the
story includes such 'Wisdom' details as Abaris, the mentor
of Pythagoras, together with astronomy, circularity and
dancing. One point suggests that Hecataeus may have
heard something authentic. He implies Hyperborean
knowledge of the nineteen-year or Metonic cycle, which
was known also in Greece, though not widely used, as a
method of regulating the calendar. This cycle was apparently employed by the Druids, the Celtic priest-magicians
who flourished in western Europe – including the British
Isles – during the last centuries before Christ.[2]

Reports of the Druids may thus account in part for
Hecataeus' notions. Distance lent enchantment. Classical
authors did eventually tend to romanticize the Druids as

noble northern philosophers, and to equate them (more or less) with the Hyperborean élite, on the basis of a geography which had become very vague indeed. This mode of thinking cannot be documented as far back as Hecataeus, but it existed, and may have existed earlier than we know. Julius Caesar wrote a fairly sober account of the Druids, much of which reflects a state of affairs before his own time. According to him the Order had its principal colleges in Britain. Earlier rumours to the same effect might help to explain Hecataeus. If the Celtic priest-magicians *were* supposedly Hyperboreans, then their island headquarters was where the Hyperboreans had to be, and all the rest of the mythos obviously belonged in the same setting.

Taken by itself, therefore, most of the passage looks like a flight of fancy, the first instance of a Hyperborean–Celtic–Druidic mix-up that went on for a long time and never had any factual basis. Perhaps, though, it did have a factual basis. The Celts reached Britain from the east; they had been in contact with wandering peoples from much further east; and the most recent scholarship suggests that the Druids actually were 'Hyperborean' in a sense (just as, according to Guthrie, Apollo was), because elements in their cult and practice came from the Asian home of shamanism.

On the strength of what little is known about them, Anne Ross in *Pagan Celtic Britain* says flatly that they were, in effect, shamans. Lacking British sources, she quotes an Irish legend of a chief Druid named Mogh Ruith, who put on a dark grey hornless bull's hide and a white-speckled bird headpiece with fluttering wings, 'a typical shamanistic appearance', and rose into the air. Stuart Piggott, while cautious on the direct shaman equation, draws attention to Celtic sacrificial deposits of animal hides and bones, which can be paralleled in Altaic shamanism. He also quotes an Irish text in which the warriors of a chief's bodyguard swear to stand firm 'though the earth should split under us and the sky above on us'. This may sound like a cliché, but in fact the only complete parallel is in an inscription found by the Orkhon river south of Lake Baikal, affirming that the power of the dominant local tribes will endure 'so long as the heaven above and the earth below have not opened'. Piggott concludes that a 'curious link' between the Celts and Central Asia – hence between Druids and shamans, between Britons and Hyperboreans – does show signs of having existed.[3]

All of which might tend to make Britain a spiritual colony of the Altaic centre. Our near-ignorance of the Druids' more advanced teachings (if they had any) precludes any checking by comparison with, say, Kalachakra. But Hecataeus' placing of a Hyperborean priesthood in Britain may not be pure fantasy; it may reflect the shamanistic succession travelling west with Celtic migration, and evolving into Druidism en route, with colleges in Britain.

Of some interest here is Avalon, the equivocal Otherworld of the British Celts. It is sometimes said to be an island, just as Shambhala sometimes is, and it has a decidedly Hyperborean air, being a blissful place where the climate is always gentle and there is never any snow or strong wind. Its name is thought to be derived from a Celtic word for 'apple'. Several scholars have proposed a direct link with Apollo, arguing that 'Apollo' means applegod.[4]

As Shambhala has its subterranean extension, Agharti, so had Avalon. It merged into an underworld known as Annwn. That fact raises the question of the name Avalon as applied to Glastonbury in Somerset, which was a holy place of the Celts. However Avalon came to be fixed on the map of Somerset, Glastonbury Tor certainly seems to have been regarded in folklore as an entrance to Annwn. This being so, it is a striking coincidence at least that a septenary spiral track has been reconstructed on the Tor (see page 89 above). Several of the motifs we have associated with the world-centre – the spiral itself, the numinous mountain, the paradisal place which is both above and below ground – do appear to come together at this obscurely hallowed spot, with its roots in an antiquity where Celts and Druids and Hyperboreans blend into one another, and Apollo himself is an honorary Briton.[5]

For a sidelight from (so to speak) the other end I am

indebted to Stephen Jenkins, who held a teaching post in Mongolia during 1970, and is one of the few Western initiates into Kalachakra. The Mongolian Communist regime has almost destroyed organized Buddhism, but a number of lamas survive as individual scholars, on good terms with the State. According to Mr Jenkins, those who expound Kalachakra still connect it with Shambhala. But their Shambhalic teaching has taken a curious turn – or perhaps, a curious tradition which was always present has now risen to the surface.

They persist in the old apocalyptic beliefs, predicting a world upheaval and the return of Gesar. They also repeat that the Buddha was a Shambhalic initiate, and taught doctrines originating there. However, they add a further claim which seems to have escaped Evans-Wentz and Roerich. In about 543 B.C., when, according to their (unusual) dating, the Buddha was near the end of his life, a European came to him to be taught the Shambhalic doctrines. This visitor's name is given as Sucandra. The lamas think that Sucandra was a Celt, probably from Britain, and that in some sense Shambhala is *in* Britain. Presumably that strange place has bilocated. 'Sucandra' means 'white (or beautiful) moon'. Mr Jenkins tells me that it could correspond to a credible Welsh name.

He suggests further that the atmosphere of the Gesar epic is rather like that of early Welsh tales of Arthur. As a matter of fact, one could be more specific. It has been argued quite seriously that 'Gesar' is the same as 'Caesar', and in Welsh tradition Arthur is called 'the Emperor' before he is called a king. Moreover, Arthur has departed to Avalon and will some day return from there, just as Gesar will return from Shambhala. Could a single myth have gone into the making of both heroes?

But at this point I think the mists, having tantalizingly parted to reveal unexplored country, close in again.

Notes

Short headings only are given here. The full title of a work may be found by referring to the Bibliography. For instance, 'French' refers to Peter J. French's book *John Dee*.

Chapter One: A Posture of Defiance
1 See French, Yates. These authors discuss Paracelsus also.
2 McGuire and Rattansi, *passim*.
3 Besides von Däniken, see e.g. Drake, Kolosimo, Le Poer Trench.
4 Campbell, Vol. 1, pp. 146–7; Cumont (1), pp. 2–5; Guthrie (1), p. 13.
5 Ouspensky, p. 302.
6 Castle and Thiering, *passim*.

Chapter Two: Secret Doctrine?
1 For short accounts of Madame Blavatsky, and criticism of her ideas, see Camp, pp. 228–32; Francis King (2), pp. 46–58; Wilson, pp. 329–37.
2 Blavatsky (2), *passim*, and especially Vol. 2, pp. 590–641.
3 Ouspensky, pp. 71–2, 82, 122, 205.
4 Dodds, pp. 246–7, 293; C. G. Jung, Vol. 14 (*Mysterium Coniunctionis*), p. 93; Thompson, pp. 16–24, 31–5, 38.
5 N. Roerich (1), pp. 191–2.
6 *Cultural Heritage of India*, Vol. 3, p. 476; Eliade, p. 274 n. 65; Evans-Wentz (2), p. 287; Santillana, p. 123 n. 16.
7 C. G. Jung, Vol. 9 Part 1 (*The Archetypes and the Collective Unconscious*), fig. 4 and pp. 362–3; Vol. 12 (*Psychology and Alchemy*), p. 63.
8 Cumont (2), p. 120; C. G. Jung, Vol. 5 (*Symbols of Transformation*), p. 45 n. 8; Vol. 7 (*Two Essays on Analytical Psychology*), pp. 222f.; Vol. 9 Part 1 (*The Archetypes and the Collective Unconscious*), p. 136 and n.

7; Vol. 12 (*Psychology and Alchemy*), pp. 54–6, 63–5 and fig. 21; Vol. 14 (*Mysterium Coniunctionis*), pp. 11–13, 19, 117–18, 270, 287, 403–4.

Chapter Three: The Prevalence of the Heptad

1 Ashe (2), pp. 26–31 and notes. Anath was regarded as a female companion of Yahweh by heretical Jews in Egypt. Also, she was sometimes identified with Athene, the Greek goddess of wisdom. See Cassuto, pp. 64–5.

2 Genesis 2: 1–3, 7: 1–4, 21: 25–31, 29: 16–30, 41: 1–7; Exodus 20: 8–11; Leviticus 25; Exodus 25: 31–9, 37: 17–24; Numbers 23: 1–4, 14, 29–30; Deuteronomy 7: 1; I Kings 8: 65, 18: 43; II Kings 5: 10–14; Zechariah 3: 9, 4: 2, 10; Joshua 6: 1–21.

3 Deuteronomy 28: 7; Ruth 4: 15; I Samuel 2: 5; Isaiah 4: 1.

4 *Jewish Encyclopaedia*, art. 'Menorah', 'Numbers and numerals'. The angels are mentioned in Tobit 12: 15. See further *Brewer*, art. 'Seven names of God'; Campbell, Vol. 1, p. 85; Dodd (1), p. 156; Spencer, pp. 178–9.

5 Asin, pp. 88, 116; C. G. Jung, Vol. 14 (*Mysterium Coniunctionis*), pp. 386–7.

6 Cassuto, pp. 43–4, 49–50, 93, 134; Hooke, pp. 224–5 and fig. 5; James (2), pp. 194–5; C. G. Jung, Vol. 14 (*Mysterium Coniunctionis*), p. 340 and n. 318. The Christian version of the seven-headed dragon or serpent is in Revelation 12.

7 Campbell, Vol. 1, pp. 412–18; Cavendish, p. 84; L. W. King, Vol. 1, p. lxxx; Kramer, pp. 57, 130, 137, 150–1, 204, 216, 218, 219, 232, 235, 257, 271–2. Cp. Neumann (1), p. 160, and Santillana, pp. 289, 301.

8 Campbell, Vol. 1, p. 101; Dodd (1), pp. 160–1 and n. 7; Guthrie (1), p. 86n., and (2), p. 138; Herodotus III. 8; Hesiod, *Works and Days*, lines 770–1; *Man, Myth and Magic*, art. 'Orpheus and Orphism'; Murray, pp. 140–9; Spencer, p. 155.

9 *Brewer*, art. 'Jamshid'; C. G. Jung, Vol. 13 (*Alchemical Studies*), p. 337 n. 3.

10 Müller, pp. 251–3. Griffith's *Hymns of the Rigveda* is in two volumes. Each has its own index, so two counts must be made and combined. To be fair, the total of index entries for each number does not exactly reproduce the number of occurrences in the hymns, because some of the entries refer to notes and not to the text; but the relative prominence of seven, three, five and ten is sufficiently brought out.

11 Evans-Wentz (2), pp. 32, 225 n. 4; *Man, Myth and Magic*, art. 'Tantrism'; Maraini, pp. 63, 77, and cp. 110–11.

12 Cp. Neumann (1), p. 160.

13 See *The Times*, 7 March 1974, p. 8.

14 Hyginus, pp. 191–2; Seltman, pp. 71, 74–5.

15 Graves (1), sections 76c, 106, 107; Hyginus, pp. 67–9, 73. Graves maintains that Amphion's lyre had only three strings, but this seems to be a conjecture.

16 Graves (1); section 160h, and (2), p. 127; Hyginus, pp. 148–9, 210–11; Massey, Part 2, Vol. 2, p. 2; Nilsson, chapter 4, especially pp. 133, 136–8, 142. Cp. Santillana, p. 157.

17 *Brewer*, art. 'Pleiad'; Santillana, p. 301.

18 Dodds, p. 292; Graves (2), p. 285; Hyginus, p. 179; Murray, p. 142.

19 Graves (1), section 1. 4; Herodotus I. 98; Santillana, pp. 239–40; Swete, note on Revelation 17: 9. Cp. C. G. Jung, Vol. 14 (*Mysterium Coniunctionis*), p. 403.

20 *Brewer*, arts. 'Pleiad', 'Wonder'; C. G. Jung, Vol. 14 (*Mysterium Coniunctionis*), pp. 403–4.

21 C. G. Jung, Vol. 14 (*Mysterium Coniunctionis*), pp. 398–9; *Man, Myth and Magic* on various legendary heroes.

22 Campbell, Vol. 1. pp. 165, 452–3; *Man, Myth and Magic*, art. 'Mountain'; *Mahabharata*, Book VI, chapter 5, verses 3–5; Maraini, pp. 77, 109–10; N. Roerich (1), pp. 191–2; Santillana, p. 66 n. 5.

Chapter Four: Numerologists and Psychologists

1 Cavendish, pp. 83–6; Wilson, p. 310.

2 C. G. Jung, Vol. 9 Part 1 (*The Archetypes and the Collective Unconscious*), 'Concerning Mandala Symbolism' and Appendix; also Vol. 13 (*Alchemical Studies*), 'Commentary on "The Secret of the Golden Flower" '. Jung owed a debt to the orientalist Richard Wilhelm, who introduced him to the Chinese alchemic treatise discussed in the latter essay. Francis King, (1), p. 97n., asserts that neither Wilhelm nor Jung understood the book. I do not think this affects the mandalic issue.

3 See e.g. C. G. Jung, Vol. 8 (*The Structure and Dynamics of the Psyche*), pp. 456–7; Vol. 9 Part 1 (*The Archetypes and the Collective Unconscious*), fig. 38 and note on this on p. 378; Vol. 12 (*Psychology and Alchemy*), pp. 218–21.

4 Cavendish, pp. 179–80.

5 Cp. Emma Jung, p. 339, and chapter XIX. See also an astonishing poem by Walt Whitman, 'Chanting the Square Deific', in *Leaves of Grass*, 1891–2 edition, XXX.

6 C. G. Jung, Vol. 12 (*Psychology and Alchemy*), p. 218.
7 Cavendish, p. 180; Hooke, p. 27; *Man, Myth and Magic*, art. 'Twelve'.
8 Cavendish, p. 80.
9 Cavendish, p. 78.
10 James (2), pp. 213ff.; *Man, Myth and Magic*, art. 'Three'.
11 Radhakrishnan, Vol. 2, p. 75; de Riencourt, p. 107; Russell, Book I, chapter XXII.
12 Campbell, Vol. 1, pp. 142, 145, 233, 237; C. G. Jung, Vol. 12 (*Psychology and Alchemy*), fig. 110.
13 Neumann (2), p. 37; Vawter, pp. 54–6.
14 Atkinson, p. 27; Bolton, pp. 115–17; Campbell, Vol. 1, p. 452; Kramer, p. 310; Rees, p. 148; Spencer, p. 106. In Bolton's words: 'The concept of fixed cardinal points is an advanced one, formed as astronomical science and mathematical geography progressed.'
15 Bolton, pp. 115–16; L. W. King, Vol. 1, pp. 63–5. The Creation Epic, to be precise, says the god Marduk created the 'seven' winds, whereas it does not say where the 'four' came from. But this all happens before the beginning of the world, which therefore contains both sets from the start, as the author's mind does. Two of the set of seven are called 'the fourfold wind' and 'the sevenfold wind'. Four and seven seem here to be coeval in their significance. When we get back behind the Creation Epic into Sumeria, seven is paramount.
16 Harrison, pp. 184–90; Nilsson, pp. 54–73, 278. Cp. Graves (1), Introduction.
17 Russell, pp. 62, 74; Thompson, pp. 12–14.
18 Cavendish, pp. 216–17.
19 Guthrie (1), pp. 110–11; Murray, pp. 206–7; Seltman, p. 40.
20 *Man, Myth and Magic*, art. 'Twelve'.

Chapter Five: The Mandalic Universe

1 C. G. Jung. Vol. 7 (*Two Essays on Analytical Psychology*), pp. 222f.
2 Guthrie (2), p. 138; Harrison, p. 457 n. 2; Kramer, p. 128; Neumann (2), pp. 8–11; Pedersen, Vols. 1–2, pp. 453–4; Seltman, p. 15; Vawter, pp. 39–41. Cp. Herodotus' ridicule (IV. 36) of Greek cartographers who, in the fifth century B.C., still 'made the ocean-stream to run all round the earth, and the earth to be an exact circle, as if described by a pair of compasses'.
3 See Unger. The interpretation has been challenged, but there

is no doubt as to the design. Cp. Neumann (2), illustration 3.

4 *Jewish Encyclopaedia*, art. 'Menorah'; *Mahabharata*, Book VI, chapters 5–12.

5 On the conception of the centre, see further Eric Burrows in Hooke, pp. 45–59; Pedersen, Vols. 3–4, pp. 262–3; Santillana, pp. 219–20, 304 n. 45. Jung's observations are in Vol. 9 Part 1 (*The Archetypes and the Collective Unconscious*), p. 146, and Vol. 14 (*Mysterium Coniunctionis*), p. 447 n. 326. It must be acknowledged that the Bible also mentions the earth's 'corners', but not, I think, with a strictly literal intent.

Other cities have been regarded as the centre of the earth such as Peking and Cuzco. American Indians have the same idea, sometimes identifying a spot as the centre not only of the earth but of the whole universe (e.g. Waters, p. 42). As will presently appear, however, those discussed in this chapter have special features and interrelations which set them apart.

6 Burrows in Hooke, pp. 46–50; Eliade, pp. 266–9; Kramer, p. 136.

7 Burrows in Hooke, pp. 52–7; Santillana, p. 220.

8 Burrows in Hooke, p. 56; Dodds, pp. 75, 222–3; Guthrie (1), pp. 80, 184–8, 201–2; Harrison, pp. 385, 396ff., 399, 401ff.; Santillana, p. 304 n. 45.

9 Guthrie (1), p. 86n.; Harrison, p. 411, fig. 123; Kramer, pp. 309–13; Nilsson, pp. 343, 363, 366–9; Seltman, p. 115.

10 Kramer, pp. 206–25.

11 Campbell, Vol. 1, pp. 305–10; Guthrie (1), p. 59; James (2), p. 173.

12 On the whole topic of mazes and labyrinths as reviewed here, see Campbell, Vol. 1, pp. 65–6, 69–70; C. N. Deedes in Hooke, pp. 3–42; Dudeney, p. 128; *Man, Myth and Magic*, art. 'Maze', and p. 2758; Matthews, pp. 44 (with figs. 20–31), 46, 67–9, 92–4, 147–9, 157–8; Purce, pp. 111, 113; Santillana, p. 290. Cp. Graves (2), pp. 102–11. The school of Jung can fairly claim that the maze is mandalic in their sense, with the centre as the vital 'self' point, which a person slowly nears as he achieves integration or self-realization. In Jung's own words: 'We can hardly escape the feeling that the unconscious process moves spiral-wise round a centre, gradually getting closer, while the characteristics of the centre grow more and more distinct.' Vol. 12 (*Psychology and Alchemy*), p. 217.

13 In Hooke, pp. 41–2. It should perhaps be emphasized that

211

this passage appeared in a book published in 1935, and more recent scholarship might be inclined to soften the tone. Cp. Waters, p. 31.

14 Deedes in Hooke, pp. 22–41; Dudeney, pp. 128–9; Graves (2), p. 328; *Man, Myth and Magic*, art. 'Dance'; Matthews, pp. 92–4, 156–9.

15 Hadingham, pp. 98–103; Hooke, pp. 10, 34, 68, and cp. 39; Kramer, p. 130; Matthews, pp. 92–4, and cp. 193; Purce, p. 113. For Glastonbury Tor, see Geoffrey Russell in Williams, pp. 16–19, and the *Central Somerset Gazette*, 6 July 1973.

16 Campbell, Vol. 1, pp. 69–70; Graves (2), pp. 105–11; Guthrie (1), pp. 230–1; Neumann (1), pp. 176–7.

17 *Man, Myth and Magic*, art. 'Dragon'.

18 See the Talmud, Hag. 69.

Chapter Six: The High Place

1 Cited in Williams, p. 16.

2 Burrows in Hooke, pp. 53–5.

3 Ashe (1), p. 103; Burrows in Hooke, p. 66 and note 2. Isaiah 2: 2 and other prophetic texts show an expectation that 'the mountain of the house of the Lord' – i.e., unequivocally, the hill of Zion with the Temple on it – will one day reveal its true nature by rising *visibly* above all others.

4 Campbell, Vol. 1, p. 148; Daniélou, pp. 316–19; Eliade, pp. 266–9; Guénon, pp. 58–9, 65–7, 70; Macdonell and Keith, pp. 115–17; *Mahabharata*, Book VI, chapter 6, verses 12 and 21, and Book XVII, chapter 2, verse 2; *Man, Myth and Magic*, art. 'Mountain', and pp. 2366, 2758; Santillana, pp. 76–7, 301 and n. 37.

5 Burrows in Hooke, pp. 50, 65–6; Campbell, Vol. 1, pp. 144, 148, 150; Eliade, pp. 264, 266–9; Kramer, p. 139; Santillana, pp. 59, 221.

6 Asin, pp. 114–25; Burrows in Hooke, p. 70.

7 Bolton, p. 101; Cook, Vol. 2, pp. 459–501; Dodds, pp. 69–70 and note 32 on p. 86; Graves (1), section 125 and note 2; Guthrie (1), pp. 73–87; Nilsson, pp. 366–9; Seltman, pp. 109–10. Pindar's reference to the 'wondrous way' is in his tenth Pythian Ode.

8 Dodds, p. 71, and cp. 140–1 and note 36 on pp. 161–2; Eliade, pp. 388–9; Graves (2), pp. 177–8; Guthrie (1), p. 73 n. 2, and pp. 193–6, 204; Seltman, pp. 109–10.

9 Bolton *passim*, and especially pp. 2–4, 7, 8, 74–6, 93–6, 100, 101, 114, 116, 118, 141.

Chapter Seven: Inhabited Skies
1 Burrows in Hooke, pp. 60–4; Cumont (1), pp. 16–17; Nilsson, pp. 112–13, 116–17, 121ff., 128.
2 Cumont (1), pp. 7–15, 56ff.; Dodd (1), pp. 102, 138–40, and (2), p. 118; Dodds, pp. 245–6; Josephus, V. 5. 5; Murray, pp. 140–9.
3 Campbell, Vol. 1, pp. 146–50, 438.
4 Cumont (1), pp. 1–15.
5 Burrows in Hooke, p. 68; *Cultural Heritage of India*, Vol. 3, pp. 347, 476; Evans-Wentz (2), p. 287; Eliade, p. 274 n. 65.
6 Cumont (1), pp. 24, 45, 164–5; Dio Cassius, Vol. 3, XXXVII, 17–18; Murray, pp. 142–3; Seltman, pp. 29–30.
7 *Encyclopaedia Britannica*, arts. 'Calendar', 'Week'; *Jewish Encyclopaedia*, art. 'Week'; Nilsson, pp. 324–36.
8 See his *Summa Theologica*, Part I, Question 74, Article 2.
9 Vawter, pp. 47–8.
10 Philo, *On the Allegories of the Sacred Laws*, I. 4. Cp. Swete, p. cxxxv and n. 2.
11 Cavendish, pp. 84–5. The phrasing is perhaps a little misleading. The Sumerians based their calendar on 'this cycle', i.e. the lunar month, simply; they did not use a seven-day period within it.
12 Nilsson, p. 148.
13 Cavendish, pp. 84–5; *Man, Myth and Magic*, art. 'Moon'.
14 Robert Graves's translation (Penguin Books, 1969), p. 268.
15 Nilsson, pp. 329–31.
16 Harrison, pp. 188–90, 389; Nilsson, pp. 155–6, 168, 170–2, 330. Graves in *The Greek Myths* (section 1.d and notes) maintains that early in the second millennium B.C. pre-Hellenic inhabitants of Greece did have a seven-day week, associating the days with the seven Titans. The invading Zeus-worshippers abolished all this. But Graves's classical references do not adequately support him.

Chapter Eight: The Primary Image
1 Hyginus, pp. 182–3.
2 Hyginus, p. 137; Le Poer Trench, pp. 46–7; Nilsson, pp. 41, 115–16, 118–19; Santillana, pp. 98–9, 101, 266, 383–4, 404–5.
3 Santillana, p. 384. Homer's allusion to the Great Bear is in the *Iliad*, XVIII, lines 486ff.
4 Santillana, pp. 3, 138, 236. Cp. Nilsson, p. 113.
5 Dodd. (1), p. xiv, and (2), pp. 12, 20; C. G. Jung, Vol. 5 (*Symbols of Transformation*), pp. 102–5; Le Poer Trench, p. 83; Mead, Vol. 1, p. 122 n. 1, Vol. 2, p. 66, and

Vol. 3, p. 31. The Hermetic texts quoted are in the dialogues entitled 'Though Unmanifest God is Most Manifest' and 'Of the Decans and the Stars'. The Hebrew star-names in Job 38: 32 are variously given in English Bibles – 'Mazzaroth and Arcturus' (King James), 'the Mazzaroth and the Bear' (Revised Standard Version), 'the signs of the Zodiac and the Bear' (Moffatt), 'the day star and the evening star' (Knox).

6 Blavatsky (2), Vol. 2, p. 631; Le Poer Trench, p. 50; C. G. Jung, Vol. 14 (*Mysterium Coniunctionis*), p. 205 n. 492; Massey, Part 2, Vol. 1, p. 219.

7 Blavatsky (2), Vol. 2, p. 631; Daniélou, pp. 316–19; Le Poer Trench, p. 49; Macdonell and Keith, pp. 115–18; *Mahabharata*, Book VI, chapter 6, verse 21; Santillana, pp. 3, 301, 451.

8 Burrows in Hooke, pp. 49–50, 60–62; Santillana, pp. 266, 301, 451.

9 Aratus, p. 18; *Man, Myth and Magic*, art. 'Nymphs'.

10 Hyginus, pp. 137, 181–3. His account of the Bears is in Book II, sections 1 and 2. See also *Man, Myth and Magic*, art. 'Diana'.

11 Farnell, Vol. 2, pp. 435–7; Guthrie (1), pp. 99–106, especially 104; Hyginus, p. 13; *Man, Myth and Magic*, art. 'Nymphs'; Seltman, pp. 127–8.

12 Farnell, Vol. 2, p. 467; Graves (1), section 77; Guthrie (1), pp. 82–6; Harrison, pp. 99–100 and fig. 16; Hyginus, pp. 31–2, 67–9; Seltman, pp. 110–11. Homer's allusion to the joint temple is in the *Iliad*, V: 445–8. The number of Niobe's children is not unanimously agreed, but since there is no doubt as to the seven gates, this seems likely to have been the original number of daughters; and the sons matched them.

13 Hyginus, pp. 13, 137, 148–9, 151, 210–11, 237; Santillana, pp. 385–6; Seltman, p. 136; Walters, art. 'Hyades'.

14 Cook, Vol. 2, pp. 453, 465; Farnell, Vol. 2, pp. 465–6; Graves (1), section 125; Harrison, p. 236 n. 3; Herodotus IV. 35. The story of Hercules pursuing the hind to Hyperborean land is found only in Pindar, with very muddled particulars. Farnell, however, in the notes to his translation of Pindar, accepts that Artemis was 'at home' there as well as Apollo.

15 Macdonell and Keith, p. 107.

Chapter Nine: Myth, Reality or Both?

1 Graves (2), p. 412.

2 *Purgatorio*, XXV. 131–2, XXIX. 43–51, XXX. 1–6.

3 C. G. Jung, Vol. 9 Part 1 (*The Archetypes and the Collective Unconscious*), pp. 195–6.

4 Cook, Vol. 2, p. 455; Guthrie (1), pp. 84, 193–8.

5 Campbell, Vol. 1, pp. 335–46; Czaplicka, pp. 45–6, 51, 153, 271, 295–7; Eliade, pp. 89–90, 93–4, 156, 166, 458–61, 503; Harrison, pp. 140–1, 206, 328–9, 450; James (2), p. 21; Le Poer Trench, pp. 83–5; *Man, Myth and Magic*, art. 'Bear', 'Lapland'; Neumann (2), p. 94. Cp. Dodds, p. 144 and note 61 on p. 166.

6 Eliade, p. 265, and cp. 67.

7 Campbell, Vol. 1, pp. 238, 251–3, 265; Chadwick, pp. 17–19, 88; Czaplicka, pp. 169–73, 191, 243; Eliade, pp. 4, 13, 29–30, 42; *Man, Myth and Magic*, art. 'Shaman'.

8 Bolton, pp. 97–8, 100; Campbell, Vol. 1, p. 257; Czaplicka, p. 221; Eliade, pp. 122 n. 26, 152–3, 168–9, 173, 200–1, 259, 261, 262, 266–9, 274 9; *Man, Myth and Magic*, art. 'Shaman'. Cp. Santillana, pp. 111, 121ff., 130, 382.

9 Eliade, pp. 266–9, 274–9, 388–9; N. Roerich (1), p. 349.

10 Bolton, pp. 81–2, 92.

11 Campbell, Vol. 1, pp. 315–25; Chadwick, pp. 2–3, 17–18, 93; Czaplicka, pp. 198, 244 n. 2; Eliade, p. 81.

12 Campbell, Vol. 3, p. 292; Czaplicka, pp. 199, 211, 243, 249–50; Eliade, pp. 257–8, 470–4; Neumann (1), p. 296; Santillana, p. 128.

13 Campbell, Vol. 1, pp. 329–31; James (1), pp. 13–14; Purce, pp. 100–1 and figs, 13, 14, and p. 111; Waters, pp. 29–32. Waters notes a number of other sevens in Hopi mythology, and in American Indian lore which may be related to it: see pp. 3, 142, 177, 183, 193, 222. These also may be part of a 'package' brought from Siberia; Hopi legend stresses an ancient migration from the west. On the other hand, the mention of seven Pleiades might suggest influence from the white man.

14 In *A Book of the Beginning*, see for instance: Part 1, Vol. 1, pp. 312, 314, 320, 358–9; Vol. 2, pp. 75, 129, 134, 137–8, 149, 520; Part 2, Vol. 1, pp. 6, 219, 286–91, 358–9; Vol. 2, pp. 2, 5, 15, 52, 82, 166–7, 221–2.

Chapter Ten: The Hidden Kingdom

1 N. Roerich (1), pp. 337–8, 406, and (2), pp. 108–10.

2 David-Neel (2), pp. 46–7; Evans-Wentz (1), pp. xvii-xviii, 59–60, and (2), pp. 99–100 and n. 2, 155–6; Maraini, pp. 117, 129; G. Roerich, pp. 156–8; N. Roerich (2), pp. 13, 21, 104, 118–23. It has been claimed that the Indian element in Kalachakra allows the supposition that Sham-

bhala is much further south than the Altai area, perhaps
even in the Himalayas, because 'Chang Shambhala' need
only mean north from India where the system – at least in
its documented form – took shape. But Shambhala does
not appear in Indian legend. It is 'north' from Tibet or
Mongolia. In a Tibetan legend, when the hero is banished,
the countries considered as his place of exile are Shambhala, India, China and Persia. These obviously represent
north, south, east and west from Tibet. See Evans-Wentz
(1), p. 117.

3 *Cultural Heritage of India*, Vol. 2, p. 220; Evans-Wentz (1),
   pp. xvii–xx, 59–60, 122, 135, 136; Santillana, pp. 373–6.
4 David-Neel (2), p. 47; Evans-Wentz (1), pp. xviii–xx; N.
   Roerich (1), pp. 15, 35, 49, 110–11, 114, 372, and (2), pp.
   28, 73, 78–9, 86–7, 110ff., 118–23.
5 Guénon, p. 63; Ossendowski, pp. 118, 177–9, 284, 301–12; G.
   Roerich, pp. 156–8; N. Roerich (1), pp. 37–8, 62, 256, 337,
   354, 398, and (2), pp. 80, 83ff.
6 David-Neel (1), p. 244; Evans-Wentz (1), p. xviii.
7 Ossendowski, pp. 3, 238–41, 247–9, 259, 265–6, 269–70, 294,
   296, 315–16.
8 Evans-Wentz (1), p. xviii; Maraini, pp. 129–30; Ossendowski,
   p. 310; G. Roerich, pp. 156–8; N. Roerich (1), pp. 44, 66,
   112, 116–18, 143, 149, 337, 353, 391–6, and (2), p. 80.
9 David-Neel (2), pp. 7, 14–15, 33–5, 43–8, 283–4; G. Roerich,
   pp. 156–8; N. Roerich (1), pp. 111, 117, 215, 353–4, 401,
   and (2), pp. 65, 71.
10 Pauwels and Bergier, pp. 193–9; Ravenscroft, pp. 254–7. Cp.
   also Brennan, pp. 85–8.
11 *Man, Myth and Magic*, art. 'Swastika',
12 Ossendowski, pp. 313–14.
13 N. Roerich (1), pp. 41, 112, 289, 303–4, 306, 314, 354.
14 David-Neel (2), pp. 19–20; Evans-Wentz (2), p. 290. On the
   shamanistic and Bön background, cp. David-Neel (1), p.
   9, and Maraini, pp. 120–1, 124, 163, 166–7.

Chapter Eleven: What Was the Ancient Wisdom?
1 Bolton, pp. 120–41; Dodds, pp. 135, 139–46; Eliade, pp.
   388–9; Guthrie (1), pp. 193–6; Herodotus IV. 94–5;
   Piggott, pp. 79–80.
2 Bolton, pp. 142–74; Dodds, pp. 140–7 and notes 59–61 on
   pp. 165–6, also note 75 on p. 168; Eliade, p. 388; Guthrie
   (1), pp. 195–8; Piggott, p. 82; Wilson, p. 196.
3 On Pythagoras and considerations arising, see, for example,
   Russell, Book I, chapter III, and E. T. Bell's *Men of*

Mathematics (1937). Professor Dodds, in his discussion of Pythagoreanism as a kind of shamanism, disclaims any intention of making it out to be nothing more than that (note 63 on pp. 166–7). The number-mysticism and the speculation about cosmic harmony are, he says, manifestly important and not shamanistic. But as Eliade shows, the number-mysticism at any rate *is* shamanistic.

4 Santillana, pp. 123–4, 132. Cp. Campbell, Vol. 1, pp. 146–50.

5 Blavatsky (1), Vol. 2, pp. 615–16, and (2), Vol. 2, pp. 319, 400.

6 Alder, pp. 58–9, 92–5, 114, 155.

7 Francis King (2), p. 44; Guénon, p. 3.

8 Guénon, *passim*, especially pp. 58–9, 63, 65, 70–4, 78, 89.

9 Von Däniken, pp. 148–51; Wilson, pp. 526–7. Baxter and Atkins offer the fullest recent discussion in English, favouring the theory of a space-ship and an atomic explosion. An article by Baxter summarizing his case, published in the *Observer* (10 October 1976, magazine section, pp. 43–8), drew a reply from Ian Ridpath (24 October, p. 10) urging the rival claims of a 'small comet'.

10 For the theosophical aspect, see Adney. For Bragdon's remarks, see N. Roerich (1), p. xiii. For the obscure business of the stone, see Guénon, p. 8; Ossendowski, pp. 285, 288–9; N. Roerich (2), pp. 61, 94–5, 113–14, 125, 145, 173ff.

11 N. Roerich (1), pp. 359–62, and (2), pp. 50–1. See also G. Roerich, pp. 243–5. On the significance of a *stupa*, see Maraini, p. 60.

12 There are allusions in Drake and in Tomas's *We are not the First* (1971), but with no sign that the authors understand just how exceptional this case is.

13 N. Roerich (2), pp. 81–2.

Chapter Twelve: Possibilities

1 Blavatsky (1), Vol. 2, pp. 615–16.

2 Evans-Wentz (2), pp. xxv-xxvi.

3 David-Neel (1), pp. 200–4, 209–13; Evans-Wentz (1), pp. 166–7 n. 4; Maraini, p. 51. On lamaistic wonder-working in general, see David-Neel (1), pp. 230–4, 240–1, 245, 291, 302–3, 319–20; Maraini, pp. 52–3; Ossendowski, pp. 116–17, 179–80, 282–3. Cp. Dodds. p. 298, and note 124 on pp. 310–11.

4 David-Neel (1), pp. 120–1, 291–2, 308–15, and cp. 316–19.

5 David-Neel (1), pp. 283–7; Evans-Wentz (1), pp. 29–30 and n., 170–1, and (2), pp. xxv-xxvi, 16, 281–2; Maraini, p. 117.

6 David-Neel (1), pp. 121–2, 298, and (2), pp. 31–2.
7 David-Neel (1), pp. 114–23, and (2), pp. 283–4; Evans-Wentz (2), p. 164; Maraini, p. 120.
8 For example in *Altai-Himalaya*, pp. 387–8, where he laments the lamas' declining powers in this respect, and hints at the existence of superior agencies causing 'manifestations' of a more striking kind.
9 Wilson, pp. 527–8.
10 David-Neel (1), p. 313.

Appendix
1 Translated in Graves (2), pp. 283–4. Hecataeus' work is lost; the passage is as quoted by a later author, Diodorus Siculus.
2 Piggott, p. 105.
3 Piggott, pp. 79–87, 108, 160–4; Ross, pp. 80, 83, 86–7. In Emma Jung, pp. 359–60, Druidic and shamanistic features are detected in the Celtic story of Merlin.
4 Cook, Vol. 2, pp. 487–93; Dodds, note 36 on pp. 161–2; Piggott, pp. 80–1. Piggott credits Tennyson with the invention of an Avalon that is like Elysium and the Hyperborean Land, but it can be traced much further back, into medieval Arthurian legend with Celtic antecedents.
5 The Avalon–Annwn connection may be pursued in the Arthurian researches of R. S. Loomis. The folk-belief about Glastonbury Tor is attested by the Welsh legend of St Collen, which exists only in a late manuscript, but is undoubtedly based on early tradition.

Bibliography

Adney, Frances, and others, *'The Messenger': Roerich's Paintings*. Blavatsky Museum, Adyar, 1925.

Alder, Vera Stanley, *The Initiation of the World*. Rider, 1969.

Aratus, *A Literal Translation of the Astronomy and Meteorology of Aratus*, trans. C. Leeson Prince. Farncombe, 1895.

Ashe, Geoffrey (1), *The Land and the Book*. Collins, 1965.

Ashe, Geoffrey (2), *The Virgin*. Routledge & Kegan Paul, 1976.

Asin, Miguel, *Islam and the Divine Comedy*, trans. Harold Sunderland. John Murray, 1926.

Atkinson, R. J. C., *Stonehenge and Avebury*. HMSO, 1971.

Baxter, John, and Atkins, Thomas, *The Fire Came By*. Macdonald & Janes, 1976.

Blavatsky, H. P. (1), *Isis Unveiled*. 2 vols. Theosophical University Press, 1972.

Blavatsky, H. P. (2), *The Secret Doctrine*. 2 vols. Theosophical University Press, 1970.

Bolton, J. D. P., *Aristeas of Proconnesus*. Clarendon Press, 1962.

Brennan, J. H., *Occult Reich*. Futura, 1974.

Brewer's Dictionary of Phrase and Fable. Revised edition. Cassell, 1959.

Camp, L. Sprague de and Catherine C. de, *Citadels of Mystery*. Fontana, 1972.

Campbell, Joseph, *The Masks of God*. 3 vols. Secker & Warburg, 1960–5.

Cassuto, U., *The Goddess Anath*, trans. Israel Abrahams. Magnes Press, 1972.

Castle, Edgar, and Thiering, Barry (eds.), *Some Trust in Chariots!* Bailey Brothers & Swinfen, 1972.

Cavendish, Richard, *The Black Arts*. Pan Books, 1969.

Chadwick, N. Kershaw, *Poetry and Prophecy*. Cambridge University Press, 1942.

Cook, A. B., *Zeus*. 3 vols. Cambridge University Press, 1914–40.

Cultural Heritage of India, The. 3 vols. Sri Ramakrishna Centenary Committee (Calcutta), 1937.

Cumont, Franz (1), *Astrology and Religion among the Greeks and Romans*. Putnam, 1912.

Cumont, Franz (2), *The Mysteries of Mithra*, trans. Thomas J. McCormack. Kegan Paul, Trench & Trübner, 1903.

Czaplicka, M. A., *Aboriginal Siberia*. Clarendon Press, 1914.

Daniélou, Alain, *Hindu Polytheism*. Routledge & Kegan Paul, 1964.

Däniken, Erich von, *Chariots of the Gods?* Corgi Books, 1973.

David-Neel, Alexandra (1), *With Mystics and Magicians in Tibet*. John Lane, The Bodley Head, 1931.

David-Neel, Alexandra (2), *The Superhuman Life of Gesar of Ling*. Rider, 1933.

Dio Cassius, *Roman History*, trans. E. Cary. 9 vols. Loeb Classical Library, 1940.

Dodd, C. H. (1), *The Bible and the Greeks*. Hodder & Stoughton, 1935.

Dodd, C. H. (2), *The Interpretation of the Fourth Gospel*. Cambridge University Press, 1953.

Dodds, E. R., *The Greeks and the Irrational*. University of California Press, 1951.

Drake, W. Raymond, *Gods and Spacemen in the Ancient East*. Sphere Books, 1973.

Dudeney, H. E., *Amusements in Mathematics*. Nelson, 1917.

Eliade, Mircea, *Shamanism*. Routledge & Kegan Paul, 1964.

Encyclopaedia Britannica.

Evans-Wentz, W. Y. (1), *The Tibetan Book of the Great Liberation*. Oxford University Press, 1954.

Evans-Wentz, W. Y. (2), *Tibetan Yoga and Secret Doctrine*. Oxford University Press, 1958.

Farnell, Lewis Richard, *The Cults of the Greek States*. 5 vols. Clarendon Press, 1896–1909.

French, Peter J., *John Dee*. Routledge & Kegan Paul, 1972.

Graves, Robert (1), *The Greek Myths*. 2 vols. Penguin Books, 1960.

Graves, Robert (2), *The White Goddess*. Faber, 1952.

Griffith, Ralph T. H., *The Hymns of the Rigveda*. 2 vols. E. J. Lazarus (Benares), 1896.

Guénon, René, *Le Roi du Monde*. Les Éditions Traditionnelles (Paris), 1950.

Guthrie, W. K. C. (1), *The Greeks and their Gods*. Methuen, 1950.

Guthrie, W. K. C. (2), *Orpheus and Greek Religion*. Methuen, 1935.

Hadingham, Evan, *Ancient Carvings in Britain*. Garnstone, 1974.

Harrison, Jane Ellen, *Themis. A Study of the Social Origins of Greek Religion*. Cambridge University Press, 1912.

Herodotus, *History*, trans. G. Rawlinson, 2 vols. Dent, 1910.

Hesiod, *Theogony* and *Works and Days*, trans. Dorothea Wender. Penguin Books, 1973.

Homer, *Iliad* and *Odyssey*, trans. E. V. Rieu. Penguin Books, 1950 and 1946.

Hooke, S. H. (ed.), *The Labyrinth*. S.P.C.K., 1935.

Hyginus, *The Myths of Hyginus*, trans. and ed. Mary Grant. University of Kansas, 1960.

James, E. O. (1), *The Cult of the Mother-Goddess*. Thames & Hudson, 1959.

James, E. O. (2), *Prehistoric Religion*. Thames & Hudson, 1957.

Jewish Encyclopaedia.

Josephus, *The Jewish War*, trans. William Whiston. London and Edinburgh, 1825.

Jung, C. G., *Collected Works*. 19 vols. Routledge & Kegan Paul. Volumes and editions used: Vol. 5, 1956; Vol. 7, 1966; Vol. 8, 1972; Vol. 9 Part 1, 1971; Vol. 12, 1970; Vol. 13, 1968; Vol. 14, 1963.

Jung, Emma, and von Franz, Marie-Louise, *The Grail Legend*. Hodder, 1970.

King, Francis (1), *Ritual Magic*. New English Library, 1972.

King, Francis (2), *Satan and Swastika*. Mayflower, 1976.

King, L. W. (ed.), *The Seven Tablets of Creation*. 2 vols. Luzac, 1902.

Kolosimo, Peter, *Not of this World*. Sphere Books, 1971.

Kramer, S. N., *History Begins at Sumer*. Thames & Hudson, 1958.

Le Poer Trench, Brinsley, *Temple of the Stars*. Fontana, 1973.

Macdonell, A. A., and Keith, A. B., *Vedic Index of Names and Subjects*. 2 vols. Motilal Banarsidass (Delhi), 1967.

McGuire, J. E., and Rattansi, P. M., 'Newton and the "Pipes of Pan"', in *Notes and Records of the Royal Society*, Vol. 21 (1966), pp. 108–43.

Mahabharata, trans. M. N. Dutt. 3 vols. H. C. Dass (Calcutta), 1895–1901.

Man, Myth and Magic, ed. Richard Cavendish. 7 vols. B.P.C. Publishing Ltd, 1970–2.

Maraini, Fosco, *Secret Tibet*, trans. Eric Mosbacher. Hutchinson, 1952.

Massey, Gerald, *A Book of the Beginnings*. 4 vols. (Second part retitled *The Natural Genesis*.) Williams & Norgate, 1881, 1883.

Matthews, W. H., *Mazes and Labyrinths*. Dover (New York), 1970.

Mead, G. R. S., *Thrice Greatest Hermes*. 3 vols, Watkins, 1964.

Müller, F. Max, *Vedic Hymns*, Vol. 1. In *Sacred Books of the East*, Vol. 32. Clarendon Press, 1891.

Murray, Gilbert, *Five Stages of Greek Religion*. Clarendon Press, 1925.

Neumann, Erich (1), *The Great Mother*. Routledge & Kegan Paul, 1955.

Neumann, Erich (2), *The Origins and History of Consciousness*. Routlege & Kegan Paul, 1954.

Nilsson, Martin P., *Primitive Time Reckoning*. Lund, 1920.

Ossendowski, Ferdinand, *Beasts, Men and Gods*. Edward Arnold 1923.

Ouspensky, P. D., *In Search of the Miraculous*. Routledge & Kegan Paul, 1950.

Pauwels, Louis, and Bergïer, Jacques, *The Morning of the Magicians*, trans. Rollo Myers. Mayflower, 1971.

Pedersen, J., *Israel: its Life and Culture*. 4 vols. Oxford University Press, 1926, 1940.

Philo, *The Works of Philo Judaeus*, trans. C. D. Yonge, 4 vols. Bohn, 1854–5.

Piggott, Stuart, *The Druids*. Penguin Books, 1974.

Purce, Jill, *The Mystic Spiral*. Thames & Hudson, 1974.

Radhakrishnan, S., *Indian Philosophy*. 2 vols. Allen & Unwin, 1940.

Ravenscroft, Trevor, *The Spear of Destiny*. Corgi Books, 1974.

Rees, Alwyn and Brinley, *Celtic Heritage*. Thames & Hudson, 1961.

Riencourt, Amaury de, *The Soul of India*. Cape, 1961.

Roerich, George N., *Trails to Inmost Asia*. Yale University Press, 1931.

Roerich, Nicholas (1), *Altai-Himalaya*. Jarrolds, 1930.

Roerich, Nicholas (2), *Himalayas, Abode of Light*. David Marlowe, 1947.

Ross, Anne, *Pagan Celtic Britain*. Cardinal, 1974.

Russell, Bertrand, *A History of Western Philosophy*. Allen & Unwin, 1946.

Santillana, Giorgio de, and von Dechend, Hertha, *Hamlet's Mill*. Macmillan, 1970.

Seltman, Charles, *The Twelve Olympians and their Guests*. Max Parriser, 1956.

Spencer, Sidney, *Mysticism in World Religion*. Penguin Books, 1963.

Swete, H. B., *The Apocalypse of St John*. Macmillan, 1907.

Thompson, C. J. S., *The Lure and Romance of Alchemy*. Harrap, 1932.

Unger, Eckhard, 'Ancient Babylonian Maps and Plans', in *Antiquity*, September 1935.

Vawter, Bruce, *A Path through Genesis*. Sheed & Ward, 1957.

Walters, H. B. *A Classical Dictionary*. Cambridge University Press, 1916.

Waters, Frank, *Book of the Hopi*. Ballantine, 1969.

Williams, Mary (ed.), *Glastonbury: a Study in Patterns*. Research Into Lost Knowledge Organisation (RILKO), 1969.

Wilson, Colin, *The Occult*. Hodder & Stoughton, 1971.

Yates, Frances A., *Giordano Bruno and the Hermetic Tradition*. Routledge & Kegan Paul, 1964.

Acknowledgements

The publishers would like to thank the following for permission to reproduce their photographs which appear between pp. 120 and 121:

Acrofilms; Elsevier; The Mansell Collection; Novosti Press Agency; Photoresources.

Line drawings: p. 21 (after the Azoth of the Philosophers); pp. 37, 147 (*The Mystic Spiral* by Jill Purce, Thames & Hudson, 1947); pp. 85, 86 (*Mazes and Labyrinths* by W. H. Matthews, Dover, New York, 1970); p. 123 (after Hermes as Mystagogue from Bocchi's *Symbolicae quaestiones*).

Index

225

Trinity, 55, 61, 71
Trophonius, 90
Troy: city, 12, 40; maze lore, *86*, 88–90, 150
Tulkus, *see* Thought-forms
Tulpas, *see* Thought-forms
Tunguska, 179, 181, 186, 200
Twelve, 56–7, 69–71, 72–3

UFOs, *see* Flying saucers
Unconsciousness, in theories of Jung, 10–11, 38, 50–1, 52, 62, 93
Ursa Major, the Great Bear, *41*; constellation recognised early and widely, 40, 44; as north-indicator, 64, 121–2, 127–8; as source of seven mystique, 114, 120–33, 138; in miscellaneous folklore, 121; in mystical doctrine, 122–4; Mme Blavatsky and Massey on, 124, 150; in Jung, 124–5, 138–9; Hindu names for, 125, 142; in relation to world-centres, 125–6, 134–5; Greek myths of, 126–33; in Dante, 138; in Siberia, 138; as chariot of Time, 154; in Asian lore compiled by Roerich, 166–7; in Guérnon, 178
Ursa Minor, 121, 126, 127, 128, 133

Velikovsky, Immanuel, 15
Venus, as source of mission to Earth, 8, 176
Virgil, 88, 90
Virtues, 54, 68
Vowels, 20, 41, 113

Week, 23, 27–8, 56, 108–12, 118–19
Whitman, Walt, 209, *5n*
Wilhelm, Richard, 209 *2n*
Wilson, Colin, 197
Winds, 53, 66
Wisdom, personification in Old Testament, 28–9, 92, 136, 149–50 (*For Ancient Wisdom theory*, *see* Ancient Wisdom)
Wise Men, Seven, 41, 80, 96
Women, possible predominance in early cults, 146, 173
Wonders, Seven, 42–3
Woolley, Leonard, 12

Yeats, W. B., 14

Zalmoxis, 169–70
Ziggurats: in Babylon, *33*, 76, 79, 82–3, 98, 136, 174; in Borsippa, 89, 108
Zion, 76, 94, 95, 136
Zodiac, 21, 56, 70, 104–5, 121–2, 124